Nature and Extent of Ethical Values in Retailing Practices

/2012

PREFACE

Ethical values are indispensable in the modern business, particularly in retail sector, because retailers are last in the distribution chain and in final touch with the ultimate consumers. Retailers have to deal with several stakeholders such as customers, wholesalers, manufacturers, and regulatory bodies who have different expectations from them. Retailers are required to fulfill their expectations in an ethical manner in the form of services they deliver, so that such efforts result into high sales, huge profits, customer satisfaction and loyalty to retail stores. It is in this context, the present study is conducted empirically to examine in detail the ethical values in retailing practices from the viewpoint of aforesaid stakeholders. The study is based upon the data obtained through specifically developed schedules from different stakeholders. The whole domain of the study has been studied under nine chapters.

The first chapter presents a theoretical perspective of different relevant aspects viz., ethics in general, business ethics, marketing ethics, retailing, stakeholders in retailing, retailing ethics and customer satisfaction.

In the second chapter, literature relating to ethical values in retailing practices has been reviewed, and accordingly, research gap has also been identified. The gap that emerged became the basis to examine the perceptions of different stakeholders in retailing about the ethical retail practices in Indian context.

The third chapter summarises research design and methodology adopted in the study. It includes the need and scope of the study, hypotheses, objectives, construction of data collection forms, pre-testing, sample design, scale purification, statistical techniques applied along with the limitations of the study.

The fourth chapter presents the perceptions of customers about ethical retail practices separately for convenience, shopping and specialty goods. It also depicts the impact of ethical values on customer satisfaction.

The fifth chapter deals with the perceptions of retailers about ethical retailing practices in their dealings with customers, employees, suppliers and regulatory bodies.

The next three chapters describe the perceptions of wholesalers, manufacturers and regulatory bodies about ethical retail practices.

The last chapter depicts the major findings, perceptual gap and strategic action plan for better ethical retailing practices.

Thus, the present study is expected to be a sound and useful document for all the stakeholders, particularly, retailers, regulatory bodies, retailers' association, wholesalers, researchers and policy makers.

(Bodh Raj)

ACKNOWLEDGEMENT

First of all, my heartiest and humble gratitude to the lotus feet of **The Supreme Lord** and **The Divine Mother** for selecting me as an instrument for completing this research.

I extend my deepest regards, gratitude and respect to my supervisor **Prof. R. D. Sharma**, Department of Commerce, University of Jammu, for his profound and eternal guidance. Without his arduous efforts and direction, my success would have not been probable. To me, he is a role model, citing a living example of ethical virtues. He in fact, transformed my weaknesses into strengths.

I pay my sincere thanks to the faculty members of the Department of Commerce, University of Jammu, namely, Prof. Neetu Andotra, Prof. Hardeep Chahal, Dr. Gurjeet Kaur Dr. Jeevan Jyoti and Sh. Tarsem Lal, for providing me the needed help and cooperation.

I am grateful to Sh M. P. Raina, though Librarian, but helped me like a family member and motivated me from time to time for the research. The staff of Rattan Tata Library, School of Economics, Delhi University, also deserve thanks for providing me the relevant literature.

I acknowledge my thanks to the non teaching staff members of the Department of Commerce, University of Jammu, for their cooperation and support.

I am also obliged to Sh Amarjeet Singh, J. E., Housing Development Board Jammu and Sh Yash Paul Gupta, President Retailers' Association, for supplying the required information.

I extend my thanks to Sh G. S. Manhas, Archana Manhas (Advocate), Prof. Gopal Sharma, Sh. Prem Sagar, Sh. Jagdish Raj, for their incessant assistance.

I am under obligation to appreciate the efforts of research scholars and friends who helped me, particularly Vipul, Sakshi, Naresh, Kulbir, Arun, Gudia, Shruti, Preeti, Nitasha, Vinod, Pardeep, Kapil, Jyoti and Pooja.

On the home side, I cannot forget my grandfather late Sh. Munshi Ram, who always encouraged me for higher studies. My parents **Smt. Chanchla and Sh. Charan Dass Sharma** deserve special thanks for supporting me in all respects since my childhood. I offer my thanks to my sisters, Shashi Bala, Chander Prabha and Aishlesha for their inspirations and brothers, Suresh and Aurvind, for making me free from domestic responsibilities and other family members for their blessings.

I dedicate my Ph. D thesis to Sri Aurobindo and The Divine Mother, Sri Aurobindo Ashram, Pondicherry. It is with Their Grace that such a big job became possible.

Dated: **(Bodh Raj)**

Place: Jammu

INDEX

Contents	Page No
Certificate	i
Preface	ii-iii
Acknowledgement	iv-v
List of Tables	vii-viii
List of Figures	ix
List of Abbreviations	x
Chapter 1 Theoretical Perspective of Ethical Values in Retailing Practices	1-17
Chapter 2 Review of Literature	18-50
Chapter 3 Research Design and Methodology	51-65
Chapter 4 Ethical Retail Practices – Perceptions of Customers	66-128
Chapter 5 Ethical Retail Practices – Perceptions of Retailers	129-151
Chapter 6 Ethical Retail Practices - Perceptions of Wholesalers	152-169
Chapter 7 Ethical Retail Practices –Perceptions of Manufacturers	170-186
Chapter 8 Ethical Retail Practices – Perceptions of Regulatory Bodies	187-200
Chapter 9 Major Findings and Strategic Action Plan	201-216
Bibliography	217-226
Annexures	227-238

LIST OF TABLES

Table No.	Title	Page No.
4.1	Respondent Profile	112
4.2.1	Split Half Reliability and Cronbach Alpha	112
4.2.2	Factor Analysis regarding Legal Provisions	112
4.2.3	Factor Analysis regarding Ethical Values	113
4.2.4	Factor Analysis regarding Customer Satisfaction	113
4.2.5	Factor Analysis regarding Other Issues	113
4.2.6	Factorial Profile in Convenience Goods	114
4.2.7	Confirmatory Factor Analysis: Convenience Goods	116
4.2.8	Demographic Profile wise ANOVA Results in Convenience Goods	117
4.2.9	Demographic Group wise Factorial Mean Values in Convenience Goods	117
4.3.1	Split Half Reliability and Cronbach Alpha	118
4.3.2	Factor Analysis regarding Legal Provisions	118
4.3.3	Factor Analysis regarding Ethical Values	118
4.3.4	Factor Analysis regarding Customer Satisfaction	118
4.3.5	Factor Analysis regarding Other Issues	118
4.3.6	Factorial Profile in Shopping Goods	119
4.3.7	Confirmatory Factor Analysis: Shopping Goods	121
4.3.8	Demographic Profile wise ANOVA Results in Shopping Goods	122
4.3.9	Demographic Profile Group Wise Factorial Mean Values in Shopping Goods	122
4.4.1	Split Half Reliability and Cronbach Alpha	123
4.4.2	Factor Analysis regarding Legal Provisions	123
4.4.3	3 Factor Analysis regarding Ethical Values	123
4.4.4	Factor Analysis regarding Customer Satisfaction	123
4.4.5	Factor Analysis regarding Other Issues	123
4.4.6	Factorial Profile of Specialty Goods	124
4.4.7	Confirmatory Factor Analysis: Specialty Goods	126
4.4.8	Demographic Profile wise ANOVA Results in Specialty Goods	127
4.4.9	Demographic Profile Group wise Factorial Mean Values in Specialty Goods	127
4.5	Result of Various CFA Indices	128
4.6	SEM Model for Convenience Goods	128
4.7	SEM Model for Shopping Goods	128
4.8	SEM Model for Specialty Goods	128
4.9	Validity and Reliability	128
5.1	Demographic Profile of Retailers	146
5.2	Split Half Reliability	146
5.3	Process of Data Reduction	146
5.4	Factorial Profile of Ethical Retail Practices	147
5.5	Demographic Profile wise ANOVA Results	148

5.6	Age and Qualification wise Factorial Mean Values	148
5.7	Experience wise Factorial Mean Values	149
5.8	Type of Retail Store wise Factorial Mean Values	149
5.9	Difference in the Perceptions of Stakeholders about Ethical Retail Practices (ANOVA)	149
5.10	Perceptions of Stakeholders about Ethical Retail Practices	150
5.11	Age and Ethical Retail Practices (Independent t- test)	150
5.12	Qualification and Ethical Retail Practices (ANOVA)	150
5.13	Difference in the Perceptions of Regulatory Bodies (ANOVA)	150
5.14	Ethical Retail Practices (One sample t- test)	150
5.15	Discriminant Validity	151
6.1	Demographic Profile of Wholesalers	164
6.2	Split Half Reliability	164
6.3	Factor Analysis	164
6.4	Factorial Profile of Ethical Retail Practices: Wholesalers' Perspective	165
6.5	ANOVA (Age wise)	166
6.6	Age and Qualification wise Factorial Mean Values	166
6.7	ANOVA (Qualification Wise)	167
6.8	ANOVA (Experience wise)	168
6.9	Experience Wise Factorial Mean Values	168
6.10	ANOVA (Product wise)	169
6.11	Type of Product Wise Factorial Mean Values	169
6.12	Discriminant Validity	169
7.1	Demographic Profile of Manufacturers	181
7.2	Split Half Reliability	181
7.3	Factor Analysis	181
7.4	Factorial Profile of Ethical Retail Practices: Manufacturers' Perspective	182
7.5	ANOVA (Age wise)	183
7.6	ANOVA (Qualification Wise)	184
7.7	ANOVA (Experience wise)	185
7.8	ANOVA (Product wise)	186
7.9	Discriminant Validity	186
8.1	Respondent Profile	198
8.2	Split Half Reliability	198
8.3	Factor Analysis	198
8.4	Factorial Profile of Ethical Retail Practices	198
8.5	Perceptions about Legal Provisions	199
8.6	ANOVA (Agency wise)	200
8.7	Agency wise Factorial Mean Values	200
8.8	Discriminant Validity	200
9.1	Perceptual Gap of Ethical values between Retailers and Customers	215
9.2	Perceptual Gap of Ethical Values between Retailers, Wholesalers and Manufacturers	215
9.3	Perceptual Gap of Ethical Values between Retailers and Regulatory Bodies	216

LIST OF FIGURES

Fig. No.	Title	Page No.
1.1	Stakeholders in Retailing	12
4.1	Measurement Model of Ethical Values in Convenience Goods	77
4.2	Measurement Model of Customer Satisfaction in Convenience Goods	78
4.3	Measurement Model of Ethical Values in Shopping Goods	89
4.4	Measurement Model of Customer Satisfaction in Shopping Goods	90
4.5	Measurement Model of Ethical Values in Specialty Goods	99
4.6	Measurement Model of Customer Satisfaction in Specialty Goods	100
4.7	Structural Model of SEM for Convenience Goods	106
4.8	Structural Model of SEM for Shopping Goods	106
4.9	Structural Model of SEM for Specialty Goods	107

LIST OF ABBREVIATIONS

EV	=	Ethical Values
CS	=	Customer Satisfaction
EFA	=	Exploratory Factor Analysis
CFA	=	Confirmatory Factor Analysis
SEM	=	Structure Equation Modelling
VE	=	Variance Explained
M	=	Mean
SD	=	Standard Deviation
MD	=	Mean Difference
Df	=	Degree of Freedom

PREFACE

Ethical values are indispensable in the modern business, particularly in retail sector, because retailers are last in the distribution chain and in final touch with the ultimate consumers. Retailers have to deal with several stakeholders such as customers, wholesalers, manufacturers, and regulatory bodies who have different expectations from them. Retailers are required to fulfill their expectations in an ethical manner in the form of services they deliver, so that such efforts result into high sales, huge profits, customer satisfaction and loyalty to retail stores. It is in this context, the present study is conducted empirically to examine in detail the ethical values in retailing practices from the viewpoint of aforesaid stakeholders. The study is based upon the data obtained through specifically developed schedules from different stakeholders. The whole domain of the study has been studied under nine chapters.

The first chapter presents a theoretical perspective of different relevant aspects viz., ethics in general, business ethics, marketing ethics, retailing, stakeholders in retailing, retailing ethics and customer satisfaction.

In the second chapter, literature relating to ethical values in retailing practices has been reviewed, and accordingly, research gap has also been identified. The gap that emerged became the basis to examine the perceptions of different stakeholders in retailing about the ethical retail practices in Indian context.

The third chapter summarises research design and methodology adopted in the study. It includes the need and scope of the study, hypotheses, objectives, construction of data collection forms, pre-testing, sample design, scale purification, statistical techniques applied along with the limitations of the study.

The fourth chapter presents the perceptions of customers about ethical retail practices separately for convenience, shopping and specialty goods. It also depicts the impact of ethical values on customer satisfaction.

The fifth chapter deals with the perceptions of retailers about ethical retailing practices in their dealings with customers, employees, suppliers and regulatory bodies.

The next three chapters describe the perceptions of wholesalers, manufacturers and regulatory bodies about ethical retail practices.

The last chapter depicts the major findings, perceptual gap and strategic action plan for better ethical retailing practices.

Thus, the present study is expected to be a sound and useful document for all the stakeholders, particularly, retailers, regulatory bodies, retailers' association, wholesalers, researchers and policy makers.

(Bodh Raj)

ACKNOWLEDGEMENT

First of all, my heartiest and humble gratitude to the lotus feet of **The Supreme Lord** and **The Divine Mother** for selecting me as an instrument for completing this research.

I extend my deepest regards, gratitude and respect to my supervisor **Prof. R. D. Sharma**, Department of Commerce, University of Jammu, for his profound and eternal guidance. Without his arduous efforts and direction, my success would have not been probable. To me, he is a role model, citing a living example of ethical virtues. He in fact, transformed my weaknesses into strengths.

I pay my sincere thanks to the faculty members of the Department of Commerce, University of Jammu, namely, Prof. Neetu Andotra, Prof. Hardeep Chahal, Dr. Gurjeet Kaur Dr. Jeevan Jyoti and Sh. Tarsem Lal, for providing me the needed help and cooperation.

I am grateful to Sh M. P. Raina, though Librarian, but helped me like a family member and motivated me from time to time for the research. The staff of Rattan Tata Library, School of Economics, Delhi University, also deserve thanks for providing me the relevant literature.

I acknowledge my thanks to the non teaching staff members of the Department of Commerce, University of Jammu, for their cooperation and support.

I am also obliged to Sh Amarjeet Singh, J. E., Housing Development Board Jammu and Sh Yash Paul Gupta, President Retailers' Association, for supplying the required information.

I extend my thanks to Sh G. S. Manhas, Archana Manhas (Advocate), Prof. Gopal Sharma, Sh. Prem Sagar, Sh. Jagdish Raj, for their incessant assistance.

I am under obligation to appreciate the efforts of research scholars and friends who helped me, particularly Vipul, Sakshi, Naresh, Kulbir, Arun, Gudia, Shruti, Preeti, Nitasha, Vinod, Pardeep, Kapil, Jyoti and Pooja.

On the home side, I cannot forget my grandfather late Sh. Munshi Ram, who always encouraged me for higher studies. My parents **Smt. Chanchla and Sh. Charan Dass Sharma** deserve special thanks for supporting me in all respects since my childhood. I offer my thanks to my sisters, Shashi Bala, Chander Prabha and Aishlesha for their inspirations and brothers, Suresh and Aurvind, for making me free from domestic responsibilities and other family members for their blessings.

I dedicate my Ph. D thesis to Sri Aurobindo and The Divine Mother, Sri Aurobindo Ashram, Pondicherry. It is with Their Grace that such a big job became possible.

Dated: **(Bodh Raj)**

Place: Jammu

INDEX

Contents	Page No
Certificate	i
Preface	ii-iii
Acknowledgement	iv-v
List of Tables	vii-viii
List of Figures	ix
List of Abbreviations	x
Chapter 1 Theoretical Perspective of Ethical Values in Retailing Practices	1-17
Chapter 2 Review of Literature	18-50
Chapter 3 Research Design and Methodology	51-65
Chapter 4 Ethical Retail Practices – Perceptions of Customers	66-128
Chapter 5 Ethical Retail Practices – Perceptions of Retailers	129-151
Chapter 6 Ethical Retail Practices - Perceptions of Wholesalers	152-169
Chapter 7 Ethical Retail Practices – Perceptions of Manufacturers	170-186
Chapter 8 Ethical Retail Practices – Perceptions of Regulatory Bodies	187-200
Chapter 9 Major Findings and Strategic Action Plan	201-216
Bibliography	217-226
Annexures	227-238

LIST OF TABLES

Table No.	Title	Page No.
4.1	Respondent Profile	112
4.2.1	Split Half Reliability and Cronbach Alpha	112
4.2.2	Factor Analysis regarding Legal Provisions	112
4.2.3	Factor Analysis regarding Ethical Values	113
4.2.4	Factor Analysis regarding Customer Satisfaction	113
4.2.5	Factor Analysis regarding Other Issues	113
4.2.6	Factorial Profile in Convenience Goods	114
4.2.7	Confirmatory Factor Analysis: Convenience Goods	116
4.2.8	Demographic Profile wise ANOVA Results in Convenience Goods	117
4.2.9	Demographic Group wise Factorial Mean Values in Convenience Goods	117
4.3.1	Split Half Reliability and Cronbach Alpha	118
4.3.2	Factor Analysis regarding Legal Provisions	118
4.3.3	Factor Analysis regarding Ethical Values	118
4.3.4	Factor Analysis regarding Customer Satisfaction	118
4.3.5	Factor Analysis regarding Other Issues	118
4.3.6	Factorial Profile in Shopping Goods	119
4.3.7	Confirmatory Factor Analysis: Shopping Goods	121
4.3.8	Demographic Profile wise ANOVA Results in Shopping Goods	122
4.3.9	Demographic Profile Group Wise Factorial Mean Values in Shopping Goods	122
4.4.1	Split Half Reliability and Cronbach Alpha	123
4.4.2	Factor Analysis regarding Legal Provisions	123
4.4.3	3 Factor Analysis regarding Ethical Values	123
4.4.4	Factor Analysis regarding Customer Satisfaction	123
4.4.5	Factor Analysis regarding Other Issues	123
4.4.6	Factorial Profile of Specialty Goods	124
4.4.7	Confirmatory Factor Analysis: Specialty Goods	126
4.4.8	Demographic Profile wise ANOVA Results in Specialty Goods	127
4.4.9	Demographic Profile Group wise Factorial Mean Values in Specialty Goods	127
4.5	Result of Various CFA Indices	128
4.6	SEM Model for Convenience Goods	128
4.7	SEM Model for Shopping Goods	128
4.8	SEM Model for Specialty Goods	128
4.9	Validity and Reliability	128
5.1	Demographic Profile of Retailers	146
5.2	Split Half Reliability	146
5.3	Process of Data Reduction	146
5.4	Factorial Profile of Ethical Retail Practices	147
5.5	Demographic Profile wise ANOVA Results	148

5.6	Age and Qualification wise Factorial Mean Values	148
5.7	Experience wise Factorial Mean Values	149
5.8	Type of Retail Store wise Factorial Mean Values	149
5.9	Difference in the Perceptions of Stakeholders about Ethical Retail Practices (ANOVA)	149
5.10	Perceptions of Stakeholders about Ethical Retail Practices	150
5.11	Age and Ethical Retail Practices (Independent t- test)	150
5.12	Qualification and Ethical Retail Practices (ANOVA)	150
5.13	Difference in the Perceptions of Regulatory Bodies (ANOVA)	150
5.14	Ethical Retail Practices (One sample t- test)	150
5.15	Discriminant Validity	151
6.1	Demographic Profile of Wholesalers	164
6.2	Split Half Reliability	164
6.3	Factor Analysis	164
6.4	Factorial Profile of Ethical Retail Practices: Wholesalers' Perspective	165
6.5	ANOVA (Age wise)	166
6.6	Age and Qualification wise Factorial Mean Values	166
6.7	ANOVA (Qualification Wise)	167
6.8	ANOVA (Experience wise)	168
6.9	Experience Wise Factorial Mean Values	168
6.10	ANOVA (Product wise)	169
6.11	Type of Product Wise Factorial Mean Values	169
6.12	Discriminant Validity	169
7.1	Demographic Profile of Manufacturers	181
7.2	Split Half Reliability	181
7.3	Factor Analysis	181
7.4	Factorial Profile of Ethical Retail Practices: Manufacturers' Perspective	182
7.5	ANOVA (Age wise)	183
7.6	ANOVA (Qualification Wise)	184
7.7	ANOVA (Experience wise)	185
7.8	ANOVA (Product wise)	186
7.9	Discriminant Validity	186
8.1	Respondent Profile	198
8.2	Split Half Reliability	198
8.3	Factor Analysis	198
8.4	Factorial Profile of Ethical Retail Practices	198
8.5	Perceptions about Legal Provisions	199
8.6	ANOVA (Agency wise)	200
8.7	Agency wise Factorial Mean Values	200
8.8	Discriminant Validity	200
9.1	Perceptual Gap of Ethical values between Retailers and Customers	215
9.2	Perceptual Gap of Ethical Values between Retailers, Wholesalers and Manufacturers	215
9.3	Perceptual Gap of Ethical Values between Retailers and Regulatory Bodies	216

LIST OF FIGURES

Fig. No.	Title	Page No.
1.1	Stakeholders in Retailing	12
4.1	Measurement Model of Ethical Values in Convenience Goods	77
4.2	Measurement Model of Customer Satisfaction in Convenience Goods	78
4.3	Measurement Model of Ethical Values in Shopping Goods	89
4.4	Measurement Model of Customer Satisfaction in Shopping Goods	90
4.5	Measurement Model of Ethical Values in Specialty Goods	99
4.6	Measurement Model of Customer Satisfaction in Specialty Goods	100
4.7	Structural Model of SEM for Convenience Goods	106
4.8	Structural Model of SEM for Shopping Goods	106
4.9	Structural Model of SEM for Specialty Goods	107

LIST OF ABBREVIATIONS

EV	=	Ethical Values
CS	=	Customer Satisfaction
EFA	=	Exploratory Factor Analysis
CFA	=	Confirmatory Factor Analysis
SEM	=	Structure Equation Modelling
VE	=	Variance Explained
M	=	Mean
SD	=	Standard Deviation
MD	=	Mean Difference
Df	=	Degree of Freedom

CHAPTER 1
INTRODUCTION

1.1. Background

Ethics plays a significant role in an individual's life and its role is more pivotal for a business, profession and progress of the society. As the need of ethics in each and every walk of life has been gaining momentum day by day, business ethics has also been gaining universal attention, particularly of business houses, business schools, consumer organisations, researchers, media etc. (Lau, 2010; Valenzuela et al., 2010; Freyne, 2009; Fernando, 2009; Oumlil and Balloun, 2009; Sharma and Sharma, 2009; Pettijohn et al., 2008; Desplaces et al., 2007 and Mc Cabe et al., 2006). This is due to more consumer awareness (Mulki and Jaramillo 2011), globalisation, competition and active role of consumer organisations, business associations, research institutes and the media (Yicel et al., 2009). In fact, the present period can be described as 'ethics era' (Smith, 1995) because ethics alone and no other regulation can regulate and protect the society. The American Marketing Association has framed a code of ethics for its members that every member is required to follow. Many companies are also framing ethical codes for their employees and are conducting seminars, workshops and providing training to their employees to face the ethical dilemma in the modern complex, competitive and global business (Zolingen and Honders, 2010; Stohl, et al., 2009; Dominguez, 2009). Business schools have introduced business ethics in their curriculum (Abratt and Penman 2002). They think that their students are future managers and the spirit of ethical values should be inculcated at the very beginning of their career (Yoo and Donthu, 2002). Researchers are taking keen interest in studying ethics due to its universal acceptance. Several international journals have been specifically focusing on ethical values, like *Journal of Business Ethics*, *Business Ethics: A European Review* etc. Media has been also playing an active role by highlighting the unethical practices of some business houses like Satyam. These unethical acts are not new as these issues came up with the origin of business (Trevino and Brown, 2004). But in the past little attention was given to control these unfair acts. No doubt some laws were framed but could not be implemented properly and followed by the businessmen. Presently, unethical acts have been increasing enormously as modern businessmen want to earn huge profit with high turnover and market share. For meeting these objectives, some of the marketers do unfair acts. But these acts may gain in short run but in long run it would have a serious consequences. The businesses which act legally and ethically enjoy more sales volume, profitability and strong image, that too with increasing and sustainable market share (Kurt and Hasioglu, 2010; Lavorata and Pontier, 2005). On the contrary, businesses which do illegal and unethical practices reduce their turnover, profitability, image (Lee et al., 2010; Orlitzky et al., 2003) and even the survival of business may be in danger (Grant and Visconti 2006, Mazzola et al., 2006). The aim of every business, however, is to earn a reasonable profit by satisfying the expectations of various stakeholders in a truthful manner (Park-Poaps and Rees, 2010; Fernando, 2009; Mitchell, 2009; Kaptein 2008; Napal, 2003; Kujala, 2001 and Whysall, 2000). Accordingly, the business firms have become conscious about the role of media and other consumer welfare organisations. They are focusing their attention towards business ethics and making ethics as a part of their corporate strategy so as to combat competition and the attainment of objectives.

1.2. Ethics

The word 'ethics' is derived from the Greek word, 'ethikos' meaning custom or character (Fernando, 2009). The Webster dictionary defines ethics as, 'the discipline dealing with what is good and bad or right and wrong or with moral duty and

(2009) provides that business ethics facilitates and promotes good to society, improves profitability, fosters business relations and employee productivity, protects business against unscrupulous employees and competitors, protects employees from harmful action by employer and allows people in business to act consistently with their personal ethical beliefs. Business ethics is based on the principles of integrity, honesty and fairness and concentrates on the benefits to the stakeholders. Mitchell (2009) remarks that business ethics based on broad principles of integrity and farness, tends to focus on issues such as product quality, employee wages as well as local community and environmental issues and how a company integrates its core values such as honesty, trust, fairness and respect into its policies, practices and decisions and it of course involves a company's compliance with legal standards and adherence to internal rules and regulations.

Among all the functional areas of business, marketing, receives the greater criticism for unethical practices (Dubinsky et al., 2004; Abratt and Penman, 2002 and Vitell et al., 1993). Since marketing managers are responsible for enhancing revenues, cutting edge competition and achieving sales quotas pressurise them and lead to illegal and unethical acts. Marketing ethics is the application of moral principles in the field of marketing. Singhapakdi and Vitell (1990) remarked marketing ethics as, 'an inquiry into the nature and grounds of moral judgements, standards and rules of conduct relating to marketing situations'. In marketing, the ethical issues, in fact, emerge from marketing professionals' relationships with different stakeholders like consumers, employees, competitors, suppliers, government and the general public. A marketer has duties and responsibilities towards each party and to the extent that the fulfillment of these duties and responsibilities conflict, this creates an ethical problem. These problems may be product quality and quantity, price discrimination, cheating consumers, deceptive advertising, unfair sales promotion, bad working conditions, environmental pollution, child and woman labour harassment, black-marketing and evasion of taxes (Rowwas, 1996).

1.3. Retailing

The word 'retail' has been derived from the French word 'retaillier' which means 'to cut off a piece' or 'to break bulk'. Retailing has been defined by different people at different periods of time (Sasikumar and Cleetus, 2008 and Pradhan, 2007). According to Kotler (2005), 'Retailing includes all the activities involved in selling goods or services to the final consumers for personal or non business use'. Retailing in simple words, connotes the selling of goods in small quantity to the ultimate or final consumers. Any organisation selling to final consumers whether it is a manufacturer, wholesaler or retailer is doing retailing. A retailer is a dealer who buys goods from wholesalers or manufacturers and sells them to the ultimate consumers. A retailer provides the feedback to the manufacturers through wholesalers about the need, taste and preferences of the consumers. He also provides the information of new products to the consumers.

Retail sector has been growing day by day. In the past, most of the retail stores were of small size with limited products but now the trend has been changed (Vedamani, 2008). At present the consumers are very busy having less time for shopping. They prefer all types of products in one store. Due to this the new type of modern big stores like departmental stores and malls have been emerged and the retail sector has been growing day by day with the increase in consumers' disposable income, high spending habits and change in consumers' tastes and preferences (Bajaj et al., 2007, Nicholls, 2002; and Whysall, 1998). Keeping in view such changes, many big business houses like Reliance, Vishal Marts etc have been investing in retailing by opening their shopping malls in different parts of India. The retail sector has shown tremendous progress and has become a prominent sector all over the world including India. Its share to the world GDP is about 27% from both organised and unorganised retail business (Vedamani 2008). Though in developed countries like USA and UK organised retailing is dominating, yet in developing countries like India, unorganised retailing is still dominating with over 12 million retail outlets of different types and sizes. Only about 6% outlets are in organised retail sector and remaining (94%) outlets are part of unorganised retail business. In the year 2007, the retail business in India was US$ 385 billion and Mc Kinsey study estimated this increase of about US$ 1.52 trillion by the year 2025 (Vedamani 2008). Indeed, the retail business in India is the second largest employer after agriculture.

1.4. Retailing Ethics

Retailing ethics originates from the concept of marketing itself, which not only starts with the consumer (Kotler, 2005) but revolves around the consumer, the nucleus around whom all other marketing activities revolve. The aim of the marketer is not only selling but to satisfy the consumers and all other stakeholders (Fassin, 2009). It is in this context, the retailers being the last point in the distribution chain (Cox and Brittain, 2006), are in direct touch with ultimate consumers. The behaviour of retailers is more significant than other intermediaries because they affect the lives of ultimate consumers i.e. the whole of the society (Abratt et al., 1999). Ethics plays a very significant role in retailing (Sharma and Sharma, 2011; Kurt and Hacioglu, 2010; Sarma, 2007; Dubinsky et al., 2004; Whysall, 2000, 1998). This is because the retailers are associated with different stakeholders like consumers, employees, suppliers, financers, government agencies, media and community at large (Sharma and Sharma, 2009; Fassin, 2009; Berman and Evans, 2007; Reynolds et al., 2006; Kujala, 2001; Whysall, 2000), who are directly or indirectly associated with them. The retailers have much more moral obligation to act ethically while dealing with different stakeholders, particularly consumer because a single unfair act leads to consumer dissatisfaction and switching to other stores. A retailer is said to be ethical when he acts fairly, honestly and with a sense of respect and trustworthiness with each stakeholder and fulfills his/her expectations in legal and ethical manner. The retailers need to provide safe and good quality products with no adulteration. He is also required to charge the fair price of goods from customers with fair advertising and sales promotion. He is in obligation to issue the bills to the customers for goods purchased by them. While dealing with salesmen, he is required to treat them as human beings by respecting employees' rights, timely payments of adequate salary and maintaining proper working hours and ambiance in retail store. While dealing with other stakeholders like wholesalers, manufacturers, government, financers and society, his dealings should be based on trust, commitment, integrity, honesty, fairness, co-operation and truthfulness like providing timely payment of bills on time, accurate information, payment of proper taxes, no employment of child labour, protection of the environment and so on. If the retailer deals with different stakeholders in ethical manner, it definitely enhances the turnover, profitability and reputation of the retailer and customer satisfaction (Sarma, 2007, Whysall, 2000). Moreover, the employees work with enthusiasm and zeal and contribute much for the retail store. The other parties also feel contented and help the retailer in all circumstances. Thus, it is much obligatory for a retailer also, to do the retail practices ethically, which definitely pay him a lot in the long run (Sarma, 2007 Dubinsky et al., 2004 and Whysall, 1998).

1.5. Customer Satisfaction

Customer satisfaction can be described as an essence of success in today's highly competitive and global world of business and thus, the significance of customer satisfaction in strategy development for a 'market oriented' and 'customer focused' firm cannot be underestimated (Kohli and Jaworski, 1990). Customer satisfaction is generally described as the full meeting of customers' expectations. Customer satisfaction is the feeling or attitude of a customer towards a product or service after it has been used. Customer satisfaction is a major outcome of marketing activity whereby it serves as a link between the various stages of consumer buying behaviour. For instance, if customers are satisfied with a particular service offering after its use, then they are likely to engage in repeat purchase and try line extensions (Valenzuela et al., 2010). It is widely recognised as a key influence in the formation of customers' future purchase intentions (Taylor and Baker, 1994). Satisfied customers are also likely to tell others about their favourable experiences and thus, engage in positive word of mouth advertising (File and Prince, 1992). But dissatisfied customers are more likely to switch to other brands and engage in negative word of mouth advertising. Furthermore, behaviour such as repeat purchase and word-of-mouth directly affect the viability and profitability of a firm. Hence, when the perceived performance equals to a customer's expectation, the customer feels satisfied and if the perceived performance falls short of a customer's expectations, then the customer feels dissatisfied. The retailing sector has been changing with the change in customer's behaviour. Customers have become more rational, conscious and sophisticated with the increased consumerism and consumer organisations. The retailers need to become more customers oriented for gaining more and more market share and competitive advantage by applying various strategies. This requires turning their vision from maximisation of sales and profit towards customer satisfaction. A customer is satisfied when he gets the expected performance of the product (Lin and Lin, 2006). When a customer visits a retail store, he has some expectations from the retailer like good quality products, convenient location, availability of brands, parking facilities, after sales services etc. If his expectations are fulfilled, he is satisfied and contrary to this, if his expectations fall short of performance, he would be dissatisfied. Satisfaction leads to customer loyalty and the dissatisfaction leads to customer dissonance.

1.6. Stakeholders in Retailing

Retailing comprises of various stakeholders or constituencies viz., customers, wholesalers, employees, competitors, manufacturers, financers, government and community etc. (Reynolds et al., 2006, Kujala, 2001 and Whysall, 1998). Retailers take finance from banks and other financial institutions for establishing their retail stores, then acquire merchandise from wholesalers or manufacturers either on credit or cash and finally, sell these goods to ultimate customers in small quantity They employ salesmen to handle the large number of customers and retailing activities. They are also liable to the government for paying taxes and supplying the necessary information to the departments like Excise and Taxation Department, Food and Supply Department, Labour and Employment Department, Weight and Measures Department etc. In addition to this, they are also associated with society or community as a whole. It is the duty of the retailers to serve all the stakeholders with trust, commitment truthfulness and fairness. Their interconnectedness and nature of consideration required while dealing with other members in the distribution chain are of utmost significance and the same are presented in fig. 1.1.

1.7. Conclusion

From the above conceptual analysis it is clear that the scope of retailing ethics has been widening day by day. The retailers have understood that ethics does not cause any harm to them rather helps them in the long run in terms of customer satisfaction and better business performance. If the retailers follow ethical values, the consumers are satisfied and build positive word of mouth and become loyal to the stores and bring new customers to the stores. This increases the sales volume and profitability of the retailers. Moreover, the image of the store depends on the ethical values, customer satisfaction and business performance. If the ethical values are followed and customers are satisfied, the retail store enjoys good image in the eyes of all the stakeholders. On the other hand, if unethical or unfair means are used, consumers are dissatisfied and create negative word of mouth and harm the business performance and image of the retail store in the eyes of all the stakeholders. Thus, the present study considers the ethical values in retail sector from the perceptions of several stakeholders. Many studies have been conducted on business and marketing ethics and examined the retailing ethics partially but not holistically and empirically. No research work has studied the retailing ethics empirically from the perceptions of various stakeholders together. Some of the major studies have been reviewed in the next chapter.

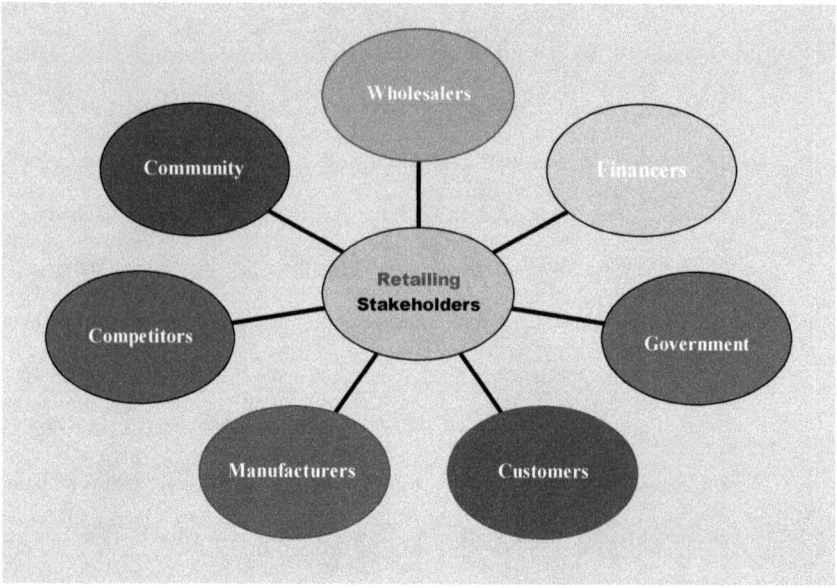

Fig. 1.1 Retailing Stakeholders

Source: Whysall, Paul (2000), "Stakeholder Mismanagement in Retailing: A British Perspective", *Journal of Business Ethics*, Vol. 23, pp. 19-28

References

Abratt, Russell and Neale Penman (2002), "Understanding Factors Affecting Salespeople's Perceptions of Ethical Behaviour in South Africa", *Journal of Business Ethics*, Vol. 35, pp. 269-280

Abratt, Russell; M. Bendixen and K. Drop (1999), "Ethical Perceptions of South African Retailers, Management and salespersonnel", *International Journal of Retail and Distribution Management*, Vol. 27, No.2, pp. 91-105

Bajaj, Cretan; Rajneesh Tulip and Niche V. Srivastava (2007), Retail Management, Seventh Edition, Oxford University Press, New Delhi, pp. 3, 4 and 9

Banerjee, Bani P. (2005), Foundations of Ethics in Management, First Edition, Excel Books, New Delhi, pp. 2, 36, 110

Barry, Richmon (1979), "Can We Prevent Questionable Foreign Payments?", *Business Horizons*, Vol. 22 (June), pp. 14-19

Beauchamp, Tom L. and Norman E. Bowie (1983), Ethical Theory and Business, Second Edition, Prentice Hall, Inc., Englewood cliffs

Berman, Berry and Joel R. Evans (2007), Retail Management, Tenth Edition, Prentice Hall of India Pvt. Ltd, New Delhi, pp. 44

Boatright, John R. (2009), Ethics and the Conduct of Business, Fifth Edition, Pearson Education, New Delhi, pp. 26

Cox, Roger and Paul Brittain (2006), Retailing, Fifth Edition, Pearson Education, New Delhi, pp. 32

De George, Richard R. (1982), *'Business Ethics'*, Second Edition, Macmillan Publishing, New York, pp. 13, 15

Desplaces, D. E.; D. E. Melcher, L. L. Beauvais, and S. M. Bosco (2007) "The Impact of Business Education on Moral Judgment Competence: An Empirical Study", *Journal of Business Ethics*, Vol. 74 (1), pp. 73-87

Dominguez, Luis Rodriguez; Isabel Gallego-Alvarez and Isabel Maria Garcia-Sanchez (2009), "Corporate Governance and Codes of Ethics", *Journal of Business Ethics*, Vol. 90, pp. 187–202

Dubinsky, Alan J.; Rajan Nataraajan and Wen-Yeh Huang (2004), "The Influence of Moral Philosophies on Retail Salespeople's Ethical Perceptions", *The Journal of Consumer Affairs*, Vol. 38, No. 2, pp. 297-317

Fassin Yves (2009), "The Stakeholder Model Refined", *Journal of Business Ethics*, Vol. 84, pp. 113-135

Fernando, A. C. (2009), Business Ethics, An Indian Perspective, First Edition, Dorling Kindersley, Pearson Education, New Delhi, pp. 4, 5, 6

File, K. M. and R. A. Prince (1992), "Positive Word of Mouth: Customer Satisfaction and Buyer Behaviour'', *International Journal of Bank Marketing*, Vol. 10, No. 1, pp. 25-29

Freyne, P. (2009), "Are Ethics Back in Business?", *Journal of Business & Finance*, Vol. 15, pp 46–47

Grant, R. M. and M. Visconti (2006), "The Strategic Background to Corporate Accounting Scandals", *Long Range Planning*, Vol. 39, pp. 361-383

Jones, T. M. (1991), "Ethical Decision Making by Individuals in Organisations: An Issue-Contingent Model", *Academy of Management Review,* Vol. 16, pp. 366-395

Kaptein, Muel (2008), "Developing a Measure of Unethical Behaviour in the Workplace: A Stakeholder Perspective", *Journal of Management,* Vol. 34, No. 5 (October), pp. 978-1008

Kohli, A. K. and B. J. Jaworski (1990), "Market Orientation: the Construct, Research Propositions, and Managerial Implications", *Journal of Marketing*, Vol. 54, (April), pp. 20-35

Kotler Philip (2005), Marketing Management, Eleventh Edition, Pearson Education Indian branch, Delhi, pp. 411

Kujala, Johanna (2001), "Analysing Moral Issues in Stakeholder Relations", *Business Ethics: A European Review,* Vol. 10, pp. 233-247

Kurt, Gizem and Gungor Hacioglu (2010), "Ethics as a Customer Perceived Value Driver in the Context of Online Retailing", *African Journal of Business Management,* Vol. 4 (5), pp. 672-677

Lau, Cubie L. L. (2010), "A Step Forward: Ethics Education Matters!", *Journal of Business Ethics*, Vol. 93, pp. 565-584

Lavorata, Laure and Suzanne Pontier (2005), "The Success of a Retailers' Ethical Policy: Focusing on Local Actions", *The Journal of Academy of Marketing Science Review*, Vol. 2005, No.12, pp. 1-9

Lee, Monle; Anurag Pant and Abbas Ali (2010), "Does the Individualist Consume More? The Interplay of Ethics and Beliefs that Governs Consumerism Across Cultures", *Journal of Business Ethics*, Vol. 93, pp. 567–581

Lin, Grace Tyng-Ruu and Jerry Lin (2006), "Ethical Customer Value Creation: Drivers and Barriers", *Journal of Business Ethics*, Vol. 67, pp. 93-105

Marnburg, E. (2000), "The Behavioural Effects of Corporate Ethical Codes: Empirical Findings and Discussion", *Business Ethics: A European Review,* Vol. 9 No. 3, pp. 200-210

Mazzola, P.; D. Ravasi and C. Gabbioneta (2006), "How to Build Reputation in Financial Mrkets", *Long Range Planning*, Vol. 39, pp. 385-407

Mc Cabe, A. Catherine; Rhea Ingram and Mary Conway Dato-on (2006), "The Business of Ethics and Gender", *Journal of Business Ethics*, Vol. 64, pp. 101-116

Mitchell, Charles (2009), International Business Ethics, Third Edition, Atlantic Publishers and Distributors, World Trade Press, New Delhi, pp. 9, 10

Mulki, Jai Prakash and Fernando Jaramillo (2011), "Ethical Reputation and Value Received: Customer Perceptions", *International Journal of Bank Marketing*, Vol. 29 (5), pp. 358-372

Napal, Geetanee (2003), "Ethical Decision Making in Business: Focus on Mauritius", *Business Ethics: A European Review*, Vol. 12, No.1, pp. 54-63

Nicholls, Alexander James (2002), "Strategic Options in Fair Trade Retailing", *International Journal of Retail and Distribution Management,* Vol. 30, No 1, pp. 6-17

Orlitzky, M.; F. L. Schmidt and S L Rynes (2003), "Corporate Social and Financial Performance: A Meta Analysis", *Organisation Studies,* Vol. 24, pp. 403-441

Oumlil, A. Ben and Joseph L. Balloun (2009), "Ethical Decision Making Difference between American and Moroccan Managers", *Journal of Business Ethics,* Vol. 84, pp. 457-478

Park-Poaps, Haesun and Kathleen Rees (2010), "Stakeholder Forces of Socially Responsible Supply Chain Management Orientation", *Journal of Business Ethics*, Vol. 92, pp.:305–322

Pettijohn, Charles, Linda Pettijohn and A. J. Taylor (2008), "Salesperson Perceptions of Ethical Behaviour: Their Influence on Job Satisfaction and Turnover Intentions", *Journal of Business Ethics*, Vol. 78, pp. 547–557

Pradhan, Swapna (2007), Retailing Management, Second Edition, Tata McGraw Hill, New Delhi, pp. 4

Reynolds, J. Scott; Frank C. Schultz and David R. Hekman (2006), "Stakeholder Theory and Managerial Decision Making: Constraints and Implications of Balancing Stakeholders' Interests", *Journal of Business Ethics*, Vol. 64, pp. 285-301

Rowwas, Mohammed Y. A. (1996), "Consumer Ethics: An empirical Investigation of Austrian Consumers", *Journal of Business Ethics,* Vol. 15, pp. 1009-1019

Runes Dagoberr D. (1964), Dictionary of Philosophy, Adams and Co, Patterson, pp. 98, 100

Sarma, Nripendra Narayan (2007), "Ethics in Retailing-Perception of Management and Sales Personnel", *(http:// dspace.iimk.ac.in/bitstream/2259/388/1/61-68.pdf),* last accessed on March, 20, 2012

Sasikumar, K. and Regina Sibi Cleetus (2008), "Impact of Corporate Retailing on Small Retail Outlets", *The Indian Journal of Commerce*, Vol. 61, No. 4, (October-December) pp. 68-77

Sharma R. D. and Bodh Raj Sharma (2011), "Legal Provisions and Ethical Values in Retail Sector: Study of Convenience Goods", *Arash, A Journal of ISMDR*, Vol. 1, No. 1, January, pp. 1-9

Sharma, R. D. and Bodh Raj Sharma (2009), "Ethics in Retailing: Perceptions of Consumers", *Saaransh RKG Journal of Management*, Vol. 1, No. 1 (July), pp. 43-55

Singhapakdi, A. and S. J. Vitell, (1990), "Marketing Ethics: Factors Influencing Perceptions of Ethical Problems and Alternatives", *Journal of Macro marketing (Spring)*, pp. 4-18

Sivananda, Swami (2004), Ethical Teachings, Sixth Edition, The Divine Life Society, Uttarakhand, pp. 3

Smith, N. Craig (1995), "Marketing Strategies for the Ethics Era", *Sloan Management Review,* Vol.36 (Summer), pp. 85-97

Stohl, Cynthia; Michael Stohl and Lucy Popova (2010), "A New Generation of Corporate Codes of Ethics", *Journal of Business Ethics,* Vol. 90, pp. 607–622

Taylor, Paul W. (1975), '*Principles of Ethics: An Introduction,* Dickerson Publishing Co., Inc., Encino, California, pp. 1

Taylor, S. A. and, T. L. Baker (1994), "An Assessment of the Relationship between Service Quality and Customer Satisfaction in the Formation of Consumers' Purchase Intentions", *Journal of Retailing*, Vol. 70, No. 2, pp. 163-78

Trevino, L K and M E Brown (2004), "Managing to be Ethical: Debunking Five Business Ethics Myths', *Journal of Academy of Management Executive* Vol. 18, pp. 69–81

Valenzuela, Leslier M.; Jay P. Mulki and Jorge Fernando Jaramillo (2010), "Impact of Customer Orientation, Inducements and Ethics on Loyalty to the Firm: Customers' Perspective", *Journal of Business Ethics*, Vol. 93, pp. 277-291

Vedamani, Gibson G. (2008), Retail Management, Third Edition, Jaico Publishing House, Mumbai, pp. 3-4.

Vitell, Scott J.; Kumar C. Rallapalli and Anusorn Singhapakdi (1993), "Marketing Norms: The Influence of Personal Moral Philosophies and Organizational Ethical Culture", *Journal of the Academy of Marketing Science*, Vol. 21, No.4, pp. 331-337

Whysall, Paul (2000), "Stakeholder Mismanagement in Retailing: A British Perspective" *Journal of Business Ethics*, Vol. 23, pp. 19-28

Whysall, Paul (1998), "Ethical Relationship in Retailing: Some Cautionary Tales", *Business Ethics: A European Review*, Vol. 7, No.2, pp.103-110

Yoo, Boonghee and Naveen Donthu (2002), "The Effects of Marketing Education and Individual Cultural Values on Marketing Ethics of Students", *Journal of Marketing Education,* Vol. 24 No. 2, pp. 92-103

Yücel, Recep; Halil Elibol and Osman Dağdelen (2009) "Globalisation and International Marketing Ethics Problems", *International Research Journal of Finance and Economics*, Vol. 26, pp. 93-104

Zolingen, Simone J. van; Hakan Honders (2010), "Metaphors and the Application of a Corporate Code of Ethics", *Journal of Business Ethics*, Vol. 92, pp. 385–40

CHAPTER 2

REVIEW OF LITERATURE

The literature on business and marketing ethics is wide and extensive. Several research studies on ethics in business have been conducted during the past four decades. Most of these studies examined the ethical beliefs and practices of managers (Lee et al., 2010; Lam and Shi, 2008; Higgins, 2005; Napal, 2003; Kujala, 2001; Deshpande, 1997; Singhapakdi and Vitell, 1993; Singhapakdi and Vitell, 1990; Izrali, 1988; Kidwell et al., 1987 and Ferrell and Weaver, 1978) and the perceptions of students about marketing ethics (Ruegger and King, 1992; Mc Nicholos and Zimmerer, 1985 and Goodman and Crawford, 1974) But only a few studies have focused attention specifically on ethics in retail practices (Kurt and Hacioglu 2010; Robinson, 2010; Sarma, 2007; Lavorata and Pontier, 2005; Dubinsky et al., 2004; Whysall, 2000, 1998; Deshpande, 1997; Levy and Dubinsky, 1983; Dornoff and Tankersley, 1976, 1975). Some of the major studies are reviewed in as under:-

Ardichvili et al. (2012) focused on comparative analysis of perceptions of ethical business cultures in large business organisations from four largest emerging economies, commonly referred to as the BRICs (Brazil, Russia, India, and China) and from the US. The data were collected from 13,000 managers and employees of business organisations in five countries. The study found significant differences among BRIC countries. The respondents from India and Brazil provided more favorable assessments of ethical cultures of their organisations than their counterparts from China and Russia. Overall, highest mean scores were accorded by the respondents from India, USA, and Brazil. There were significant similarities in ratings between the US and Brazil. To test the hypotheses, MANOVA was conducted with country as the independent variable and the items of ethical practices as the dependent variables. The authors opined that indigenous multinational corporations (MNCs) from BRIC countries had gained increasing presence and influenced global trade due to the fact that these countries were following unique paths, determined by specific combinations of internal culture and institutional conditions and legacies and influenced by societal norms and behaviour.

Davies et al. (2012) explored the extent to which consumers consider ethics in luxury goods consumption and whether there was a significant difference between consumers' propensity to consider ethics in luxury versus commodity purchase and whether consumers were ready to purchase ethical-luxury. They argued that prior research in ethical consumption focused on low value, commoditised product categories such as food, cosmetics and high street apparel and it has been debatable if consumers follow similar ethical consumption patterns in luxury purchases. They concluded that consumers' propensity to consider ethics was significantly lower in luxury purchases when compared to the commoditised purchases and explored some of the potential reasons for this reduced propensity to identify or act upon ethical issues in luxury consumptions.

Lii and Lee (2012) investigated the efficacy of three corporate social responsibility (CSR) initiatives viz., sponsorship, cause-related marketing (CRM), and philanthropy on consumer–company identification and brand attitude and, in turn, consumer citizenship behaviour. CSR reputation was proposed as the moderating variable that affects the relationship between CSR initiatives, consumer-company identification, and brand attitude. A total of 492 students were contacted, and 447 of them provided valid responses. The linear relationships among consumer company identification, brand attitude and behavioral responses (extra-role behaviour and in-role behaviour) were examined by employing a linear structural equation modeling analysis. For the measurement model, the GFI (0.919), AGFI (0.871), NFI (0.930) and CFI (0.942) values were satisfactory. The scale reliability was assessed by applying the internal consistency method. Cronbach alpha provided a reasonable estimate of internal consistency as its value ranged from 0.855 (extra-role behaviour) to 0.885 (in-role behaviour) which were greater than 0.7. The standardised loadings and average percentage of variance extracted (AVE) were used to measure convergent validity and to assess discriminant validity, the square root of the average variance extracted (AVE) in each construct was compared to the correlation coefficients between the two constructs. The results showed that all three CSR initiatives had a significant effect on consumer company identification and brand attitude.

Casali (2011) opined that in order to reduce the likelihood of unethical business practice, organisations, governments and managers are seeking new ways to better understand what guides management for ethical decision making. The study examined the development of the managerial ethical profile (MEP) scale. The MEP scale is a multilevel, self-reporting scale measuring the perceived influence that different dimensions of common ethical frameworks has on managerial decision making. The MEP scale measured on eight sub scales viz., economic egoism, reputation egoism, act utilitarianism, rule utilitarianism, self-virtue of self, virtue of others, act deontology, and rule deontology. The MEP scale was converted into an online instrument and linked to an e-mail message, sent to the members of a professional association of health care managers in Australia with 2,473 members. On the whole, 441 usable questionnaires were returned with a response rate of 18%. Confirmatory factor analysis (CFA) was used to provide evidence of scale validity. The finding of the study indicated eight factor model appeared to be the best theoretical construct suggesting ethical framework as multidimensional.

Limbu (2011) studied the effects of consumers' perceptions concerning the ethics of online retailers on web site customer satisfaction and loyalty. An online survey instrument was administered to a sample of 220 students who were enrolled in various business undergraduate classes at a mid size university located in the south western USA. The participants completed a questionnaire based on their latest online purchase. The measurement model and structural relationships were estimated using AMOS 18. They found non-deception, fulfillment and security as significant predictors of web site satisfaction. Only privacy was related directly with loyalty. While direct effects of fulfillment and non-deception on loyalty were not significant; satisfaction mediates these relationships. Results provided a strong support for the web site satisfaction-loyalty relationship. The study suggested that internet retailers must address ethical issues surrounding their web sites by protecting financial and personal information, delivering accurate products and avoiding deceptive practices.

Mulki and Jaramillo (2011) studied the role played by ethical reputation in amplifying the positive impact of value received by the customer on satisfaction with the supplier and ultimately loyalty. The responses were taken from 299 customers, concerning two large financial institutions within Chile. The study aimed at testing the relationships among ethical perceptions, customer value, satisfaction, and loyalty. The results showed that ethical perceptions about the organisation amplify the impact of customer value on customer satisfaction and eventually loyalty. The study contributed to the existing literature by showing that ethical perceptions from customers can help financial institutions in achieving higher levels of satisfaction and loyalty. The study however, relied on customer survey responses collected in one country and one industry and generalisability of findings is yet to be tested.

Nygaard et al. (2010) examined the effect of social power on corporate ethical values from a sample of 225 retailers. The results indicated a strong link between social power, ethics and commitment and these affected output performance. They found that brand owner's use of power affected corporate ethical values and both coercive and non-coercive sources of social power affected ethical outcomes. Coercive power deteriorated ethical values and referent power and expert power have the opposite effect. Further, ethical values have an impact on performance through retail company commitment among managers and employees.

Valenzuela et al. (2010) found customer orientation and development of long-term relationships with customers as significant for the growth and profit sustainability from 299 customers of financial institutions in Chile. They were of the opinion that businesses use special treatments, inducements and personal gestures to show their appreciation to customers. However, there were concerns about whether these inducements really create the right perceptions in customers' mind. They suggested that when customers believed firm as ethical and the inducements and special treatments received seen in a positive light and could help in developing customer loyalty.

Oumlil and Balloun (2009) investigated the ethical perceptions, religion, personal moral philosophies, corporate ethical values and ethical intentions of 172 US and Moroccan business managers. They also assessed the impact of cultural factors on business ethical decision making. The results demonstrated significant difference between the perceptions of managers of both countries regarding two personal moral philosophies, viz., idealism and relativism. Moroccan managers were more idealistic than the U.S. managers. The findings also presented a strong positive relationship between religion and idealism and female respondents found to be more ethical than their male counterparts.

Singhapakdi et al. (2008) examined the influences of personal characteristics and the organisational environment underlying the Thailand business people's ethical perceptions from 798 managers enrolled in executive MBA from eight public and five private universities. Corporate ethical values and idealism have positive influence on managers' perceptions about ethics. The ability to perceive the existence of an ethical problem was negatively influenced by relativism but positive relationship existed between ethics and perceived ethical problems with ethical intention.

Roman and Cuestas (2008) examined the conceptualisation and measurement of consumers' perceptions regarding the ethics of online retailers (CPEOR) and assessed the relationship between CPEOR, consumers' general Internet expertise and reported positive word of mouth (WOM). Results from a convenience sample of 357 online shoppers suggested that CPEOR could be operationalised as a construct composed of four dimensions viz. security, privacy, fulfillment, and non-deception. The findings through CFA and SEM indicated that consumers' general Internet expertise significantly improved CPEOR and CPEOR strong predictor of positive word of mouth.

Pettijohn et al (2008) evaluated salespeople's perceptions of the ethics of businesses in general, their employer's ethics, their attitudes as consumers, and the relationships existing between these perceptions and the sale force's job satisfaction and turnover intentions by obtaining data from 156 salespeople of 14 retailers dealing in shopping goods. The results indicated positive relationship between salesperson perceptions of business ethics, his/her employer's ethics, consumer attitudes, and the salesperson's job satisfaction and reduced turnover intentions. The attitudes as a consumer was significantly ($p < 0.001$) related to salespersons' perceptions of their employers' ethics and ethical behaviour significantly affected their sales force's satisfaction with their jobs and their likelihood of staying on their positions. The study suggested that all businesses need to behave ethically and promote their ethical behaviour as a means of building job satisfaction and reducing unwanted turnover. The study however considered the retail salespeople engaged in the sale of shopping goods and therefore, the generalisability of results was limited to this type of salesperson, i. e., shopping goods.

Li et al. (2008) conducted a survey of 316 respondents from Chinese enterprises and found the level of their work values as more likely in line with increasing age and education, and associated with employment position and gender. The authors found the older employees having the higher work values and the higher the education one receives, the higher the work values he/ she counts. Managers rated higher work values than the employees did, and male employees showed higher work value perceptions than their female counterparts. The results indicated that the employees' age, education, position and gender are important antecedents of work values, and these demographic effects could be a good revelation to enterprise management in both theory and practice.

Lam and Shi (2008) examined the effects of various demographic variables like age, gender, education and religion on ethical attitudes of working persons from the respondents from China and Hong Kong who provided the needed information through a questionnaire. The questionnaire comprised of two sections. The first section contained 26 items, divided into two dimensions, viz., rule based issues and social concerns. The second section contained information on demographic variables. It was found that gender difference was not significant in China, while in Hong Kong, females have a lower acceptability of unethical behaviour related to both dimensions, namely, rule based norms and social concerns. It was also viewed that respondents of the age of 45 years and above have lower acceptability of rule based norms in China. The study concluded that respondents who had university degree did not have higher ethical standards than counterparts who had no university degree. Moreover, religion has significant effect on ethical attitudes and Christianity was found to be most favourable to higher ethical standards.

Sarma (2007) in his research study entitled, "Ethics in Retailing-Perceptions of Management and Sales personnel", examined the ethical practices of retailers and the ethical beliefs of salespeople, through a questionnaire containing situations or practices which were considered to be ethically troublesome for retail salespeople. The situations were divided into customer related, peer related and work related. A total of 62 salespersons out of eight major retail outlets in Guwahati were approached. The study found that salespeople did face ethical dilemmas in relation with different stakeholders. The findings provided that only four out of thirty three situations were regarded as ethical issues by one third of respondents. The respondents wanted company guidelines on at least half of the situations evaluated by them. The results also highlighted that retailers had no clear policies and code of ethics for guiding their salespeople. They had developed some norms which they communicated at the time of induction which might not guaranteed ethical behaviour. The study suggested for the establishment of clear policies by the retail managers for their staff and communication of the same to them effectively so that they can do their work in an ethical manner. The study conducted in Guwahati, however, did not have strong organised retailing and the sample size was too small.

Roman and Munuera (2005) highlighted several key determinants and consequences of ethical behaviour of salespeople. The determinants of ethical behaviour were, reward system, control system, age and education. On the other hand, the consequences were role conflict, performance and job satisfaction. A total of 280 financial service salespeople were approached for their responses to the questionnaires provided to them. It was found that education had no influence on ethical behaviour and methods of compensation and control system were the important determinants of ethical behaviour. Moreover, a salesperson's ethical behaviour led to lower level of role conflict and higher level of job satisfaction but not higher performance. The main drawback of this study was less sample size. The study felt the need for further analysis of the relationship between ethical behaviour and other relevant behaviours that may take place during the interaction with the customers.

Lavorata and Pontier (2005) identified the ethical practices of convenience retailers and also assessed the ultimate relevance of ethical marketing for a retailer. The data were gathered through interviews of three types of stakeholders at French Consumer Research Organisation, 'Dia Mart'. The three stakeholders were management of major retailers, a firm specialising in consumer behaviour and environment specialists. They used 'Ethical Assessment Criteria' to analyse the traditional retailers' ethical actions. The criteria has six dimensions, viz., relation with civil society, relation with customers and suppliers, the environment, business facilities and subcontracting in emerging countries, relation with shareholders and labour and management relations. The findings suggested that ethics must be integrated into the marketing strategies of the retailers.

Higgins and Kelleher (2005) conducted comparative study on the ethical orientation of functional managers like marketing finance and human resource. A total of 30 managers were selected from ten Irish financial institutions. Three managers were taken from each institution of whom, one was marketing manager, another finance manager and third was human resource manager. A questionnaire containing seven ethical dilemmas was presented to them in a face to face interview. The respondents were asked to respond on a six point Likert scale ranging from 1 = 'extremely unacceptable' and 6 = 'extremely acceptable'. The findings showed a mean score of 2.54 indicating that the respondents regarded the behaviour dilemmas as more 'unacceptable'. The results also revealed that finance and human resource managers were more ethically oriented than their marketing counterparts.

Valentine and Fleischman (2004) evaluated the impact of ethics training on employees' perceptions about organisational ethics. A questionnaire was supplied to 1700 accounting, 850 human resource and 850 marketing and sales managers. The responses however, were received from 313 respondents with a response rate of 9.3%. Various statistical techniques like mean, standard deviation, correlation and MANCOVA were used for the purpose of data analysis. MANCOVA considered two variables, viz., 'corporate ethical values' and 'ethical environment' as dependent variables; 'presence of ethics training' as independent variable and 'years of job tenure' and 'job satisfaction' as covariates. The results provided that most of the respondents replied that their employers were 'moderately ethical' and they were relatively satisfied with their job. MANCOVA results indicated that respondents employed in organisations with formalized ethics training have more positive perceptions of organisational ethics than their counterparts who were working in organisations that have no such ethics training. Moreover, job satisfaction was significantly associated with corporate ethical values and ethical environment. However, the study obtained data from respondents through a mailed questionnaire, so chances of some biasness could not be ruled out.

Dubinsky et al. (2004) investigated the relationship between retail salespersons' moral philosophy (idealism and relativism) and their perceptions about ethically troublesome situations. The authors suggested some guidelines to retail managers regarding how to address the ethical issues of their salespeople. The sample size for the study comprised of 224 salespeople of 70 specialty stores. The respondents were provided with a questionnaire which was developed by using the scales of Dubinsky and Levy (1985) Factor analysis was used to extract different factors out of 29 items relating to ethical practices. Meanwhile, five factors emerged, namely, psychological pressure on customers, salesperson deception, poor customer service, price related items and salesperson excuses. The analysis was done with regression analysis, t-test, ANOVA and MANOVA. The results provided that relativism was not associated with all five factors of ethical retail practices however, idealism was negatively associated with retail salespeople' attitude towards four out of five factors. The study finally suggested that retail managers should provide training to their salespeople and should lead by giving their own example. The study however, examined solely specialty stores' sales people and thus, ignored the sales persons of other types of stores as well as retail managers.

Napal (2003) explored the impact of organisational size and structure on ethical conduct by obtaining data from 350 respondents, who were contacted through interviews and mailing. The findings revealed that both organisational size and structure have impact on the ethical conduct. It was reported that large organisations due to their bureaucratic nature and rigid structure have more tendency to engage in unethical behaviour. While the centralised organisations felt in a better position for ensuring rigid control in the form of code of ethics and corporate ethical policies. The study provided that 78% of the respondents considered the rule of fairness as extremely helpful to ethical conduct and same number of participants believed that participative style of management encourages an ethical approach in decision making. Moreover, majority of respondents (82%) reported that a code of ethics positively guided the business persons in the pursuit of their objectives. Finally, the behaviour of top management was reported to be significantly ethical than middle management and their co-workers.

Valentine and Barnett (2002) attempted to find out the relationship between existence of formal ethics code in organisations and employees' perceptions of organisations' ethical values. The overall sample size was 3000 marketing professionals, out of them, only 373 responded. The respondents were asked to indicate whether their organisations had a formal code of ethics. MANCOVA was used to examine the relationship between ethical code and perceptions of sales professionals of their organisations' ethical values. The findings revealed that one third of respondents' organisations have a formal code of ethics. The results indicated that sales professions whose organisations had ethics code have more positive perceptions of organisations' ethical values than their counterparts.

Thomas et al. (2002) examined the effects of ethical and unethical cues on customers' evaluations of the ethics of a service provider and their subsequent satisfaction with the service. They found customers responding to unethical cues in the environment through lower ethical assessments and satisfaction ratings, but that ethical cues may not necessarily increase satisfaction scores when compared to a neutral situation. The study suggested that ethical cues and an honest service provider lead to satisfaction with the service encounter, while unethical cues create dissatisfaction.

Ergeneli and Ankan (2002) in their study based on the perceptions of salespeople working in clothing and medical equipment sectors in Turkey, examined the differences between male and female salespersons' perceptions of ethical issues and the effect of demographic factors, like age and income etc. The responses were received from 248 salespeople who responded on a five point Likert scale based questionnaire. The analysis was done by using various statistical tools like mean, standard deviation, correlation and t-test etc. The findings revealed no significant difference in ethical perceptions based on gender. However, female salespeople had more ethical score than their male counterparts at two age groups viz. below 20 years of age and age group of 40-49 years.

Peterson et al. (2001) investigated the relationship of demographic factors like age and gender with ethical beliefs of business professionals. The study found that business professions in the younger age group exhibited a lower standard of ethical beliefs. However, in the younger age groups, the female demonstrated a higher level of ethical beliefs, while in the senior age group the male had higher level ethical beliefs. The results showed the influence of external factors like people at work, people at home and supervisor on ethical beliefs between age and gender by providing that business professionals above the age of 30 years were less influenced by external factors than those under the age of 30 years regardless of sex. The study also suggested for the preparation of code of ethics and development of ethical culture, which are essential for shaping employees' behaviour.

Kujala (2001) in his paper entitled, "Analysing moral issues in stakeholders' relations," presented a framework for analysing managers' attitude towards moral issues in stakeholder relations. The framework has various types of stakeholders, viz., customers, employees, competitors, owners, suppliers, community, government, financers and the environment, which were based upon the interviews of five top managers and from review of literature. Each stakeholder relation has some moral issues, which were discussed in the framework. There were seven moral issues in relation with consumers viz. advertising, information, product safety and product quality etc. and ten moral issues in relation with employees such as right to just wages, participation, hiring and firing policies, discrimination and working conditions etc. The relationship with competitors have moral issues like fair play, price cutting, bribery, co-operation, consistency and stability etc. and the relation between suppliers and dealers facilitates fair business practices, paying the bills on time and extending all co-operation. He also explained the moral issues in relation with other stakeholders like community and government, financers and environment such as compliance with laws, tax base, risk evaluation and long term relations, pollution, product recycling and extinction of species. The framework assists the present research for exploring the ethical issues in retailing, keeping in view the expectations of all the stakeholders.

Honeycutt et al. (2001) explored the perceptions of automobile salespeople regarding legal and ethical behaviour and its relationship with age, education and method of compensation. A total of 184 salespeople responded through a questionnaire. The findings indicated that ethical perception was significantly associated in all five situations, while legal perception was significant only in two situations. The method of compensation was significantly associated at five percent level in four situations, but age was significantly associated with one situation and finally, education was insignificantly associated with ethical behaviour. The respondents were, however, selected conveniently, so the findings could not be generalised.

Whysall (2000) in his research article suggested that all companies expect to meet ethical norms in their dealings with their stakeholders as stakeholder groups tend not to stand in isolation. He cited examples of stakeholder mismanagement in British retailing with a view to drawing lessons from them and finally, developed a stakeholder model of a retail business.

Whysall (2000) presented a framework of stakeholders in retailing and discussed the significance of these stakeholders by citing several ethical issues in retailing to demonstrate the benefits that accrue from applying a stakeholder approach. The study suggested that such a framework offers a broader perspective and in particular, that rising concern for ethical issues in retailing is better articulated through such a framework. The study provided that customers might be exploited by retailers by pricing strategies and deceptive promotion; the suppliers felt threatened when imported loss leaders destabilise national markets; sourcing might raise political opposition and boycotts and government's relations with retailers were complex and operated on many levels. The study suggested that responsible retailers should obey the laws framed by the government.

Whysall (2000) in his study entitled, "Retailing and the Internet: a review of ethical issues," emphasised that internet has important ethical connotations for retailing. The study cited examples of retailers' difficulties in this respect, before considering use of the internet for ethical scrutiny of retailers by a spectrum of activists and agencies. The author focused on the positive use of the internet to publicise retailers' social responsibility contrasts with questionable exploitation of the Web's anonymity and the internet not only offers freedom of speech, but also widens opportunities for irresponsible activity. Ethical issues relating to e-commerce were identified and privacy was highlighted both as central to the ethics of e-retailing and as a critical factor in its development. The study argued that retail interest in the internet has focused around e-commerce but its impact on retailer image both positive and negative needs to be recognised.

Deshpande et al. (2000) studied the perceptions of proper ethical conduct of male and female Russian managers by obtaining data from 200 managers through a questionnaire consisting of 17 variables relating to business practices. A total of 129 managers responded out of which 54 were male and 75 were female. The findings provided that female managers considered various items, viz., doing business on company time, falsifying time, quality and quantity reports, calling in sick to take a day off and the acceptance of gifts and favours in exchange for professional treatment as more unethical than male managers.

Bone and Corey (2000) examined differences among packaging professionals, brand managers and consumers with respect to ethical sensitivity, values, perceived consequences of business practices and perceived industry norms from the responses of a random sample of 3000, i. e., packaging professional, brand managers and consumers, 1000 each. The study found that managers and consumers differed with respect to several important factors regarding ethical decision making, viz., ethical sensitivity, industry norms and perceived consequences of business practices. The results also revealed no difference among consumers and businesspeople with respect to moral values.

Abratt et al. (1999) in their study "Ethical Perceptions of South African Retailers: Management and Sales Personnel", explored the ethical beliefs of executives, managers and retail salespeople in South Africa. The data were collected through a 38 statements based questionnaire, divided into two categories, viz., work related and customer related issues. In total, 3000 questionnaires were handed out, while 570 people gave their responses out of which 86 were working as executives, 230 as managers and 263 as salespeople. Factor analysis was used to reduce the large number of variables into comprehensive dimensions, viz., work related statements into –dishonest non adherence, socialising and self indulgence and customer related statements into-dishonesty, dissonant communication and dishonest executives. Analysis was done through statistical tools like mean and ANOVA. The results highlighted the difference in the ethical beliefs of executives, managers and salespeople and indicated salespeople as doing something more unethical than managers and executives regarding both work related and customer related factors. It was suggested that retailers must formulate ethical policies and procedures for their salespeople and communicate them so that they can solve the ethical dilemmas in the retail practices.

Whysall (1998) studied ethical relationship in retailing by quoting examples of British companies facing problems of ethical nature. The study remarked that ethical retailing is adequate if it considers wide range of interactions with all stakeholders such as customers, employees, suppliers, government and community. He opined that retailers must be aware of the ethical dimension and ethical retailing involves justice, equity, honesty, integrity and respect in relation with all stakeholders in retailing.

Dawson (1997) looked at ethical differences between men and women in the sales profession by mailing 550 questionnaires to the employees of two firms, who were in the sales department. But only 203 responses were received of which 109 were male and 94 were female respondents. The data so collected were analysed with the help of ANOVA. The ANOVA results indicated a significant difference between male and female responses on eight out of twenty statements. The findings also provided that the ethical standards did change with age and years of experience for both men and women. It was found that as age and experience progressed, ethical levels became higher for both sexes. Moreover, the ethical differences between men and women were highest at younger age and earlier experience levels and vise-versa. However, the sample size was relatively small which might not be representative of the sales profession as a whole.

Burns and Bready (1996) studied the perceptions of students regarding retail ethics by selecting two samples from Malaysia and USA and compared the perceptions of respondents from two cultures by applying t test. They used the scale developed by Dubinsky and Levy (1985). The scale comprised of 38 items relating to ethical retail practices having Alpha value of 0.8. The authors found significant mean differences in the perceptions of students regarding ethical retail practices. The Malaysian students have lower ethical perceptions than their USA counterparts.

Verbeke et al. (1996) examined the effect of organisation's environment, climate and personality traits on the ethical decision making of salespeople. For data collection questionnaires were distributed among 190 sales managers. Each manager got five questionnaires and who were asked to give those questionnaires to their salespeople.

One questionnaire to one of their best salesmen, another to a less productive salesman and the remaining three to other staff and one of them must be a woman. The study had a response rate of 19.5%. The findings revealed that two factors of organisation environment, viz., 'control orientation' and 'internal communication' positively affected ethical decision making. In addition to this, organisation climate and personality traits also affected ethical decision making. But another factor of organisation environment (competitiveness of the market) did not affected ethical decision making.

Schwepker and Ingram (1996) examined the relationship between salespersons' moral judgement and their job performance. They defined moral judgement as, 'an individual's decision as to whether something is considered ethical or unethical'. For data collection, 314 questionnaires were distributed among salespeople of 33 firms in USA of which 152 responses were received. The relationship between moral judgement and job performance was observed with the help of regression analysis. The results depicted significant relationship between moral judgement and job performance for three out of four dimensions. It was also found that those salespeople who took ethical decisions had higher job performance. Only one dimension of job performance, viz., 'providing information' was not related with moral judgment. Moreover, moral judgement had a positive effect on performance for men than women, while, the performance of salespeople above 40 years was affected by their moral judgement. Finally, those respondents who had college degree, felt that their performance was enhanced with moral judgments and vise-versa.

Rowwas (1996) scrutinised the ethical beliefs of 200 Austrian consumers through a questionnaire. MANCOVA was performed with the four dimensions of the consumer ethics scale as dependent variables with machiavellianism as co-variate and gender as an independent variable. The results revealed that respondents considered one dimension of consumer ethics scale, viz., 'actively benefiting from illegal activity' as unethical. It was found that Austrian customers accepted machiavellianism (egoism) more than their counterparts American customers did. Moreover, Austrian customers gave little weight to idealism than to relativism while making ethical decisions. Finally, Austrian women were more ethical than Austrian men in terms of their ethical beliefs.

Cole and Smith (1996) assessed the perceptions of business students and of business practitioners regarding ethics in business. A survey consisting of a series of brief ethical situations was completed by 537 senior business majors and 158 experienced business people. They responded to the situations, first, as they believed the typical business person would respond and, second, as they believed the ethical response would be. The results revealed that both students and business people perceived a significant gap between the ethical response to the given situations and the typical business person's response. Students were significantly more accepting than business people of questionable ethical responses, and they also had a more negative view of the ethics of business people than did the experienced business people. It was also found that female students scored significantly higher than their male counterparts on ethical response to eight of the ten statements, but on the other hand, no significant difference was discovered between male and female business people. Moreover, business people of the age group of 20-35 years scored significantly lower to half of the statements. The study finally, suggested that businesses need to increase their efforts to promote ethical conduct and to make 'ethics' a well known priority in all actions and policies.

Singhapakdi et al. (1995) examined the marketing practitioners' perception regarding the importance of ethics and social responsibility in achieving organisational effectiveness. They analysed the relative influence of corporate ethical values and personal moral philosophies, viz., idealism and relativism on a marketer's perceptions regarding the ethics and social responsibility. A total of 2000 professional members of American Marketing Association were randomly selected for the survey and out of which only 453 people responded on nine point Likert scale based questionnaire ranging from 1 = strongly disagree to 9 = strongly agree. The results provided that respondents believed ethics and social responsibility as somewhat important in achieving organisational effectiveness. The findings indicated that two moral philosophies, viz., idealism and relativism, the former influenced positively and the latter negatively, a marketer's perceptions regarding the importance of ethics and social responsibility in achieving organisational effectiveness. The study however, focused entirely on the perceptions of marketing managers, thus, ignoring the perceptions of other stakeholders like consumers.

Takala and Uusitalo (1995) investigated ethical issues by focusing on various ethical theories, viz., utilitarianism, deontology and virtue ethics in the context of retail business in Finland. They opined that deontological theory suggests prima facie ideals which can direct our thinking regarding right and wrong and the utilitarian focuses on 'the greatest good for the greatest number', by performing a social cost/benefit analysis and acting on it. All benefits and costs of a particular act are being considered and summarised as the net of all benefits minus all costs. If the net result is positive, the act is morally acceptable and vice versa. Virtue ethics ensures that all professional activities can be understood as guided by some special artificial virtues. They found that there prevailed among retailers some kind of confusion about what was ethical and what was unethical in their daily professional practices. To avoid ethical dilemmas, four main principles were put forth by the Finnish retailers namely: freedom versus rules; principles versus moralising; boundaries versus transition; economy and moral versus subjective judgment and felt the need to follow the laws and regulations set by authorities as an important prerequisite for the success of business concern.

Sautar et al. (1994) in their study examined the impact of work environment factors on ethical decision making. The study determined the frequency with which employees facing an ethical conflict, the general areas in which employees experience ethical conflicts and how they response to these ethical conflicts. The data were collected from a sample of 301 companies drawn from a list of Westren Australian companies listed in stock exchange. Three questionnaires were sent to the managing directors for distribution to an employee from each of the three levels of management, viz., top, middle and supervisory. But only 105 usable questionnaires were returned. The findings provided that about 40% of the respondents reported no instances of ethical conflict over the past five years. The areas in which the ethical conflicts were mostly common were dealing with the internal stakeholders such as superiors and dealing with external stakeholders such as customers and suppliers. The authors also highlighted the practices which cause the ethical conflicts like concealment of information, lack of concern for long term and being unfair to individuals. In response to a question, 'how they response to these ethical conflicts?', about 42 percent of the total respondents replied that they did what they thought was right according to their personal ethics and the rest of the respondents reported that they did what the company expected. However, most of the respondents were top managers and the number of lower level employees who face more ethical conflicts was small.

Rowwas et al. (1994) investigated the ethical beliefs, ethical ideologies and degree of machiavellianism (egoism) of consumers from two countries viz. Egypt and Lebanon. The former was a peaceful country at that time and the latter had suffered from civil unrest and terrorism. The data obtained from 1000 respondents were analysed by using

MANOVA and discriminant analysis. The former was used to determine whether the ethical beliefs of two sample groups differ with regard to the variables of interest and the latter was used to determine the direction and intensity of relationships. It was found that two samples differ significantly in terms of ethical beliefs, ethical ideologies and machiavellianism. The results provided that Egyptian consumers viewed all types of questionable statements as more unethical than the Labanese consumers. Moreover, Labanese consumers were less sensitive to consumer ethical issues, less idealistic, more relativistic and more machiavellianism as compared to their Egyptian counterparts, who were more sensitive, more idealistic, less relativistic and less machiavellianism. The study however, used the convenience sampling which might have led to biasness and faulty interpretations.

Rallapalli et al. (1994) in their exploratory research studied the relationship between consumers' ethical beliefs and their personality traits. The primary data were collected 295 students of a major University in USA through a questionnaire. Two statistical techniques, viz., simple correlation and canonical correlation were used for data analysis. The former was used to examine the relationship between each personality trait and each dimension of consumer ethics scale and the latter determined the associations of all the four dimensions of consumer ethics scale with the personality traits. The results demonstrated that only 14 out of 40 personality traits and consumer ethics pairs had significant relationship. The 'need for autonomy', one of the personality traits was strongly and positively correlated with 'actively benefiting from an illegal action', while 'or social desirability was negatively correlated with 'actively action' one of the dimensions of consumer ethics scale.

'oped a scale to measure the marketing related norms of considering codes of ethics of American Marketing

Association (AMA). The scale consisted of five dimensions, viz., price distribution; information and contracts; product and promotion; obligation and disclosures and general honesty and integrity. A random sample of 2000 managers were drawn from mailing list of AMA but only 542 people responded The reliability of the scale was tested by using co-efficient alpha and the validity of the dimensions of marketing norms scale was tested by correlating the five dimensions of norms scale with the two dimensions of Ethical Position Questionnaire, viz., idealism and relativism. As an additional test of the validity of the scale, standard multiple regression analysis was performed with each dimensions of marketing norms scale as dependent variable and ethical climate, moral philosophy and demographic variables such as gender and income as independent variables. It was found that moral philosophy; income and gender were significant predictors of marketers' price and distribution norms, obligation and disclosure norms and general honesty and integrity. The ethical climate has little effect on one's acceptance of these marketing norms. The main drawback of the study was that it has taken a sample from AMA only, the further research work is needed to test the marketing norms scale by using other national and international sample of marketing managers.

Singhapakdi and Vitell (1993) explored the relative influence of personal and professional values underlying the ethical Judgements of marketing practitioners. A self made questionnaire was used for collecting data from 2000 marketing practitioners, who were the members of American Marketing Association (AMA), but only 492 respondents responded with response rate of 24.6%. The findings indicated that the ethical judgements of marketing practitioners were partially explained by his/her professional and personal values. The study suggested that individual firms profession in general must establish professional norms/codes of ethics to guide the conduct of its members.

Vogel (1992) found business ethics as not universally similar, but vary by country to country by arguing that Americans are more sensitive to and concerned with issues of business ethics than other countries because the values of business civilisation are so engrained in the national psyche. He presented three critical differences in business ethics between Americans and Europeans. Firstly, he argued that Americans make ethical decisions based on individual values, while Europeans refer to the norms of the community, labeled as 'communicative' or 'consensual' business ethics. Secondly, Americans use laws and formal rules as opposed to the informal mechanisms of social control in Europe. A third critical difference was the American preoccupation with universal application of American rules and procedures.

Trawick et al. (1991) found purchasing agents tend to avoid unethical salespersons. The sample consisted of members of a purchasing agents' association. Twenty-two items related to different salespersons' behaviour, such as giving gifts to purchasing agents and giving preferential treatment to certain purchasing agents, were examined. The results provided that as salesperson's actions were rated more unethical, purchasing agents' intentions to choose that supplier declined. The agent also felt that the salespersons' unethical behaviour would harm his/her career more as the behaviours were rated more unethical. The authors were of the opinion that two forces were acting on the intentions of the agent to purchase from the unethical salesperson – an external reward/ punishment consideration and an internal self- reward.

Norris and Gifford (1988) Collected both comparative and longitudinal data between 1976 and 1986 from retail store managers and retail students concerning their perceptions of ethical retail practices. Contrary to the popular belief that ethics have eroded over time, the results indicated significant increase in the ethical level of retail store managers, while a significant decrease in the perceptions of ethics of retail students.

The study conducted by **Dubinsky and Levy (1985)** suggested that retail salespeople apparently did not consider many situations as ethical. Only four of the eight situations which pose ethical problems were believed to be covered by company policies in most respondents' organisations. They opined that in some instances where policies existed, salespeople did not see the situations involving ethical issues and in other cases, situations which were seen ethically troublesome were not believed to be addressed by stated policies. They found that retail salespeople wanted more policy help than they presently had. Also when testing whether salespeople's sex, retail sales experience, and time in company were related to their ethical beliefs, no significant mean differences were found. They opined that retail salespeople like other boundary-spanning personnel face some ethical dilemma. They suggested that to deal with ethical issues, salespeople should benefit from company policies which address to situations posing ethical problems and a concerted effort by the management to examine, formulate, and execute policies that serves as help, not hindrance, to the sales staff.

Levy and Dubinsky (1983) conducted studies with retail sales personnel from a major department store chain and a national specialty store chain. Two kinds of stores were selected as the sampling frame because of the high degree of selling activities inherent in their sales positions. It was believed that such sales jobs have more potential for ethically troubling situations to arise than positions where the employee was primarily a checkout clerk or some other kind of "non-sales" retail sales person. One of the major purposes was to provide the researchers and retail managers with a fairly comprehensive list of potentially ethically troublesome situations. The comparisons between two organisations were included so that an examination could be made of the similarities and differences between the ethical perceptions of department store and specialty store sales people. They were of the opinion that unless retail salespeople know how to address ethically troublesome situations which may arise, they may engage in behaviour which run counter to their personal and organisational objectives. They identified 31 situations which may be ethically troublesome to the retail salespeople. For each situation, respondents were asked whether the situation should be addressed to by a policy and whether their company had such a policy that did so. The department store and specialty store salespeople, generally agreed on which situations required a company policy and which were currently addressed to by a policy. Both groups, however, were apparently confused by the existence of policies for some situations which were not believed to be ethically troublesome.

Ferrell and Weaver (1978) examined the personal beliefs of marketing practitioners about ethical behaviour of managers, their peers and top management, on the basis of data collected through a systematic random sample of 280 marketing managers of American Marketing Association (AMA). A self made questionnaire, consisting six response areas and 17 behaviour related statements, was utilised for data collection. A total of 133 respondents gave their responses on five point Likert scale ranging from "not at all unethical" to "very unethical". The findings indicated marketing managers as more ethical in comparison with their peers and top management and they have higher ethical standards of conduct than their existing enforced corporate policy.

Dornoff and Tankersley (1975) studied social responsibility perceived by retail store managers and whether these perceptions vary with different types of retailers. Three types of retail establishments were chosen to be sampled: discount house, specialty stores and department stores. Although one would expect that most retailers interested in protecting their consumer franchise by guarding against actions causing customer dissatisfaction. The results of retailers' responses to the actions taken in the situations clearly demonstrated that retailers were more often concerned with increasing profit than with their role as a socially responsible institution. In most situations, the retailers' objectives of consumer satisfaction and profitability were not regarded as harmonious and significant perceptual differences between retailers toward the actions taken in purchase conflict situations. Except for few cases, there were significant differences between the perceptions of retailers and there involved misleading promotion of product use and the handling of finance charges. The main wrong doer found to be the discount houses, followed by the department stores, and then by the specialty stores.

Research Gap

The review of literature indicates that nature and extent of ethical values in retailing practices has not been studied extensively. Most of the studies conducted so far in retailing ethics are theoretical in nature and even those who studied empirically; studied just the perception of one group of stakeholders in retailing, i. e., salespeople or retailers or consumers. Further, most of the studies have been done in developed countries like USA and UK and developing countries like India has dearth of research on retailing ethics. All this indicates a gap in literature about the perceptions of ethical retail practices from the perceptions of various stakeholders, viz. customers, retailers, wholesalers, manufacturers and regulatory bodies. Hence, the focus of the present study has been on the perceptions of ethical values in retailing practices from the view points of all the stakeholders in Indian context. Moreover, the impact of ethical values on customer satisfaction has also been not studied yet. The present study also examines the impact of ethical values on customer satisfaction.

References

Abratt, Russell; M. Bendixen and K. Drop (1999), "Ethical Perceptions of South African Retailers: Management and Salespersonnel", *International Journal of Retail and Distribution Management*, Vol. 27, No. 2, pp. 91-105

Ardichvili, Alexandre; Douglas Jondle; Brenda Kowske; Edgard Cornachione; Jessica Li and Thomas Thakadipuram (2012), "Ethical Cultures in Large Business Organisations in Brazil, Russia, India, and China", *Journal of Business Ethics*, Vol. 105, pp. 415-528

Bone, Paula Fitzgerald and Robert John Corey (2000), "Packaging Ethics: Perceptual Difference among Packaging Professionals, Brand Managers and Ethically-Interested Consumers", *Journal of Business Ethics*, Vol. 24, pp. 199-213

Burns David J. and John T. Brady (1996), "Retail Ethics as Appraised by Future Business Personnel in Malaysia and United States", *The Journal of Consumer Affairs*, Vol. 30, No. 1, pp. 195-217

Casali, Gian Luca (2011), "Developing a Multidimensional Scale for Ethical Decision Making", *Journal of Business Ethics*, Vol. 104, pp. 485-497

Cole C. Barbara and Dennie L. Smith (1996), "Perceptions of Business Ethics: Students versus Business People", *Journal of Business Ethics*, Vol. 15, pp. 889-896

Davies, Iain A.; Zoe Lee and Ine Ahonkhai (2012), "Do Consumers Care about Ethical-Luxury?", *Journal of Business Ethics*, Vol. 106, pp. 37-51

Dawson, Leslie M. (1997), "Ethical Differences between Men and Women in the Sales Profession", *Journal of Business Ethics*, Vol. 16, pp. 1143-1152

Deshpande, S. P.; Jacob Joseph and V. V. Maximov (2000), "Perceptions of Proper Ethical Conduct of Male and Female Russian Managers", *Journal of Business Ethics*, Vol. 24, pp. 179-183

Deshpande, S. P. (1997), "Managers Perception of Proper Ethical Conduct: The Affect of Sex, Age and Level of Education", *Journal of Business Ethics*, Vol. 16, pp.79-85

Dornoff, R. J. and C. B. Tankersley (1976), "Do Retailers Practice Social Responsibility", *Journal of Retailing*, Vol. 51 (Winter), pp. 33–42

Dornoff, R. J. and C. B. Tankersley (1975), "Perceptual Differences in Market Transactions: A Source of Consumer Frustration", *Journal of Consumer Affair*, Vol. 9, pp. 97–103

Dubinsky, A J.; Rajan Nataraajan and Wen-Yeh Huang (2004), "The Influence of Moral Philosophies on Retail Salespeople's Ethical Perceptions", *The Journal of Consumer Affairs*, Vol. 38, No. 2, pp. 297-317

Dubinsky, A. J. and M. Levy (1985), "Ethics in Retailing Perceptions of Retail Salespeople", *Journal of Academy of Marketing Science*, Vol, 13 (1), pp. 1-16

Ergeneli, Azize and Semra Ankan (2000), "Gender Difference in Ethical Perceptions of Salespeople: An Empirical Examination in Turkey", *Journal of Business Ethics*, Vol. 40, pp. 247-260

Ferrell, O. C. and K. Mark Weaver (1978), "Ethical beliefs of marketing managers", *Journal of Marketing*, Vol. 42 (July), pp. 69-73

Goodman, Charles S. and Merle C. Crawford (1974), "Young Executives: A Source of New Ethics?", *Journal of Personnel*, Vol. 53, pp. 180-187.

Higgins, Eleanor O. and Bairbre Kelleher (2005), "Comparative Perspective on the Ethical Orientations of Human Resources, Marketing and Finance Functional Managers", *Journal of Business Ethics*, Vol. 56, pp. 275-288

Honeycutt, Jr. Earl D.; Myron Glassman; M. T. Zugelder and Kiran Karande (2001), "Determinants of Ethical Behaviour: A Study of Autosalespeople", *Journal of Business Ethics*, Vol. 32, pp. 69-79

Izraeli, D. (1988), "Ethical Beliefs and Behaviour among Managers: A Cross Cultural Perspective", *Journal of Business Ethics*, Vol. 7, pp. 263-271

Kidwell, J. M.; R. E. Stevens and A. L. Bethke (1987), "Differences in the Ethical Perceptions between Male and Female Managers: Myth or Reality", *Journal of Business Ethics*, Vol. 6, pp. 489-493

Kujala, Johanna (2001), "Analysing Moral Issues in Stakeholder Relations", *Business Ethics: A European Review*, Vol. 10, pp. 233-247

Kurt, Gizem and Gungor Hacioglu (2010), "Ethics as a Customer Perceived Value Driver in the Context of Online Retailing", *African Journal of Business Management*, Vol. 4, No. 5), pp. 672-677

Lam, Kit-Chun and Guicheng Shi (2008), "Factors Affecting Ethical Attitudes in Mainland China and Hong Kong", *Journal of Business Ethics*, Vol. 77, pp. 463-479

Lavorata, Laure and Suzanne Pontier (2005), "The Success of a Retailers' Ethical Policy: Focusing on Local Actions", *The Journal of Academy of Marketing Science Review*, Vol. 2005, No.12, pp.1-9

Lee, Monle; Anurag Pant and Abbas Ali (2010), "Does the Individualist Consume More? The Interplay of Ethics and Beliefs that Governs Consumerism across Cultures" *Journal of Business Ethics*, Vol. 93, pp. 567–581

Levy, M. and A. J. Dubinsky (1983), "Identifying and Addressing Retail Salespeople's Ethical Problems', *Journal of Retailing* Vol. 59, pp. 46–66

Li, Wanxian, Xinmei Liu andWeiwu Wan (2008), "Demographic Effects of Work Values and Their Management Implications", *Journal of Business Ethics*, Vol. 81, pp. 875-885

Lii, Yuan-Shuh and Monle Lee (2012), "Doing Right Leads to Doing Well: When the Type of CSR and Reputation Interact to Affect Consumer Evaluations of the Firm", *Journal of Business Ethics*, Vol. 105, pp. 69-81

Limbu Yam B.; Marco Wolf and Dale L. Lunsford (2011), "Consumers' Perceptions of Online Ethics and its Effects on Satisfaction and Loyalty", *Journal of Research in Interactive Marketing*, Vol. 5 No. 1, pp. 71-89

Mc Nichols, C. W. and T. W. Zimmerrer (1985), "Situation Ethics: An Empirical Study of Differentiators of Students' Attitudes", *Journal of Business Ethics*, Vol. 4, pp. 175-180

Mulki, Jay Prakash and Fernando Jaramillo (2011), "Ethical Reputation and Value Received: Customer Perceptions", *International Journal of Bank Marketing*, Vol. 29 No. 5, pp. 358-372

Napal, Geetanee (2003), "Ethical Decision Making in Business: Focus on Mauritius", *Business Ethics: A European Review*, Vol. 12, No.1, pp. 54-63

Norris, Donald G. and John B. Gifford (1988), "Retail Store Managers' and Students' Perceptions of Ethical Retail Practices: A Comparative and Longitudinal Analysis (1976–1986)", *Journal of Business Ethics*, Vol. 7, pp. 515-524

Nygaard, Arne and Biong, Harald (2010), "The Influence of Retail Management's Use of Social Power on Corporate Ethical Values, Employee Commitment, and Performance", *Journal of Business Ethics*, Vol. 97, pp. 87-108

Oumlil, A. Ben and Joseph L. Balloun (2009), "Ethical Decision Making Difference between American and Moroccan Managers", *Journal of Business Ethics*, Vol. 84, pp. 457-478

Peterson, D.; Rhoads, A. and Vaught, B. C. (2001), "Ethical Beliefs of Business Professionals: A Study of Gender, Age and External Factor", *Journal of Business Ethics*, Vol. 31, pp.225-231

Pettijohn, Charles, Linda Pettijohn and A. J. Taylor (2008), "Salesperson Perceptions of Ethical Behaviours: Their Influence on Job Satisfaction and Turnover Intentions *Journal of Business Ethics*, Vol. 78, pp. 547–557

Rallapalli C. Kumar; Scott J. Vitell; Frank A. Wiebe and James H. Barnes (1994), "Consumer Ethical Beliefs and Personality Traits: An Exploratory Analysis", *Journal of Business Ethics*, Vol. 13, pp. 487-495

Robinson, Pamela K. (2010), "Responsible Retailing: The Practice of CSR in Banana Plantations in Costa Rica", *Journal of Business Ethics*, Vol. 91 pp. 279–289

Roman, Sergio and Pedro J Cuestas (2008), "The Perceptions of Consumers Regarding Online Retailers' Ethics and Their Relationship with Consumers' General Internet Expertise and Word of Mouth: A Preliminary Analysis", *Journal of Business Ethics,* Vol. 83, pp. 641-651

Roman Sergio and J L Munuera (2005), "Determinants and Consequences of Ethical Behaviour: An Empirical Study of Salespeople", *European Journal of Marketing,* Vol. 39, No. 5/6, pp. 473-495

Rowwas, Mohammed Y. A. (1996), "Consumer Ethics: An empirical Investigation of Austrian Consumers", *Journal of Business Ethics,* Vol. 15, pp. 1009-1019

Rowwas, Mohammed Y. A.; Scott J. Vitell and Jamel A. Al-Khatib (1994), "Consumer Ethics: The Possible Effect of Terrorism and Civil Unrest on the Ethical Values of Consumers", *Journal of Business Ethics*, Vol. 13, pp. 223-231

Ruegger, D. and S. W. King (1992), "A Study of the Effects of Age and Gender upon Students Business Ethics" *Journal of Business Ethics,* Vol. 11, pp. 179-186

Sarma, Nripendra Narayan (2007), "Ethics in Retailing-Perception of Management and Sales Personnel", *(http:// dspace.iimk.ac.in/bitstream/2259/388/1/61-68.pdf)*, last accessed on March 20, 2012

Sautar, Geoffrey; M. M. Mc Neil and Caron Molster (1994), "The Impact of the Work Environment on Ethical Decision Making: Some Australian Evidence", *Journal of Business Ethics,* Vol. 13, pp. 327-339

Schwepker, Jr. harles H. and Thomas N. Ingram (1996) Improving Sales Performance through Ethics: The Relationship between Salesperson Moral Judgment and Job Performance", *Journal of Business Ethics*, Vol. 15, pp. 1151-1160

Singhapakdi, A. and S. J. Vitell, (1990), "Marketing Ethics: Factors Influencing Perceptions of Ethical Problems and Alternatives", *Journal of Macro marketing (Spring)*, pp. 4-18

Singhapakdi, Anusorn; Kenneth L. Kraft; Scott J. Vitell and Kumar C. Rallapalli (1995), "The Perceived Importance of Ethics and Social Responsibility on Organisational effectiveness: A Survey of Marketers", *Journal of Academy of Marketing Science*, Vol. 23, No. 1, pp. 49-56

Singhapakdi, Anuson and Scott J. Vitell (1993), "Personal and Professional Values Underlying the Ethical Judgements of Marketers", *Journal of Business Ethics*, Vol. 12, pp. 525-533

Singhapakdi, Anusorn, Mahesh Gopinath, Janet K. Marta and Larry L. Carter (2008), "Antecedents and Consequences of Perceived Importance of Ethics in Marketing Situations: A Study of Thai Businesspeople", *Journal of Business Ethics*, Vol. 81, pp. 887-904

Takala, Tuomo and Outi Uusitalo (1995), "Retailers' Professional and Professio-Ethical Dilemmas: The Case of Finnish Retailing Business, *Journal of Business Ethics*, Vol. 14, pp. 893-907

Thomas, James L., Scott J. Vitell, Faye W. Gilbert, Gregory M. Rose (2002), "The Impact of Ethical Cues on Customer Satisfaction with Service", *Journal of Retailing*, Vol. 78, pp. 167–173

Trawick, I. Frederick; John E. Swan, Gail W. Mc Gee and David R. Rink (1991), 'Influence of Buyer Ethics and Salesperson Behaviour on Intention to Choose a Supplier', *Journal of the Academy of Marketing Science*, Vol. 19 (1), pp. 17–23.

Valentine, Sean and Gary Fleischman (2004), "Ethics, Training and Businesspersons' Perceptions of Organisational Ethics", *Journal of Business Ethics*, Vol. 52, pp. 381-390

Valentine, Sean and Tim Barnett (2002), "Ethics Codes and Sales Professionals' Perceptions of their Organisations' Ethical Values", *Journal of Business Ethics*, Vol. 40, pp. 191-200

Valenzuela Leslier M.; Jay P. Mulki and Jorge Fernando Jaramillo (2010), "Impact of Customer Orientation, Inducements and Ethics on Loyalty to the Firm: Customers' Perspective" *Journal of Business Ethics*, Vol. 93, pp. 277–291

Verbeke, William; Cok Ouwerkerk and Ed Peelen (1996), "Exploring the Contextual and Individual Factors on Ethical Decision Making of Salespeople', *Journal of Business Ethics*, Vol. 15, pp. 1175-1187

Vitell, Scott J; Kumar C. Rallapalli and Anusorn Singhapakdi (1993), "Marketing Norms: The Influence of Personal Moral Philosophies and Organisational Ethical

Culture", *Journal of the Academy of Marketing Science*, Vol. 21, No.4, pp. 331-337

Vogel, D. (1992), "The Globalisation of Business Ethics: Why America Remains Distinctive?", *California Management Review*, Vol. 35 (1), pp. 30–49

Whysall, Paul (2000), "Retailing and the Internet: A Review of Ethical Issues", *International Journal of Retail & Distribution Management*, Vol. 28 (11), pp. 481-489

Whysall, Paul (2000), "Addressing Ethical Issues in Retailing: A Stakeholder Perspective", *International Review of Retail, Distribution and Consumer Research*, Vol. 10 (3), July, pp. 305–318

Whysall, Paul (2000), "Stakeholder Mismanagement in Retailing: A British Perspective", *Journal of Business Ethics*, Vol. 23, pp. 19-28

Whysall, Paul (1998), "Ethical Relationship in Retailing: Some Cautionary Tales", *Business Ethics: A European Review*, Vol. 7 (2), pp. 103-110

CHAPTER 3
RESEARCH DESIGN AND METHODOLOGY

The chapter examines in detail the nature, scope and need of the study, particularly in the form of hypotheses and objectives formulated within the framework of research gap which emerged out of the existing literature reviewed and ongoing retailing practices in India. Moreover, determination of sample size; generation of scale items, and the statistical tools used in the study have also been summarised along with limitations of the study. These are as under:-

3.1 Nature and Scope of the Study

The present study entitled, "Nature and Extent of Ethical Values in Retailing Practices," is chain type and exploratory vis-à-vis evaluative in nature. It aims both to bridge up the gap in the literature and to find out strategic action plan for policy making. The study examines empirically, retailing ethics from the perspectives of different stakeholders in retailing, viz., retailers, customers, wholesalers, manufacturers and regulatory agencies together by unearthing the ethical issues in the given research domain. Finally, it examines the impact of retailing ethics on customer satisfaction and also suggests strategic action plan for better ethical retail practices so as to satisfying the customers and making them loyal to the retail store for better business.

3.2 Need of the Study

Ongoing process of globalisation, privatisation and liberalisation of Indian economy has resulted into sharp rise in retail sector, that too in the form of collaboration with various foreign companies. Retailing, being emerging as strong integral part of Indian business in a big way, is the second largest employer after agriculture and contributing about 14% of GDP of Indian economy. The retail industry is the first link in the distribution chain from customers' point of view. It is therefore, vital for the retailers to act in an ethical manner because they affect the lives of many people rather the whole of the society. The study of ethics is an integral part of development of durable relationship between companies and their customers and, thus, is an inescapable approach for retailers as well. But little is known about ethical practices of retailers despite the fact that it plays such a vital socio- economic role in the economy. No doubt, several studies have been conducted on business and marketing ethics, particularly in affluent countries like USA and UK, but only a few of them have touched the area of retailing ethics in Indian context. Even those worked on retailing ethics, studied it partially and theoretically (Sarma, 2007; Lavorata and Pontier, 2005; Dubinsky et al., 2004; Whysall, 2000; Abratt et al., 1999; Whysall, 1998; Bellizzi and Hite, 1989). In fact, none has yet studied the nature and extent of ethical retail practices empirically from all possible angles in Indian context. So, the present study investigates the nature and extent of ethical retail practices on the basis of perceptions of retailers, customers, wholesalers, manufacturers and regulatory agencies. A strategic action plan has also been worked out to strengthen the ethical values in Indian retail business (Sharma and Sharma, 2011, 2009). Besides its academic value, the present research will be helpful to all the stakeholders in retailing.

3.3 Hypotheses and Objectives

Retailing involves several stakeholders such as consumers, suppliers, employees and regulatory bodies etc. (Sharma and Sharma, 2011, 2009; Sarma, 2007; Lavorata and Pontier, 2005; Dubinsky et al., 2004; Whysall, 2000, 1998 and 1995) who are directly or indirectly associated with retailing processes and activities. They have different expectations from retailers which need be fulfilled in an ethical manner (Kaptein, 2008 and Kujala, 2002). While dealing with these stakeholders, retailers' dealings need to be based on trust, commitment, integrity, honesty, fairness, co-operation and truthfulness

(Whysall, 1998). This creates a favourable attitude of these groups towards retailers. Different stakeholders have different perceptions of ethical practices in retailing (Kaptein, 2008; Kujala, 2001 and Whysall, 2000). This leads to the development of first hypothesis and objective:-

> H_1 *There is wide ranging difference of opinion with regard to ethical practices in retailing among different stakeholders.*
>
> O_1 *To examine the perceptions of different stakeholders about ethical retail practices.*

The ultimate consumer is one of the most important stakeholders whom retailers supply goods with all planned and meaningful efforts. The aim of modern retailer is not sale and profit only, but to satisfy customers on continual basis. When a customer gets performance equals to expectations, he/she is satisfied and vice versa. In a retail store, the customer is satisfied if he gets desired products at right place, time and reasonable price. If a retailer behaves ethically, the customer is satisfied from that retailer (Valenzuela et al., 2010 and Kenhova et al., 2003). Customer satisfaction inherent to a specific transaction represents an immediate post-purchase evaluation, indicating affective reaction toward the experience with the product or service. Costumers experience some satisfaction when they perceive sales behaviour as fair (Oliver, 1993). Ròman and Ruiz (2005) also opined that customer satisfaction increases when a customer perceives a seller's behaviour as ethical. Bejou et al., (1998) found ethics as a determinant of customer satisfaction and Roman (2003) found a salesperson's ethical behaviour leading to higher customer satisfaction. Hassan et al. (2008) developed a contingency restrictive model of Islamic ethical sales behaviour on customer satisfaction and emphasised that ethical sales behaviour as perceived by the customer, directly influences customer satisfaction. The results from the exploratory study of Jamal and Naser (2003) showed that the perceived ethical standard of the customer relationship advisors had a positive impact on customer satisfaction. It indicates that ethics has direct and positive impact on customer satisfaction. Thus, the second hypothesis and objective are:-

> **H₂ *Ethical values positively influence customer satisfaction.***
> **O₂ *To find out the impact of ethical values on customer satisfaction.***

Perceptions of different age groups of retailers about ethical values have been examined by many researchers (Rugger and King, 1992; Serwinek, 1992; Browning and Zabriskie, 1983). Deshpande (1997) reported a significant relationship between age and ethical behaviour. Serwinek (1992) found workers senior in age having stricter interpretations of ethical standards, while Ruegger and King (1992) were even more precise in their findings that respondents falling in the 40 plus year age group are more ethical. Dawson, (1997) also found the age and education having influence over ethical values. He concluded that with higher age and education, the ethical values also increase and vice versa. Thus, younger people tend to be less ethical than those of senior in age people. Browning and Zabriskie (1983) in a sample of industrial buyers found respondents with less education viewing taking gifts and favours to be less unethical than those with more education. Serwinek (1992) in a sample of insurance employees found that the level of education of the respondents did not significantly affect ethical conduct. This leads to the development of next hypothesis and objective:-

> **H₃ₐ *There is significant difference in the ethical retail practices of younger and senior in age retailers.***
> **H₃ᵦ *Highly educated retailers are more ethical than their less educated counterparts.***
> **O₃ *To find out the effect of age and education on ethical retail practices.***

A regulatory body is a public authority/government department which is responsible for exercising autonomous authority over some area of human activity in a regulatory/supervisory capacity. Regulatory bodies take care of legal and regulative activities (codifying and enforcing rules and regulations and imposing supervision for the benefit of the public at large). Regulatory bodies are set up to enforce standards and safety, oversee use of public goods and regulate trade and commerce. There are different regulatory bodies for regulating the retailing sector such as Food and Supply Department, Taxation Department, Labour and Employment Department, Weights and Metrology Department and Retailers' Associations as self regulating agencies. The Food and Supply Department examines the quality and safety of products in retail stores through sampling methods. Taxation Department collects taxes from retailers and controls tax evasion. Labour and Employment Department focuses on issues of child labour, fair pay, working conditions etc. and Weight and Metrology Department checks the measures of weights used by the retailers. Retailers have framed their associations for their own welfare and better support from regulating agencies and these associations guide the members from time to time and make them aware about the new trends in retail sector by organising seminars and workshops (Botero et al., 2004). These regulatory bodies do influence the ethical retail practices. Thus, the next hypothesis and objective are:-

> **H$_4$** *The regulatory bodies differ in their perceptions about ethical retail practices.*
> **O$_4$** *To find out the significant difference in the perceptions of regulatory bodies.*

Sarma (2007) found retailers having developed certain norms of behaviour which may not guarantee ethical practices. The ethical values at retail level are not so high in the present time due to cut throat competition and unfair trade practices by competitors for immediate sales and quick profits. Some retailers try to become ethical to some extent like giving due respect and recognition to customers, dealing politely but to some areas they seem to be less ethical like adulteration, payments to suppliers, evasion of tax and not disclosing true facts (Sarma, 2007; Lavorata and Pontier, 2005 and Dubinsky et al., 2004). This leads to the development of last hypothesis and objective:-

> H$_5$ *Moderate level ethical values are followed by the retailers.*
> O$_5$ *To find out the extent of ethical values in retailing practices and accordingly, work out a strategic action plan for better ethical retail practices.*

3.4 Research Methodology

The nature and extent of ethical values in retailing has been studied on the basis of the perceptions of different stakeholders. As a result, a strategic action plan has also been formulated for better retail practices and policy formulation. In the light of aforesaid hypotheses and objectives, the various aspects of the research methodology followed in the study are as under:-

3.4.1 *Nature and Sources of Information*

Both secondary and primary sources of data have been used for obtaining needed information. The secondary data have been extracted from several journals like *Journal of Business Ethics, Journal of Retailing, Journal of Marketing, Journal of Academy of Marketing Science, Journal of Business Ethics: A European Review, Journal of Personal Selling and Sales Management*. The information from the internet, books, magazines and government records etc. has also been gathered. The primary data were collected from Customers (n = 470); Retailers (200); Wholesalers (70); Manufacturers (32) and Regulatory Bodies (35) through five specifically developed data collection schedules. The schedules were developed after reviewing the literature related to the subject under study (Sarma 2007, Lavorata and Pontier, 2005 Dubinsky et al., 2004; Dubinsky and Levy, 1985) and discussions with the experts. The schedules comprised of general information such as age, qualification, religion, occupation and other items representing ethical values in retailing practices, based on five point Likert scale (5<.....>1) ranging from 5 to 1, where 5 means strongly agree and 1 means strongly disagree.

3.4.2 *Selection of Respondents*

A total of 470 customers were selected from a list of 1506 households in Gandhi Nagar colony of Jammu city through systematic random sampling, one from each house, particularly one who did most of the purchases in the family. The sample size was determined by applying the following formula

$$n = \frac{(SD)^2 * Z^2}{D^2}$$ (Malhotra, 2008, p. 371)

Retailers from whom the aforesaid customers purchased goods were contacted subsequently. In total, there have been 250 retailers in Gandhi Nagar dealing in different kinds of products like garments, grocery, stationery, utensil etc. All of them were approached for obtaining the relevant data but out of them 200 retailers responded properly. In case of suppliers, the responses were obtained from the wholesalers and manufacturers whose names figured during survey with retailers. On the whole a list of 100 wholesalers and 40 manufacturers operating in different parts of Jammu city supplying merchandise to the retailers in Gandhi Nagar area of Jammu city and other retailers in other areas. In fact, the present study, being exploratory, comparative and chain type, requires the selection of those wholesalers and manufacturers from whom the retailers under reference buy merchandise so that a whole picture of ethical values of retailers in their dealings with various stakeholders can be drawn.

3.4.3 Pre testing in case of Consumer Survey

The schedule prepared for collecting data from the customers was pre-tested by taking basic relevant response from 50 consumers from Gandhi Nagar colony of Jammu city. The schedule comprised of, 10 items of general nature, 35 items relating to legal provisions, 27 of ethical values, 28 of customer satisfaction and 13 issues of miscellaneous nature. The respondents were required to give three responses for each statement concerning their experience with ethical behaviour of all the three types of retailers dealing in convenience goods, shopping goods and specialty goods. The data so collected were analysed with the help of 17 Version of SPSS. Factor analysis was used for data reduction and purification, which resulted into the deletion of some insignificant items with factor loadings below 0.50. After applying factor analysis, the number of statements came down to 10 of general category, 28 relating to legal provisions, 25 of ethical values, 20 of customer satisfaction and 10 relating to issues of miscellaneous nature. The reliability of data was obtained by dividing the data so collected in two equal halves. The split half reliability before factor analysis has been quite satisfactory in terms of mean values (Group I = 3.37 and Group II = 3.29). It has also been proved satisfactory after factor analysis (Group I = 3.42 and Group II = 3.40) for convenience goods. Same is the case with shopping and specialty goods. Moreover, the data were found to be valid under convergent validity test also as majority of the responses for most of the statements have fallen in the above average category.

3.4.4 Statistical Tools

The data so collected through the schedules from respondents have been processed and analysed in order to bring out precise results with the help of appropriate statistical tools such as, Descriptive, Exploratory Factor Analysis, Confirmatory Factor Analysis and SEM, Correlation, ANOVA, One Sample t – test, Independent t – test.

(i) *Descriptive*: It includes Mean, Median, Standard Deviation and Range. The arithmetic mean has been used extensively in order to know the exact value of each observation (Tull and Hawkins, 1993, p. 613-616). The standard deviation examines the amount of variation in the responses. Median is used for calculating average median sales and profit and Range indicates the lowest and highest limits of sales and profit.

(ii) *Exploratory Factor Analysis*: EFA is a class of procedures primarily used for data reduction and summarisation by considering key statistics such as KMO, Bartlett's Test of Sphericity, Commonalities, Eigenvalues, Factor Loadings and Percentage of Variance Explained (Malhotra, 2008, p. 609, 612). The technique of factor analysis was used for data reduction and data purification. Factor analysis was carried out through Statistical Package for Social Sciences (SPSS, 17.0 Version). It was carried with Principal component analysis along with varimax rotation for summarisation of the total data into minimum factors. The items having factor loading less than 0.5 and Eigen value less than 1 were ignored for the subsequent analysis (Hair et al, 2009, p. 128).

(iii) *Confirmatory Factor Analysis*: CFA is used to provide confirmatory test of measurement theory, which requires that a construct first be defined and specified in terms of measurement model. It is a way of testing how well measured variables represent a smaller number of constructs. One of the biggest advantages of CFA is its ability to assess the construct validity of the measurement theory by calculating Factor Loadings, Average Variance Extracted (AVE) and Construct reliability (CR).

(iv) *Structure Equation Modelling*: SEM also known as, 'Covariance Structure Analysis' and 'Latent Variable Analysis', is family of statistical models that seek to explain the relationships among multiple variables and examines the structure of interrelationships expressed in a series of equations and which ultimately depicts all the relationships among constructs (Hair et al, 2009, p. 735). In SEM, measurement model is specified and its validity depends on goodness of fit of model. The goodness of fit is checked by using different indices such as chi square, significance of chi square, CMIN/DF, GFI, AGFI, CFI, TLI, RMSR and RMSEA (Hair et al., 2009, p. 771, 773). The present study uses SEM to examine the impact of retailing ethics on customer satisfaction.

(v) *Other Tools and Tests:* Correlation has been used to test the convergent validity. ANOVA has been used to find out the significant mean differences in the perceptions of respondents with different demographic backgrounds such as age, qualification, occupation and religion. One sample t – test and Independent t – test have been used for finding out mean differences between two samples.

3.5 Reliability and Validity

Reliability refers to the extent to which a scale produces consistent results if repeated measurements are made (Malhotra, 2008, p. 284). To examine the reliability of data, split half test and Cronbach alpha were used. The split half test divides the data into two halves to examine if the variation in both the halves is within the range of sampling error (Tull and Hawkins, 1993, p. 316). Further, Cronbach alpha is the average of all possible split half coefficients resulting from different ways of splitting the scale items. It varies from 0 to 1 (Malhotra, 2008, p. 285) and a value of greater than 0.7 indicates satisfactory internal consistency reliability. The validity of a scale may be defined as the extent to which differences in observed scale scores reflect true differences among objects on the characteristics being measured rather than systematic or random error (Malhotra, 2008, p. 286). To check the validity, three types of validity tests were applied, viz., Content, Construct and Convergent. Content validity / face validity is a subjective but systematic evaluation of how well the content of a scale represents the measurement task at hand, i. e., whether the scale items adequately cover the entire domain of the construct being measured. Further, Construct validity addresses the question of what construct/characteristic the scale is measuring. Lastly, convergent validity is the extent to which the scale correlates positively with other measures of the same construct (Malhotra, 2008, p. 287). With CFA, Composite Reliability and Convergent validity have been determined in case of customers by applying the following formulas.

$$CR = \frac{(Sum\ of\ Factor\ Loadings)^2}{(Sum\ of\ Factor\ Loadings)^2 + Sum\ of\ the\ Error\ Variances}$$

AVE = *Sum of squared Standardised Factor Loadings / No of items*

The CR should be above 0.7 and AVE greater than 0.5 (Hair et al, 2009, p. 801)

3.6 Limitations and Future Research

Though all efforts have been made to maintain the study exhaustive, objective, reliable and valid, yet it has certain limitations which must be taken care of whenever its findings are considered for implementation. These limitations are also important to be considered in future research.

- Geographically and also in terms of nature of retailing activities, the geographic domain of the study remained restricted to Jammu city only and thus, findings cannot be generalised. Hence, future research needs to take adequately larger samples of wide perspective covering different parts of the country.
- Since in Jammu city, the bigger retailing retail stores/houses like shopping malls are at nascent stage. Thus, representation to such retail selling remained out of the scope of the research.

- Every effort has been made to keep the objectivity in research but the element of subjectivity cannot be ruled out as response obtained may be actuated by personal likes and dislikes of the respondents.
- Due to the comparative and chain type of study, only those suppliers were contacted from whom retailers under study bought their merchandise. Manufacturers outside Jammu have not been taken into consideration.
- The present study examined the perceptions of all stakeholders in retailing except employees (Salesmen) of the retailers. The future research should focus on employees as well.

References

Abratt, Russell; M. Bendixen and K. Drop (1999), "Ethical Perceptions of South African Retailers: Management and Salespersonnel", *International Journal of Retail and Distribution Management*, Vol. 27, No.2, pp. 91-105

Bejou, David; Christine T. Ennew and Adrian Palmer, (1998), "Trust, Ethics and Relationship Satisfaction", *International Journal of Bank Marketing*, Vol. 16 (4), pp.170-175

Bellizzi, Joseph A. and R. E. Hite {1989), "Supervising Unethical Sales Force Behaviour", *Journal of Marketing*, Vol. 53, pp. 36-47

Botero, Juan, Simeon Djankov, Rafael La Porta, Florencio Lopez-de-Silanes and Andrei Shleifer (2004), "The Regulation of Labour," *Quarterly Journal of Economics*, Vol. 118, pp. 1339-1382

Browning, J. and N. B. Zabriskie (1983), "How Ethical are Industrial Buyers?" *Journal of Industrial Marketing Management*, Vol. 12, pp. 219-224

Dawson, Leslie M. (1997), "Ethical Differences between Men and Women in the Sales Profession", *Journal of Business Ethics*, Vol. 16, pp. 1143-1152

Deshpande, Satish P. (1997), "Managers Perception of Proper Ethical Conduct: The Affect of Sex, Age and Level of Education", *Journal of Business Ethics*, Vol. 16, pp.79-85

Dubinsky, J.; Rajan Nataraajan and Wen-Yeh Huang (2004), "The Influence of Moral Philosophies on Retail Salespeople's Ethical Perceptions", *The Journal of Consumer Affairs*, Vol. 38, No. 2, pp. 297-317

Dubinsky, A. J. and M. Levy (1985), "Ethics in Retailing Perceptions of Retail Salespeople", *Journal of Academy of Marketing Science*, Vol. 13 (1), pp. 1-16

Hair, J. F.; William C. Black; Barry J. Babin; Ralph E. Anderson and Ronald L. Tathum (2009), Multivariate Data Analysis, Sixth Ed. Pearson Prentice Publishers, New Delhi

Hassan, Abul; Abdelkader Chachi and Salma Abdul Latiff (2008), "Islamic Marketing Ethics and Its Impact on Customer Satisfaction in the Islamic Banking Industry", *JKAU, Islamic Economics*, Vol. 21 (1), pp. 27-46

Jamal, A. and Kamal, N. (2003) "Factors Influencing Customer Satisfaction in the Retail Banking Sector in Pakistan", *International Journal of Consumer Marketing*, Vol. 13 (2) pp. 20-52

Kaptein, Muel (2008), "Developing a Measure of Unethical Behaviour in the Workplace: A Stakeholder Perspective", *Journal of Management,* Vol. 34, No. 5, pp. 978-1008

Kenhova, Patrick Van; Kristof De Wulf and Sarah Steenhaut (2003), "The Relationship between Consumers' Unethical Behavior and Customer Loyalty in a Retail Environment", *Journal of Business Ethics,* Vol. 44, pp. 261-278

Kujala, Johanna (2001), "Analysing Moral Issues in Stakeholder Relations", *Business Ethics: A European Review,* Vol. 10, pp. 233-247

Lavorata, Laure and Suzanne Pontier (2005), "The Success of a Retailers' Ethical Policy: Focusing on Local Actions", *The Journal of Academy of Marketing Science Review,* Vol. 2005, No.12, pp. 1-9

Malhotra, Naresh K. (2008), "Marketing Research", Fifth Edition, Prentice-Hall of India Pvt. Ltd. New Delhi

Oliver R. L. (1993), "Cognitive, Affective, and Attribute Bases of the Satisfaction Response", *Journal of Consumer Research* Vol. 20, pp. 418-30

Roman, S. and S. Ruiz (2005), "Relationship Outcomes of Perceived Ethical Sales Behaviour: The Customers' Perspective", *Journal of Business Research,* Vol. 58, pp. 439-445

Roman S. (2003), "The Impact of Ethical Sales Behaviour on Customer Satisfaction, Trust and Loyalty to the Company: An Empirical Study in the Financial Services Industry", *Journal of Marketing Management,* Vol. 19, pp. 915-939

Ruegger, D. and S. W. King (1992), "A Study of the Effects of Age and Gender upon Student Business Ethics" *Journal of Business Ethics,* Vol. 11, pp. 179-186

Sarma, Nripendra Narayan (2007), "Ethics in Retailing-Perception of Management and Sales Personnel", *(http:// dspace.iimk.ac.in/bitstream/2259/388/1/61-68.pdf),* last accessed on March, 20, 2012

Serwinek, P. J. (1992), "Demographic and Related Differences in Ethical Views Among Small Businesses", *Journal of Business Ethics,* Vol. 11, pp. 555-566

Tull Donald S. and Del I. Hawkins (1993), Market Research: Measurement and Method, McMillan Publishing Company, New Delhi.

Valenzuela Leslier M., Jay P. Mulki and Jorge Fernando Jaramillo (2010), "Impact of Customer Orientation, Inducements and Ethics on Loyalty to the Firm: Customers' Perspective", *Journal of Business Ethics*, Vol. 93, pp. 277–291

Whysall, Paul (2000), "Stakeholder Mismanagement in Retailing: A British Perspective" *Journal of Business Ethics*, Vol. 23, pp. 19-28

Whysall, Paul (1998), "Ethical Relationship in Retailing: Some Cautionary Tales", *Business Ethics: A European Review*, Vol. 7, No.2, pp. 103-110

CHAPTER 4
ETHICAL RETAIL PRACTICES: PERCEPTIONS OF CUSTOMERS

4.1 Background

The chapter examines the nature and extent of ethical values being observed in retailing practices from the viewpoint of customers with regard to all the three types of consumer goods viz. convenience, shopping and specialty goods. It also examines the impact of ethical values on customer satisfaction.

The customer is one of the most significant stakeholders in retailing who purchases products as per his/her requirements from different types of retailers (Fassin, 2009). The retailers being in direct and front link with customer, (Dubinsky and Levy, 1985) are of utmost significance to the retailers from several perspectives (Davies et al., 2012; Roman and Cuestas, 2008, Whysall, 2000, 1998). If retailers deal with customers in an ethical manner (Dornoff and Tankersley, 1976), it would definitely enhance the turnover, profitability, customer satisfaction (Limbu et al., 2011; Kurt and Hacioglu, 2010; Roman and Ruiz, 2005 and Jamal and Kamal, 2003) and loyalty (Lii and Lee, 2012; Valenzuela et al., 2010; Lin and Lin, 2006 and Kenhova et al., 2003; Whysall, 2000). In other words, unethical practices lead to low sales, less profit or even losses, customer dissatisfaction, switching to other stores and bad image of the retailer (Lee et al., 2010; Whysall, 2000). It is thus, necessary to study their dealings in terms of legal provisions, ethical values (Mulki, and Jaramillo, 2011), and customer satisfaction (Roman, 2003; Thomas et al., 2002) so that an appropriate strategic action plan emerges for better and profitable retailing practices through ethical efforts along with continuous improvement, maintenance and monitoring.

4.2 Data Collection

The data for the present research have been obtained from both secondary and primary sources. The secondary data available in several Journals such as, *Journal of Business Ethics, Journal of Marketing and Journal of Retailing,* books and the internet were also used. The primary data have been collected from 470 consumers from Gandhi Nagar, a posh colony in Jammu city. There are 1506 houses in Gandhi Nagar in total and out of which 470 houses were selected through systematic random sampling by selecting one consumer from each house. The first house being selected at random with the help of a random table and the subsequent houses were selected after the interval of three houses which was computed by dividing the population of 1506 houses by the sample size of 470 houses. From each house, the family member who did most of the shopping and having experience of behaviour of retailers was taken as respondent. The sample size of 470 was determined through the following formula of standard error of the Mean (Malhotra, 2008, p. 371)

$$n = \frac{(SD)^2 * Z^2}{D^2}$$

Where n stands for sample size; SD for Standard Deviation; Z is confidence level (1.96) and D is the level of precision (0.05).

4.3 Data Collection Form

The primary data were collected through a specifically developed schedule on the basis of the available literature (Kaptein, 2008; Sarma, 2007; Lavorata & Pontier, 2005; Dubinsky et al., 2004; Kujala, 2001 and Whysall, 2000) and discussions with the experts on the related subject. It comprised of four Scales, viz., Legal Provisions, Ethical Values, Customer Satisfaction and 0ther Issues. It initially consisted of, 10 items of demographic nature; 35 items of legal provisions; 27 of ethical values; 28 of customer satisfaction and 13 statements relating to other related issues. The respondents were required to give three responses for each statement concerning their experience with ethical behaviour of retailers dealing in convenience, shopping and specialty goods All items other than the items relating to demographic information were based on 5 point Likert scale (5 < ----- > 1) ranging from (strongly agree) to (strongly disagree) (Malhotra, 2008, p. 274).

4.4 Pre - Testing

The schedule was pre - tested on 50 respondents selected conveniently from Gandhi Nagar colony of Jammu city. The standard deviation of pre-testing data was used for determining the sample size. For modifying the schedule, factor analysis was applied for dropping the irrelevant items. After pre- testing, the number of items for the final survey got reduced to 10 items of demographic information, 28 items of legal provisions; 25 of ethical values; 20 of customer satisfaction and 10 relating to other issues. Thus, in total, out of 103 items, 20 items were deleted and remaining 83 items came up for the final survey.

4.5 Final Survey: Profile of Respondents

After pre – testing, the final survey was conducted on 470 personally contacted consumers, selected through systematic sampling from Gandhi Nagar colony of Jammu city as already explained. The respondents who refused initially to response were approached five times and even finally those again refused, were replaced as per systematic sampling order. The respondents were required to give their responses for each item separately for convenience goods, shopping goods and specialty goods. The proportion of male respondents figured higher (60%) than their female counterparts (40%). The average age of respondents came up as 46 years and more than half of them (51%) had below average age. Majority of the respondents (83%) were married and 91% of them had Hindu as their religion. About half of the respondents (48%) were graduates, about 29% worked in service sector and 69% belonged to nuclear families. Moreover, the average expenditure and income per month came up as Rs 17, 400 and Rs 33, 350 respectively. More than half of the respondents (60%) had incurred below average expenditure and 75% of them earned below average income. Finally, about 72% of the total respondents found taking purchase decisions collectively (Table 4.1) for all types of goods.

Thus, the analysis has been done separately for convenience goods, shopping goods and Specialty goods. It is discussed as under:-

4.6 Analysis of Convenience Goods

Because of their nature of use and consumer urgency, convenience goods are purchased very frequently, within less time and without much planned efforts, e.g., pulses, rice, bread, and other grocery items (Kotler, 2005, p. 536), as consumption of such goods is immediate as and when need rises.

4.6.1 Reliability and Validity

To check the reliability, Cronbach Alpha and Split half values have been worked out (Malhotra, 2008, p. 285) twice, i. e. before and after factor analysis by dividing the respondents into two equal halves. The data were found reliable before the factor analysis as mean values of both groups (Group I = 3.25 and Group II = 3.29) are almost similar. Similarly, after factor analysis, the data have proved quite satisfactory in terms of split half reliability as mean obtained from both halves of respondents are satisfactory (Group I = 3.28 and Group II = 3.31). Moreover, Cronbach Alpha values also proved reliable before and after factor analysis as it came to be 0.941 and 0.932 respectively (Table 4.2.1). The Content / Construct validity also duly assessed, by reviewing the literature and discussions with the experts and researchers working on similar topics. With the help of CFA, Composite Reliability (CR) and Convergent Validity through

Average Variance Extracted (AVE) have been established (Table 4.9) by applying the following formulas.

$$CR = \frac{(Sum\ of\ Factor\ Loadings)^2}{(Sum\ of\ Factor\ Loadings)^2 + Sum\ of\ the\ Error\ Variances}$$

AVE = *Sum of squared Standardised Factor Loadings / No of items*

The CR should be above 0.7 and AVE greater than 0.5 (Hair et al, 2009, p. 801)

4.6.2 Exploratory Factor Analysis

The technique of exploratory factor analysis has been used through Statistical Package for Social Sciences (SPSS, 17 Version) with Principal component analysis along with varimax rotation for summarisation of the total data into minimum meaningful factors. The items having factor loading less than 0.5 and Eigen value less than 1 were ignored for the subsequent analysis (Hair et al., 1995). As stated earlier, the schedule comprised of 93 statements (10 of general information) under four scales, viz., legal provisions, ethical values, customer satisfaction and miscellaneous Issues. When the factor analysis was initially applied collectively on all the dimensions, some of the statements of each dimension got mixed with other dimensions. Thus, the factor analysis was applied separately for each dimension viz., legal provisions, ethical values, customer satisfaction and other issues. Each dimension has one master statement for studying internal objectivity and consistency. In case of legal provisions dimension, in the first exercise, within 6 iterations, data purification process resulted into the deletion of six items having loading below 0.5. Finally, five factors emerged with 21 items at 56.45% variance explained (Table 4.2.2). The first round of data processing ethical values scale resulted into the deletion of two items because of loading below 0.5. Two more items were deleted in the next round. At the end, five factors emerged having 20 items with variance of 53.07% (Table 4.2.3). The first round of data purification for customer satisfaction resulted into the deletion of four items due to loading below 0.5. The variance explained was 58.49% with KMO = .874 and Bartlett = 2882.551 with 7 iterations. The final round presented four factors with variance explained at 63.70% within 5 iterations (Table 4.2.4). For the determination of other issues, three factors emerged with a variance of 62.40% and accordingly, two items were deleted due to loading below 0.5. Finally, two factors emerged with variance explained at 67.11 percent within 3 iterations and KMO as .687 (Table 4.2.5).

The perceptions of the ultimate customers about the legal norms and ethical values being followed by the retailers dealing in convenience goods along with customer satisfaction are presented as under:-

(A) Legal Provisions

These are rules and regulations framed by the government from time to time which every retailer is expected to abide by honestly. The overall mean score of this dimension (3.13) indicates moderate level of adherence to legal provisions by the retailers. The total variance explained was 56.45% along with five factors, viz., product quantity, quality, information, pricing and social norms (Table 4.2.6). These factors are discussed in detail as below:-

Factor 1 (*Product Quantity*): The factor has nine items, viz., 'proper weight of product', 'proper records', 'proper packing', 'package contains printed quantity', 'fair advertising', 'accurate information', 'fair sales promotion', 'promise and warranty', 'no sale of out dated products' (Table 4.2.6). Proper packaging stands highly associated with this factor, reflecting proper consideration to the issue in question. The mean score of this factor (3.60) indicates a moderate level of product quantity norms being followed in convenience goods. About 78% of the total respondents observed weight of goods as proper (3.63) along with packing and (3.73) about two third of them experienced fair advertising and sales promotion.

Factor 2 (*Product Quality*): The factor comprises of four variables, viz., 'genuine quality products', 'standardised products', 'no adulteration' and 'safe products'. About 74% of the total respondents found quality of convenience goods as genuine (3.57), while half of them experienced retailers selling less standardised products (2.99).

Factor 3 (*Information*): This factor has four variables, viz., 'no claim of unbranded product as superior', 'adequate discount', 'after sales dealings', 'actual price as per advertisement'. About two third of the total respondents found retailers offering unbranded products as good as branded products (2.53) and 63% of them experienced retailers sometimes getting irritated in after sales dealings (2.67) issues. About half of the respondents found prices sometimes varying from the retail list issued by retail association (2.94).

Factor 4 (*Pricing Norms*): This factor is made up of two variables, viz., 'fair prices' and 'no price discrimination', the former having higher factor loading. About two third of the total respondents experienced retailers charging printed prices (3.33) and about 60% of them found retailers not practicing any price discrimination (3.20).

Factor 5 (*Social Norms*): This factor has two variables, viz., 'no employment of minors' and 'no environment pollution'. About 57% of the total respondents found retailers dealing in convenience goods, employing minors in their stores (2.45) but not causing any environment pollution (3.21).

(B) Ethical Values

Ethical values are the moral virtues inherited from culture, religion, family, society and ethical codes of various organisations and professional bodies. These values build up character and fair dealings with different people. While dealing with the customers, retailers need to maintain these ethical values. The overall mean score in this regard (3.07) reflects moderate level of ethical values observed by the retailers dealing in convenience goods. The total variance explained was 53.07%. The factor wise findings of the study regarding ethical values are as under:-

Factor 1 (*Honesty*): The factorial mean of 2.66 indicates retailers being less honest. This factor has five items, viz., 'truthful, sincere and honest', priority to consumer needs', 'no excuses for unstocked products', 'truth of product features', 'less profitable customers', 'no pressure for purchase'. About 73% of the total respondents found retailers not so truthful and three fourth of them experienced retailers focusing on pushing sales than satisfying the needs of the ultimate consumers. About half of them found retailers making excuses for products not in stock to retain the customer; considering the less profitable consumers and keeping no discrimination between more and less profitable consumers. About the same number of respondents experienced no pressure for making a purchase (Table 4.2.6).

Factor 2 (*Fairness*): This factor has four items, viz., 'equal and fair dealings', 'knowledge to salesmen', 'accurate information', 'access to all alternatives'. The overall mean value (3.46) reflects average level fairness in retailing practices. About 60% of the total respondents found retailers treating them equally and fairly (3.17) and about 69% of them got accurate and timely information (3.39) and about 83% had access to all alternatives available in the stores (3.70).

Factor 3 (*Respect & Recognition*): This factor has five items, viz., 'after sales dealings', 'recognition as consumer', 'cognizance to complaints', 'politeness and patience', 'courteous and respectful'. The overall mean value (3.68) reflects due respect and recognition to ultimate consumers by the retailers. Majority (91%) of the total respondents found retailers behaving politely and patiently (3.88) with the customers and giving due cognizance to their complaints (3.56) Moreover, about 86% of them observed retailers as courteous, respectful and helpful (3.80).

Factor 4 (*Openness*): This factor has two items, viz., 'don't criticise competitors' and 'don't conceal limitations'. About half of the respondents found retailers not lowering down the value of products which are not available with their competitors (3.05) and about 63% of them observed retailers not expressing their weaknesses (2.66).

Factor 5 (*Responsiveness*): This factor comprises of three items, viz., 'no false claims', 'products as per customer needs' and 'assist all customers'. About 56% of the total respondents found retailers making false claims (2.82) and about 72% of them observed products not available as per their needs (2.50). Finally, about 62% of the respondents experienced retailers not assisting all consumers fairly and satisfactorily (2.73).

(C) Customer Satisfaction

Customer is satisfied when his/her expectations are equal to the performance. Retailers are last link in the distribution chain and are in direct contact with consumers. Thus, their behaviour and dealings are critical factors for the consumer satisfaction. The overall mean score (3.21) reflects moderate level of customer satisfaction in retailing with total variance of 63.7% (Table 4.2.6). Customer satisfaction dimension has the following factors:-

Factor 1 (*Product quality and quantity*) This factor comprises of five items, viz., 'good quality products', 'authentic quantity', 'proper and safe packing', 'desired brands' and 'printed price'. Out of which, 'authentic quantity' is contributing more significantly towards the factor followed by 'good quality products', 'proper and safe packing', 'printed price', and 'desired brands'. Majority of the total respondents (80%) found themselves satisfied with quality (3.75), product quantity (3.81), packing and desired brands (3.86).

Factor 2 (*Assistance*): This factor has four items, viz., 'correct and timely information', 'availability at store', 'help in buying decision processes and 'provide needed help'.

Majority of the total respondents observed retailers supplying correct and timely information (3.75) and assisting in buying decisions (3.79).

Factor 3 *Store Facilities*): This factor has two items viz., 'proper sitting arrangement' and 'proper parking space'. The former has the highest factor loading (.846) followed by the latter (.747). Majority (85%) of the total respondents were dissatisfied with sitting facility (1.51) and parking facility (1.46).

Factor 4 (*Store Location*): This factor is made up of two items, viz., 'convenient store location' and 'no discrimination'. About 91% of the total respondents found satisfied with location (4.21) and experienced no price discrimination (3.31).

(D) Other Issues

This dimension has two factors which depict the relationship between age, education and ethical behaviour. The overall mean came to be 3.62 with 67.11% of variance explained. The factors are explained as under:-

Factor 1 (*Education and Ethics*): This factor has three items, viz., 'education contributes to ethics', 'educated retailers abide by norms and regulation' and 'educated retailers are humble, helpful and respectful', the last item has the highest factor loading (.868) providing relationship between retailers education and their ethical behaviour. Majority (88%) of the total respondents found education contributing to ethical behaviour (3.91) and educated retailers as more humble, helpful and respectful (3.80). About 72% of them observed retailers following the prescribed norms and regulations (3.53).

Factor 2 (*Age and Ethics*): This factor has three items, viz., 'age fosters polite behaviour', 'aged retailers are more honest and humble' and 'aged retailers control the unethical behaviour of salesmen'. About two third of the total respondents found age contributing to ethical behaviour (3.42) and thus, retailers who are senior in age are more honest humble and respectful (3.41) and also controlling the unethical behaviour of their employees (3.67).

4.6.3 Confirmatory Factor Analysis in case of Convenience Goods

The confirmatory factor analysis (CFA) is used to provide confirmatory test of measurement theory. One of the biggest advantages of CFA is its ability to assess the construct validity of the measurement theory by calculating Factor Loadings, Average Variance Extracted (AVE) and Construct reliability (CR).

(A) Ethical Values

EFA on Ethical Values construct resulted into five factors, viz., Honesty, Fairness, Recognition, Openness and Responsiveness. But last two factors have been dropped due to their low regression weights. CFA on Ethical Values construct with three latent factors, viz., Honesty, Fairness and Recognition having different measured variables, has been performed. All indicators in this model have factor loadings greater than 0.5 (Table 4.2.7). The model was found to be as fit (CMIN/DF = 1.644, RMR = .030, GFI = .981, AGFI = .966, CFI = .985, TLI = .979 and RMSEA = .037, Hair et al., 2009, p. 770, Table 4.5).

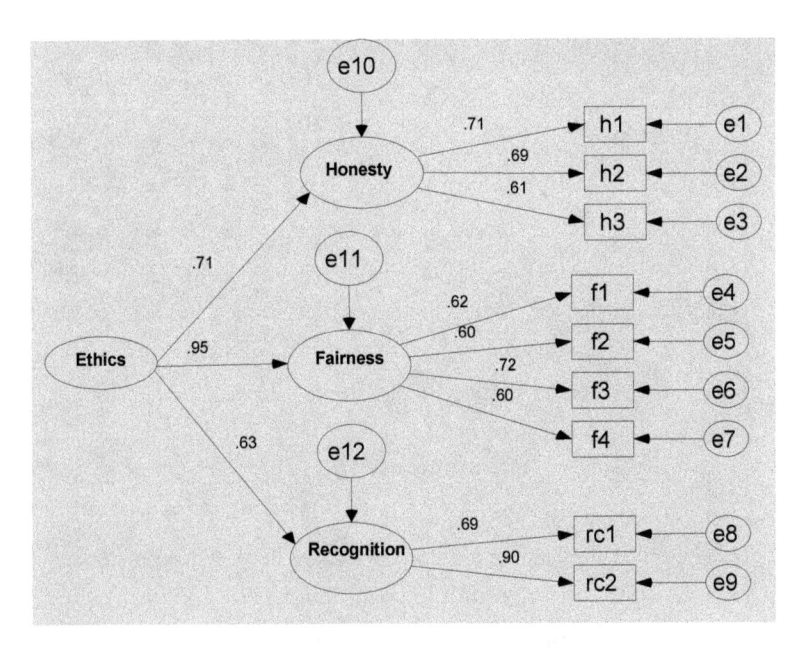

Fig 4.1 *Measurement Model of Ethical Values Construct*

(B) CFA for Customer Satisfaction

EFA on Customer Satisfaction construct resulted into four factors viz. Quality, Assistance, Facilities and Location. But as stated earlier, last two factors have not been considered due to the low regression weights of items under them. CFA on Customer Satisfaction construct has been performed by keeping two factors i.e. Quality and Assistance as latent variables having different measured indicators. All indicators in this model have factor loadings greater than 0.5 (Table 4.2.7). The model was found to be as fit (CMIN/DF = 4.720, RMR = .032, GFI = .956, AGFI =.914, CFI = .950, TLI = .922 and RMSEA = .08, Table 4.5).

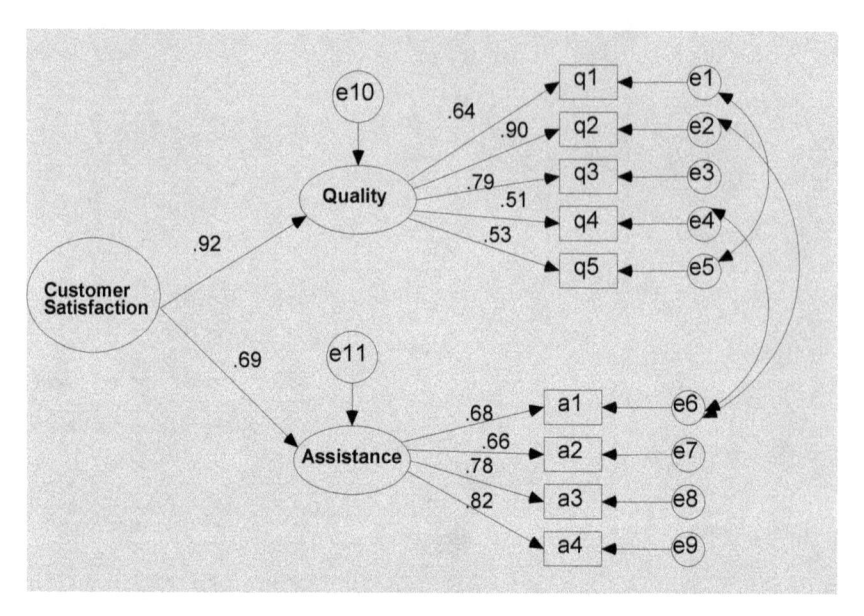

Fig. 4.2 *Measurement Model of Customer Satisfaction Construct*

4.6.4 Demographic Analysis in case of Convenience Goods

Ethical retailing practices have been studied in terms of perceptions of ultimate customers. The respondents were segregated under various groups on the basis of age, qualification, religion and occupation The analysis done on the basis of ANOVA is as under:-

(A) Age Wise Analysis

The classification of respondents into three age groups, viz., below average, average and above average finds average age of respondents as 46 years (Table 4.1). The respondents belonging to below average age group were higher (51%) in number followed by above average (47%) and average age respondents (2%). ANOVA has been used to know whether significant difference exists in the mean values of responses of these three age groups and the results came to be to be significant (F = 4.311, Sig. <.05, Table 4.2.8). Each age group has been studied in detail as under:-

(i) *Below Average Age Respondents*

The overall mean score accorded by the respondents (3.01) indicates moderate level of ethics retailing (Table 4.2.9). Majority of the below average respondents (71%) experienced equal treatment from retailers (3.04) and they are getting the needed information about the product (3.46). They found retailers providing them access to all available brands in their stores (3.62) with due respect and recognition (3.79) to their customers as valuable clients. Majority of the total respondents reported retailers dealing politely and patiently with them (3.88) and giving immediate response to their complaints (3.54).

(ii) *Average Age Respondents*

About two third of the Average age group of respondents found retailers furnishing the required information about the products (3.36) and providing them access to all available brands of products in the retail store (3.27) and retailers' behaviour as polite (3.64), courteous and respectful (3.73).

(iii) **Above Average Age Respondents**

About two third (65%) of the total respondents under this age group observed retailers treating all the customers without any partiality (3.28) and about 80% of them found retailers supplying the required and timely information about the product available in the retail store (3.48). They also found retailers displaying all the available brands in the retail stores (3.82) and solving the consumers' complaints immediately (3.54). Moreover, majority (89%) of the total respondents observed retailers dealing politely and patiently (3.89) and giving due respect and recognition to the ultimate consumers (3.97).

(B) Qualification wise Respondents

Respondents have been classified on the basis of their qualification into four groups, viz., matriculate, under graduate, graduate and post graduate respondents. The number of graduate respondents is the highest (48%) followed by matriculate (14%), under graduate (13%) and post graduate respondents (25%). ANOVA results depict significant mean differences in the responses of customers belonging to different educational backgrounds (F = 3.311, Sig. <.05, Table 4.2.8), which is discussed in detail as under:

(i) Matriculate Respondents

Moderate mean score (3.15) has been accorded by this group of respondents for ethics in retailing practices (Table 4.2.9). Majority of the matriculate respondents (95%) observed retailers behaving politely and patiently (3.91) and giving due respect and recognition to them as valuable clients (3.95). About 61% of them found retailers as unbiased in dealing with different customers as they do not give any preference to any consumer to buy first. About 81% of them found retailers having knowledge of all the brands of products in their stores and they supply the needed information to the ultimate consumers about the product and its usage (3.61). About 92% of total respondents shared that they get the desired brands of products in the retail stores (3.81) and retailers listen all their complaints (3.19) about the product usage.

(ii) Under Graduate Respondents

The majority of the undergraduate respondents (85%), by assigning lower mean scores to three factors viz., F1, F4 and F5 (Table 4.2.9) indicate retailers most often telling lies in order to increase their sale of products (1.69) and giving priority to their sales motive instead of satisfying the consumers' needs' (2.56). About 61% of them observed retailers sometimes making excuses for the products which are not available in the retail store (2.64) in order to sell other related products and not allowing consumers to shift to other retailers.

(iii) *Graduate Respondents*

The number of graduate respondents is the highest (48%) among the total respondents. About two third (64%) of the total respondents observed retailers as impartial in their dealings with different customers (3.27) as they give equal treatment to all of them. About 78% of the them found retailers possessing all the knowledge about the different brands of products they handle (3.61) and furnishing the needed information to the ultimate customers about the product and its usage (3.46) and about 84% of them opined that they get access to all the available brands of the products in the retail store (3.73). Only 30% of the total respondents found retailers as truthful because most often they tell lies in order to push sales (2.11) by giving priority to sales motive as compared to consumers' requirements (2.50).

(iv) *Post Graduate Respondents*

Majority of the post graduate respondents (92%) found retailers dealing politely and patiently with all the consumers (3.91) and about 88% of them experienced retailers as respectful and courteous (3.86) as they assist the respondents in choice making of the products to be purchased. About 71% of the total respondents found retailers having knowledge of all the brands of products available in their retail stores (3.61) and supplying the required information (3.46) to the ultimate consumers. Lastly, about 55% of the total respondents observed retailers not criticising their competitors with consumers (3.10) while convincing them for the purchase of the products available in the store.

(C) Religion wise Respondents

Respondents have been catagorised into three religious groups, viz., Hindu, Sikh and Others. Majority of the respondents were Hindu (91%) followed by Sikhs (8%) and others (1%). ANOVA depicts insignificant mean differences among consumers belonging to different religious communities (F = 1.689, Sig. >.05, Table 4.2.8). Further, factor wise analysis also reveals insignificant mean differences in all the five factors, viz., F1 (honesty: Sig. = .190), F2 (fairness: .304), F3 (respect & recognition: .596), F4 (openness: .208) and F5 (responsiveness: .884, Table 4.2.8).

(D) Occupation wise Respondents

The respondents were segregated into four categories of occupations, namely, service (29%), business (20%), retired (16%) and others (35%). ANOVA reveals insignificant mean differences among respondents belonging to different occupations (F = 0.736, Sig. >.05, Table 4.2.8). Further, factor wise analysis shows insignificant mean differences in all the five factors, viz., F1 (honesty: Sig. = .923), F2 (fairness: .211), F3 (respect & recognition: .205), F4 (openness: .237) and F5 (responsiveness: .276, Table 4.2.8).

4.7 Analysis of Shopping Goods

The shopping goods require more time and efforts for proper and valuable selection. These types of products include garments and shoes etc. which have lot of variety in the given market.

4.7.1 Reliability and Validity

The data were found reliable before the factor analysis as mean values of both groups (Group I = 3.27 and Group II = 3.34) are almost similar. Similarly, after factor analysis, the data proved quite satisfactory in terms of split half reliability as mean obtained from both halves of respondents are above average (Group I = 3.28 and Group II = 3.40). Moreover, Cronbach Alpha values before and after factor analysis came to be as 0.933

and 0.910 respectively (Table 4.3.1), indicating high reliability. The Content/Construct validity was duly assessed by review of literature and discussions with the experts and researchers of similar topics. The higher Kaiser-Meyer-Olkin Measures of Sampling Adequacy values, Bartlett's Test of Sphericity and Variance Explained represent the construct validity. Convergent Validity has also been found satisfactory.

4.7.2 Exploratory Factor Analysis

The schedule comprised of 93 items (10 of general information), under four scales, viz., Legal Provisions, Ethical Values, Customer Satisfaction and Other Issues. The factor analysis was initially applied collectively on all the dimensions but some of the statements of each dimension got mixed with other dimensions. Thus, the factor analysis was applied separately for each dimension, viz., Legal Provisions, Ethical Values, Customer Satisfaction and Other Issues. For Legal Provisions scale, in the first exercise, within 14 iterations, process resulted into the deletion of five items which had loading below 0.5 with 58.45 percent variance explained. Thus, finally six factors emerged with relation to 17 items with variance of 63.42%. The KMO is above 0.8 (Table 4.3.2). The first round of data processing in Ethical Values scale showed a variance of 54.29% within 8 iterations resulting into the deletion of five items because of loading below 0.5. One more item got deleted in the next round on the same ground. The entire process is shown in table 4.2.2. At the end, five factors emerged having 18 items with variance of 54.76 percent and KMO above 0.8 and Bartlett value of 1820.74 (4.3.3). The first round of data purification of Customer Satisfaction scale resulted into the deletion of two items due to factor loading below 0.5. The variance explained was 60.19% with KMO 0.874, Bartlett 2882.551 with 7 iterations. The final round gave four factors with variance explained at 58.44% (Table 4.3.4). Lastly, in Other Issues, three factors emerged with a variance of 62.34 percent and accordingly one item was deleted due to loading below

0.5. Finally, three factors were extracted with variance explained at 68.08% (Table 4.3.5).

The perceptions of the ultimate consumers about the legal norms and ethical values followed by the retailers dealing in shopping goods along with customer satisfaction came up as under:-

(A) Legal Provisions

The overall mean score (3.33) indicates moderate level of adherence to legal provisions by the retailers. The total variance explained for the dimension under study came up at 63.42% along with six factors, viz., Quantity, Quality, Pricing, Social Norms, Information and After sales services (Table 4.3.6). These factors are discussed in detail as below:-

Factor 1: (*Product Quantity*): This factor comprised of five items, viz., 'proper size of product', 'proper records', 'proper packing', 'package contains printed size' and 'no sale of outdated products' (Table 4.3.6). Proper packaging stands highly associated with this factor, reflecting proper consideration of the issue in question by the retailers. The mean score of this factor (3.81) indicating a moderate level of product quantity norms being followed in shopping goods. About 87% of the total respondents found the size and packing of goods always in order (3.86 and 3.80).

Factor 2 (*Product Quality*): This factor is made up of items like, 'genuine quality products', 'standardised products', 'no duplication' , safe products'. About 77% of the total respondents observed retailers to have always maintained product quality (3.63) and about half of them do claim to have provided standardised products (3.17).

Factor 3 (*Pricing Norms*): This factor comprised of items namely, 'fair prices' and 'no price discrimination', the former having higher factor loading (0.846) followed by the latter (0.826). About half of the respondents experienced dealers charging fair prices (3.08) and not practicing price discrimination (Table 4.3.6).

Factor 4 (*Social Norms*): This factor has two variables, viz., 'no employment of minors' and 'no environment pollution', latter having higher factor loading (0.737). About half (52%) of the respondents found employing minors in their stores (2.65) and however, about two third of them observed retailers not causing environment pollution (3.26).

Factor 5 (*Information Norms*): This factor comprised of two variables, viz., 'no claim of unbranded product as superior' and 'adequate discount', latter contributing more significantly towards this factor. About 62% of the total respondents found retailers trying to sell unbranded products by claiming these as superior and unique ones (2.63) and also observed the retailers particularly in garments trade, offering high discounts (2.57) by enhancing the prices (Table 4.3.6).

Factor 6 (*After sale services*): This factor has two variables, viz., 'repair during warrantee period' and 'issuance of bills on purchase'. About 71% of the total respondents found retailers repairing the products during warrantee period without any resistance and about two third of the total respondents found retailers issuing bills on purchases even without asking for the same.

(B) Ethical Values

The overall mean score of ethical values (2.99) with total variance of 54.76 percent reflects below average level of ethical values possessed by the retailers dealing in shopping goods. The findings of the study regarding different ethical values are highlighted as under:-

Factor 1 (*Honesty*): This factor has five items, viz., 'recognition as consumer' 'knowledge of salesmen', 'access to all varieties', 'politeness and patience', 'courteous'(Table 4.3.6). Majority of the respondents (92%) found retailers quite courteous (3.80), giving due recognition (3.92), and dealing politely and patiently (3.91). Majority of them observed salesmen having knowledge about the goods and helping the customers for meaningful selection of goods (3.63).

Factor 2 (*Fairness*): This factor having five items, viz., 'equal and fair dealings', 'truth of product features', 'less profitable customers', 'no pressure for purchase', 'no preference to some customers'. About 58% of the total respondents experienced equal and fair treatment by the retailers (3.13) with less truthfulness (2.72) while half of them found retailers pressurising customers for buying the products (2.84) and also giving preference to some customers (2.97).

Factor 3 (*Respect & Recognition*): This factor comprising three items, viz., 'priority to customer needs', 'low margin product', 'no excuses for unstocked products'. About two third of the total respondents observed retailers having priority of sales over the customer needs (2.47) and selling more expensive products when less expensive products are better for customers (2.49). About half of the respondents expressed retailers making lame excuses for the products which are not in stock (2.84) so that they can retain the customers (Table 4.3.6).

Factor 4 (Responsiveness): This factor has three items namely, 'no false claims', 'products as per customer needs' and 'assist all customers'. About 62% of the respondents found retailers making false claims (2.70) and about four fifth of them observed unbranded products available in the store (2.40). Finally, about 60% of the total respondents perceived retailers not assisting all consumers fairly and satisfactorily (2.75).

Factor 5: (*Openness*): This factor has two items, viz., 'after sales dealings', and 'don't conceal weakness', the former item having the higher factor loading which indicates that the retailers dealing in electronic goods focus on after sales services like repairs. About 63% of the total respondents found retailers not expressing their weaknesses (2.70).

(C) Customer Satisfaction

The overall mean score of this dimension (3.69) reflects moderate level of customer satisfaction in shopping goods. The total variance explained emerged as 58.45%. Customer satisfaction dimension has four factors which are explained as under:-

Factor 1 (*Product quality and quantity*): This factor comprised of six items, viz., 'good quality products', 'authentic quantity', 'proper and safe packing', 'desired brands' "printed price' and 'supply of goods on delivery date' (Table 4.3.6). About 80% of the total respondents found themselves satisfied with quality (3.80) and price (3.61). Majority (89%) of the total respondents were satisfied from packing (3.91) and brands of products (3.99).

Factor 2 (*Assistance*): This factor has five items, viz., 'correct and timely information', 'availability at store', 'help in buying decision processes', 'provide needed help' and 'implement suggestions'. The item 'help in buying decision process' has the highest factor loading (0.857), indicating retailers assisting customers in taking buying decision (Table 4.3.6). Majority of the total respondents found retailers giving correct information (3.76) and helping in buying decisions (3.82) and about 58% of them viewed retailers implementing their suggestions (3.25).

Factor 3 (*Store Services*): This factor has three items, namely, 'long queue', 'attractive displays' and 'no discrimination'. Majority (93%) of the total respondents found themselves highly satisfied by the displays (4.10) and two third of them experienced no price discrimination (3.29) because the price remained fixed and printed on the product.

Factor 4: (*Store Location*): This factor comprised of two items viz., 'convenient store location' and 'proper sitting arrangement', the latter having higher factor loading

(0.691). About 91% of the total respondents were satisfied with location of the store (4.21) and more than half of them found retailers not providing any sitting facility (2.75) in their stores (Table 4.3.6).

(D) Other Issues

This dimension has three factors, depicting relationship between age, education and ethical behaviour. The overall mean (3.37) with 68.09% of variance explained indicates better status of these issues. These factors are explained as under:-

Factor 1 (*Education and Ethics*): This factor has three items, viz., 'education contributes to ethics', 'educated retailers abide by norms and regulation' and 'educated retailers are humble, helpful and respectful'. The item 'educated retailers are humble, helpful and respectful' has the highest factor loading (0.841) providing thereby positive relationship between education and ethics (Table 4.3.6). Majority (87%) of the respondents found education contributing to ethical behaviour (3.89) of retailers, who become more humble, helpful and respectful (3.81). About 71% of them experienced retailers following the prescribed norms and regulations (3.52).

Factor 2 (*Age and Ethics*): This factor has three items, viz., 'age fosters polite behaviour', 'aged retailers are more honest and humble' and 'aged retailers control unethical behaviour of salesmen' (Table 4.3.6). About two third of the total respondents opined that the age contributes to ethical behaviour (3.43) and thus, retailers senior in age found to be more honest, humble and respectful (3.41) and three fourth of the respondents observed those retailers controlling the unethical behaviour of their employees (3.66).

Factor 3 (*Fairness*): This factor has two items, viz., 'young retailers do have fair practices' and 'less educated retailers are also fairing their dealings'. The latter has higher factor loading (0.783). About half of the total respondents perceived young retailers sometimes doing unfair practices (2.76) and two third of them found less educated retailers sometimes doing unfair retail practices (Table 4.3.6).

4.7.3 Confirmatory Factor Analysis in case of Shopping Goods

(A) Ethical Values

EFA resulted into five factors, viz., Honesty, Fairness, Recognition, Responsiveness and Openness. But two factors i. e. Responsiveness and Openness have not been confirmed due to the low regression weights (<.50) of items under them. CFA on Ethics Values construct with three latent factors viz. Honesty, Fairness and Recognition having different observed variables, has been performed. All indicators in this model have factor loadings greater than 0.5 (Table 4.3.7). The model was found to be as fit (CMIN/DF = 2.373, RMR = .048, GFI = .956, AGFI =.935, CFI = .943, TLI = .927 and RMSEA = .054, Table 4.5).

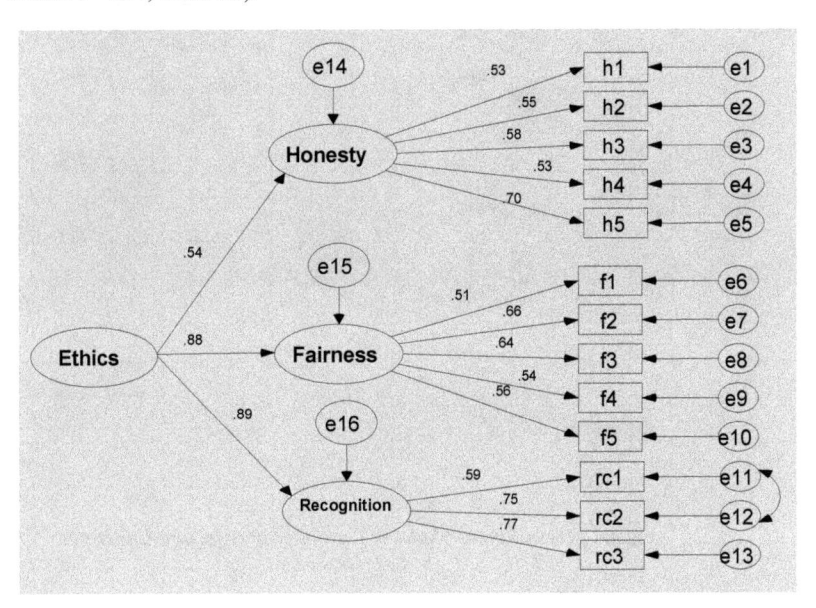

Fig 4.3 *Measurement Model of Ethical Values Construct*

(B) Customer Satisfaction

EFA on Customer Satisfaction construct resulted into four factors, viz., Quality, Assistance, Services and Location. But last two factors have not been confirmed due to the low regression weights (<.50) of items under them. CFA on Customer Satisfaction construct has been performed by keeping two factors, i. e., Quality and Assistance as latent variables, measured in terms of different indicators. All indicators in this model have factor loadings greater than 0.5 and with significance (Table 4.3.7). The model was found to be as fit (CMIN/DF = 4.156, RMR = .035, GFI = .938, AGFI = .901, CFI = .935, TLI = .913 and RMSEA = .08, Table 4.5).

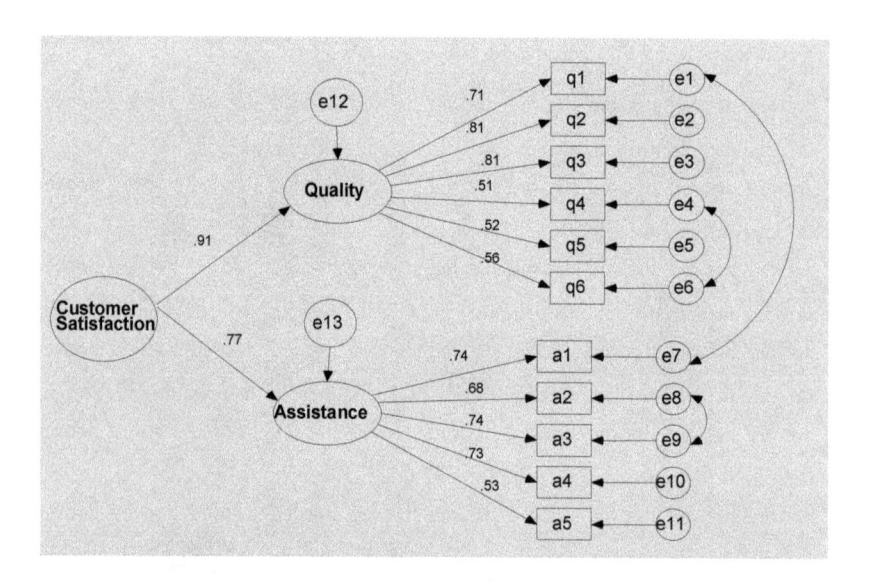

Fig 4.4 *Measurement Model of Customer Satisfaction Construct*

4.7.4 Demographic Group wise Analysis in case of Shopping Goods

(A) Age Wise Analysis

The classification of respondents into three age groups, viz., below average, average and above average finds average age of respondents as 46 years (Table 4.1). The number of respondents belonging to below average age group is the highest (51%) followed by above average (47%) and average age respondents (2%). ANOVA depicts significant differences in the mean values of the three age groups (F = 4.016, Sig. <.05, Table 4.3.8). Each age group has been studied in detail as under:-

(i) *Below Average Age Respondents*

Majority of the below average respondents (91%) found retailers of shopping goods giving due respect and recognition to them as their valuable clients (3.90) and about 71% of them observed salesmen having knowledge of the different brands of the products (3.52) and giving access to all the available brands in their stores (3.68). Moreover majority (89%) of the total respondents experienced retailers' behaviour as courteous, polite and patient (3.92) with all types of consumers.

(ii) *Average Age Respondents*

Majority (81%) of the total respondents belonging to average age group also observed retailers behaving politely and patiently (3.73) with all the consumers and about 55% of them found salesmen having knowledge of the available brands of the products in their retail stores (3.27) and providing needed information about all these brands (3.82) to the ultimate consumers.

(iii) *Above Average Age Respondents*

Majority of respondents under this age group observed retailers displaying all the available brands of shopping goods in their retail stores (3.92) and about two third (63%) of them found retailers treating all the customers equally (3.20) and not ignoring less profitable consumers (3.16). About 89% of the total respondents experienced retailers behaving politely and patiently (3.90) and not making excuses for the products which are not available in their retail store (3.00).

(B) Qualification wise Respondents

Respondents have been classified on the basis of qualification into four groups, viz., matriculate, under graduate, graduate and post graduate respondents. The number of graduate respondents is the highest (48%) followed by matriculate (14%), under graduate (13%) and post graduate respondents (25%). ANOVA portrays insignificant mean differences in the responses of different customers belonging to different educational backgrounds (F = 2.366, Sig. >.05, Table 4.3.8). The respondents belonging to different religions accorded almost same mean values towards all the five factors (Table 4.3.9).

(C) Religion wise Respondents

On the basis of religion, respondents have been catagorised into three religious groups, viz., Hindu, Sikh and Others. Majority of the respondents are Hindu (91%) followed by Sikhs (8%) and others (1%). ANOVA depicts insignificant mean differences in the mean values of the responses of the respondents belonging to different religious communities (F = 1.194, Sig. = .304, Table 4.3.8). Moreover, the respondents belonging to different religions gave almost similar responses towards five factors (Table 4.3.9).

(D) Occupation wise

The respondents were segregated into four categories of occupations, viz., service (29%), business (20%), retired personnel (16%) and others (35%). ANOVA reveals insignificant mean differences among respondents having different occupations (F = 0.817, Sig. = .465). Meanwhile, factor wise analysis also reveals insignificant mean differences in all the five factors (Table 4.3.8). The respondents belonging to different occupations awarded almost same responses towards five factors (Table 4.3.9).

4.8 Analysis of Specialty Goods

The specialty goods are purchased infrequently with more time and with much planned efforts e.g. jewelry, furniture, durable goods etc.

4.8.1 Reliability and Validity

The data were found reliable before the factor analysis as mean values of both groups (Group I = 3.38 and Group II = 3.51) are almost similar. Similarly, after factor analysis, the data proved quite satisfactory in terms of split half reliability as mean obtained from both halves of respondents are above average (Group I = 3.40 and Group II = 3.53). Moreover, Cronbach Alpha values also proved reliable before and after factor analysis as it came to be 0.936 and 0.924 respectively. (Table 4.4.1) The content/construct validity was duly assessed by review of literature and discussions with the experts. The higher Kaiser-Meyer-Olkin Measures of Sampling Adequacy values, Bartlett's Test of Sphericity and Variance Explained represent the construct validity. Convergent Validity has been found satisfactory (Malhotra, 2008, p. 286)

4.8.2 Exploratory Factor Analysis

The schedule comprised of 93 items (10 of general information) with four scales (dimensions), i. e., Legal Provisions, Ethical Values, Customer Satisfaction and Other Issues. The factor analysis was initially applied collectively on all the dimensions but some of the statements of each dimension got mixed with the other dimensions. Thus, the factor analysis was applied separately for each dimension viz., Legal Provisions, Ethical Values, Customer Satisfaction and Other Issues. Step by step process of data reduction for each dimension is as under:-

For Legal Provisions scale, in the first round, eight items got deleted due to factor loadings below 0.5 within 11 iterations. Subsequently one more item got deleted in next round. Finally, five factors emerged with relation to 18 items with variance explained at 55.24%. The KMO is 0.846 and Bartlett is 1984.394 (Table 4.4.2). The first round of data purification of Ethical Values scale resulted into the deletion of three items within 9 iterations. Finally, five factors emerged having 21 items within 8 iterations. The variance explained was 56.10%, KMO above 0.8 and Bartlett value 2948.051 (Table 4.4.3). In case of Customer Satisfaction, initially, two items got deleted due to factor loading below 0.5. Six factors emerged within 7 iterations with variance explained at 62.89%. In the subsequent rounds three more items got deleted. Finally, three factors emerged with variance explained to 56.82 percent, KMO 0.836 and Bartlett value 2026.01 (Table 4.4.4). Under Other Issues, no item got deleted and thus, 9 items clubbed under three factors with variance explained of 62.83%, KMO 0.740 (Table 4.4.5).

The perceptions of the ultimate consumers about the legal norms, ethical values and customer satisfaction from the retailers dealing in specialty goods came up as under:-

(A) Legal Provisions

The overall mean score of this dimension (3.42) and standard deviation (0.42) indicate moderate level of adherence to legal provisions by the retailers. The total variance explained for the dimension under study came to be at 55.24% along with five factors namely, Quality, Quantity, Promotion, Social norms and Pricing Table 4.4.6). These factors are explained in detail as under:-

Factor 1 (*Product Quality*): This factor comprised of items like, 'genuine quality products', 'standardised products', 'no duplication' , 'safe products' and 'no hoarding of gifts'. About 85% of the total respondents observed retailers providing qualitative (3.85) and safe (3.74) products. About two third of them found retailers selling standardised products (3.46) and giving gifts to the customers (3.33).

Factor 2 (*Product Quantity*): This factor has four items, viz., 'proper size of product', 'proper records', 'proper packing' and 'package contains specified size' (Table 4.4.6). About four fifth of the total respondents found the size (3.91) and packing (3.96) of goods always in order.

Factor 3 (*Promotion*): This factor comprised of three variables, viz., 'fair advertising', 'accurate information' and 'fair sales promotion'. About 64% of the total respondents observed retailers doing fair advertising (3.34) and sale promotion (3.57). About three fourth of them got needed and accurate information (3.59, Table 4.4.6).

Factor 4 (*Social Norms*): This factor has three items, viz., 'no price discrimination', 'No employment of child labour' and 'issuance of bills on purchase'. The last item has the highest factor loading (0.710) with above average value (3.49) made by the customers. About half of the respondents observed retailers employing minors in their stores (2.88) and two third of them experienced no price discrimination (3.35) because price remained fixed and printed on all the products (Table 4.4.6)

Factor 5 (*Pricing Norms*): This factor comprised of three variables, viz., 'adequate discount', 'proper after sales services', 'advertised price'. About 56% of the total respondents did not get adequate discount (2.79) and experienced variation in advertised prices (2.75).

(B) Ethical Values

The overall mean score of ethical values came to be as 3.24 with variation of 0.50, reflecting average level of ethical values being practiced by the retailers. The findings of the study regarding different ethical values are highlighted as under:-

Factor 1 (*Fairness*): This factor has five items, viz., equal and fair dealings', 'no exploitation of less bargainers', 'accurate information', 'truth of product features', 'less profitable customers', ''no pressure for purchase', 'no preference to some customers' and 'protect consumer rights'. About 63% of the total respondents experienced equal and fair treatment by the retailers (3.28) and about 72% of them got accurate information (3.51). But half of them found retailers not telling the complete truth about product features (2.90). Finally, 57% of the total respondents observed retailers giving importance to less profitable customers, not pressurising for purchase, giving no preference to some customers and protecting consumer rights to some extent (Table 4.4.6).

Factor 2 (*Honesty*): The factorial mean (3.89) indicates retailers as moderately honest in dealing with customers. This factor has five items, viz., 'recognition as consumer', 'knowledge of salesmen', 'access to all varieties', 'politeness and patience', 'courteous'. Majority (90%) of the total respondents observed retailers as courteous, respectful (3.86); giving due recognition to customers (4.01) and dealing politely and patiently (3.99). Majority of them found salesmen possessing knowledge about the products and also assisting customers in buying decisions (3.73).

Factor 3 (*Respect & Recognition*): This factor comprised of three items, viz., 'priority to customer needs', 'low margin product', 'no excuses for unstocked products'. About 60% of the total respondents found retailers having priority of sales over the customer needs (2.59) and 64% of them observed retailers not selling more expensive products when less expensive products are better for customers (2.61). About half of the respondents experienced retailers not making lame excuses for the products which are not in stock (3.04).

Factor 4 (_Responsiveness_): This factor has three items, viz., 'no false claims', 'products as per customer needs' and 'assist all customers'. About 61% of the respondents found retailers making false claims (2.72) and about 74% of them observed less standardised products in the stores (2.43). Finally, about 60% of the total respondents found retailers not assisting all consumers fairly and satisfactorily (2.73).

Factor 5 (_Openness_): This factor has two items, viz., 'after sales dealings', and 'cognizance to customer complaints', the former has higher factor loading (0.562). About 85% of the total respondents found retailers providing after sale services (3.81) and giving due consideration to their complaints (3.68, Table 4.4.6).

(C) Customer Satisfaction The overall mean score (3.83) reflects above average customer satisfaction in retailing. The total variance explained emerged as 56.82% (Table 4.4.6). Customer satisfaction dimension has the following factors.

Factor 1 (_Product quality and quantity_): This factor comprised of five items, viz., 'good quality products', 'authentic quantity', 'proper and safe packing', 'desired brands' and 'printed price' About four fifth of the total respondents found themselves satisfied with the quality (3.92) and price (3.85). About 89% of them found highly satisfied from packing (4.08); proper size (4.04) and desired brands (4.13).

Factor 2: (_Assistance_): This factor has five items, viz., 'correct and timely information', 'help in buying decision processes, 'provide needed assistance', 'no discrimination' and 'implement suggestions'. About four fifth of the total respondents found retailers providing correct and timely information (3.87) and helping in buying decisions (3.92) by providing the needed help (3.88). About two third of the total respondents observed retailers implementing their suggestions (3.23) and not discriminating (3.44) with them in terms of pricing of products purchased by them.

Factor 3 (*Store Services*): This factor has three items, viz., 'convenient store location', 'attractive displays' and 'no long queue'. Majority of the total respondents found satisfied by the location (4.20) and displays (4.19). About 55% of them experienced no rush (3.14) in specialty goods stores.

(D) Other Issues

This dimension has three factors depicting the relationship between age, education and ethical behaviour. The overall mean (3.39) and standard deviation (0.48) indicate positive relationship between age, education and ethics. These factors are explained as under:-

Factor 1 (*Education and Ethics*): This factor has three items, viz., 'education contributes to ethics', 'educated retailers abide by norms and regulation' and 'educated retailers are humble, helpful and respectful'. The item 'educated retailers are humble, helpful and respectful' has the highest factor loading (0.860). Majority of the respondents found education contributing to ethical behaviour (3.92) and thus, educated retailers are more humble, helpful and respectful (3.81) than their counterparts. About 73% of them observed retailers adhering to the prescribed norms and regulations (3.54) to some extent.

Factor 2 (*Age and Ethics*): This factor has four items, viz., 'age fosters polite behaviour', 'aged retailers are more honest and humble', 'young retailers do fair practices' and 'aged retailers control unethical behaviour of salesmen'. About two third of the total respondents found age contributing to ethical behaviour (3.40) and senior in age retailers are more honest humble and respectful (3.44). About fourth fifth of them observed senior in age retailers controlling the unethical behaviour of their employees (3.69) and about half of them found young retailers doing unfair practices (2.75) for increasing sales and profit.

Factor 3 (*Fairness*): This factor has two items, viz., 'less educated retailers are also fair' and 'no discrimination by less educated retailers', the latter having higher factor loading (0.625). About two third of the total respondents observed less educated retailers sometimes doing unfair practices (2.48) but not practicing price discrimination (3.50) because price remained fixed and printed in all the products (Table 4.4.6).

4.8.3 Confirmatory Factor Analysis: Specialty Goods

(A) Ethical Values

EFA provides five factors, viz., Fairness, Honesty, Recognition, Responsiveness and Openness. But two factors i. e. Responsiveness and Openness have not been confirmed due to the low regression weights (<.50) of items under them. CFA on Ethics construct with three latent factors viz. Fairness, Honesty and Recognition having different indicators has been performed. All indicators in this model have factor loadings greater than 0.5 (Table 4.4.7). The model was found to be as fit (CMIN/DF = 2.831, RMR = .05, GFI = .929, AGFI = .904, CFI = .920, TLI = .905 and RMSEA = .062, Table 4.5).

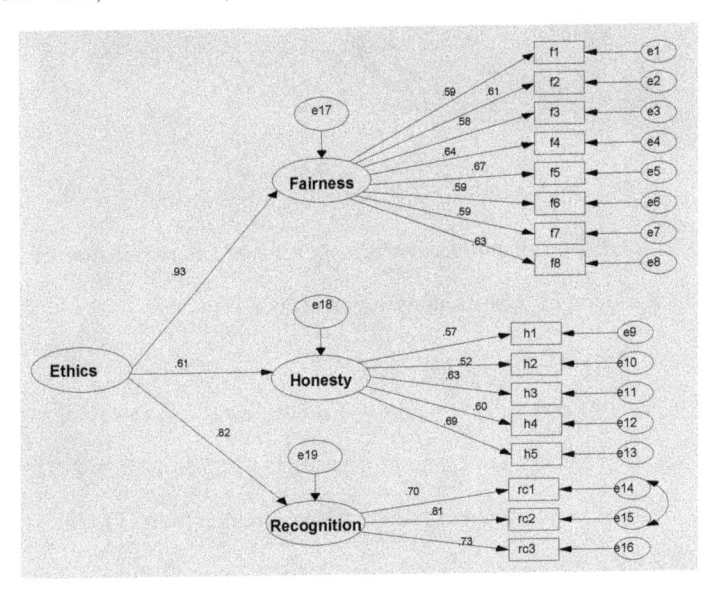

Fig 4.5 *Measurement Model of Ethical Values Construct*

(B) Customer Satisfaction

EFA on Customer Satisfaction construct resulted into three factors, viz., Quality, Assistance, and Services. CFA on Customer Satisfaction construct has been performed by keeping two factors i. e. Quality and Assistance as latent variables, while one factor having low regression weights of items in it was dropped out. All variables in this construct have factor loadings greater than 0.5 along (Table 4.4.7). The model was found to be as fit (CMIN/DF = 3.856, RMR = .032, GFI = .960, AGFI =.927, CFI = .954, TLI = .934 and RMSEA = .07, Table 4.5).

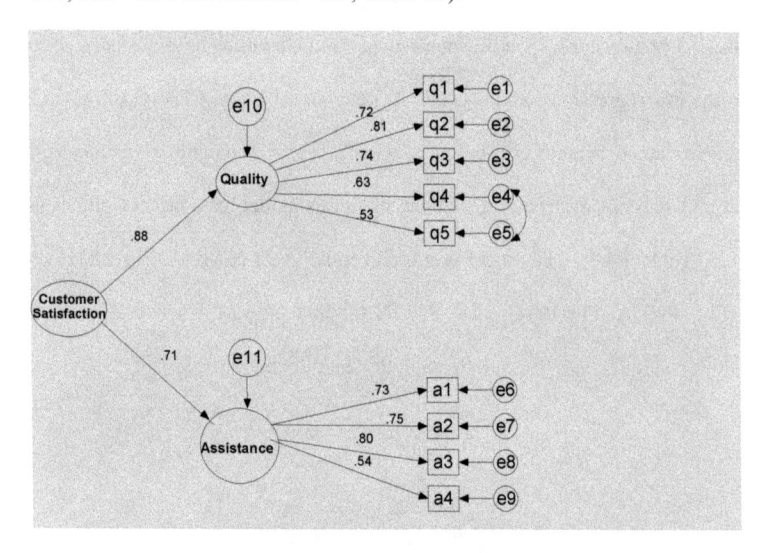

Fig 4.6 *Measurement Model of Customer Satisfaction Construct*

4.8.4 Demographic wise Analysis in case of Specialty Goods

(A) Age wise Analysis

Applying ANOVA on overall basis indicates significant mean difference in the responses of different age groups of respondents (F = 3.867, Sig. = .022). Factor wise ANOVA gives significant mean differences in three factors viz., F1 (fairness: F = 5.981, Sig. = .003), F3 (respect & recognition: F=4.238, Sig. = .015) and F5 (openness: F =

3.033, Sig. = .049) (Table 4.4.8), while other factors have insignificant mean differences. Each age group has been analysed separately.

(i) *Below Average Age Respondents*

The overall mean score of the below average age respondents is 3.18. Majority of the total respondents accorded higher mean scores to three factors, viz., F1 (Mean = 3.03), F2 (3.84) and F3 (3.77, Table 4.4.9). About 70% of the total respondents found retailers of specialty goods supplying the needed information to the consumers about the product to be purchased by them (3.46) and 59% of them observed retailers treating all consumers equally without any partiality with any of the consumer in their retail store (3.19). About half of the respondents (51%) shared that retailers protect their rights as a consumer (3.03). Majority of the respondents (92%) experienced retailers giving them due respect and recognition as valuable clients (4.00) and behaving politely and patiently (3.99) with all the consumers. Finally, about 85% of the total respondents found retailers giving adequate after sales services to the consumers by repairing the products purchased by the consumers and extending any other kind of service required after sales (3.84).

(ii) *Average Age Respondents*

The overall mean score (3.03) by the average age group of respondents indicates retailers as moderately ethical in their dealings with consumers (Table 4.4.9). About 55% of the total respondents found salesmen possessing knowledge of all the products (3.27) available in their retail store and assisting consumers in choice making (3.00) of the product to be purchased. About 73% of the total respondents got the needed information regarding the different brands of the products (3.53) and about 46% of them observed retailers treating all the consumers without any partial treatment with any of the consumer in their retail stores (3.03). Majority of the respondents (82%) experienced retailers giving them due respect as valuable clients (3.91) and behaving politely and patiently (3.82) and about half (55%) of them found satisfied from after sales services (3.18).

(iii) *Above Average Age Respondents*

The higher overall mean score (3.29) by this group of respondents indicates retailers as more ethical as compared to the respondents of other age groups. The respondents also assigned higher mean scores to three factors viz. F1 (fairness: 3.26), F2 (honesty: 3.94) and F5 (openness: 3.74, Table 4.4.9). Majority of the respondents (88%) found retailers of specialty goods giving due respect to consumers as their valuable clients (3.86) and behaving politely and patiently (3.98) in their dealings with consumers. About the same number of respondents (85%) observed retailers giving adequate after sales services to the consumers by repairing the products purchased by them (3.80) and listening to their other complaints (3.68). About 61% of the total respondents found retailers protecting consumer rights (3.19) and about 69% of them get equal treatment from retailers (3.39) while purchasing specialty products in their retail stores.

(B) Qualification wise Respondents

ANOVA shows significant mean differences in the responses of customers belonging to different educational backgrounds (F=3.809, Sig. = .010). On further analysis, out of five factors, three factors have significant mean differences, viz., F1 (fairness: F = 4.866, Sig. = .002), F2 (honesty: F=4.678, Sig. = .003) and F5 (openness: F=3.339, Sig. = .019), Table 4.4.8). On the whole, matriculate respondents awarded higher mean scores to ethical values (3.30) followed by graduate (3.28), under graduates (3.20) and post graduates (3.10, Table 4.4.9). Thus, each group has been analysed separately.

(i) *Matriculate Respondents*

The respondents assigned higher mean scores to three factors, viz., F1 (fairness: 3.28), F2 (honesty: 3.95) and F5 (openness: 3.91, Table 4.4.9). Majority of the respondents (92%) found retailers giving due respect to consumers as their valuable clients (3.95) and behaving politely and patiently (3.94) in their dealings with consumers. About the same number of respondents (95%) observed retailers giving adequate after sales services to the consumers by repairing the products purchased by them (3.95) and listening to their complaints (3.88). About 62% of the total respondents found retailers protecting consumer rights (3.22) and about 65% of them got equal treatment from retailers while purchasing specialty products in the retail stores (3.36). About 83% of them got accurate and timely information about the different brands of the product (3.67) and about 72% of them experienced no psychological pressure for buying the product (3.41).

(ii) *Under Graduate Respondents*

Majority of the under Graduate respondents (97%) found retailers as respectful and courteous (4.11) in their dealings with consumers and considering their complaints (3.57) regarding the product purchased by them. About 89% of them got adequate after sale services (3.89) from retailers dealing in specialty goods and about two third of them observed retailers protecting consumer rights (3.05) and not criticising their competitors (3.34) with consumers while convincing them for purchasing the products.

(iii) *Graduate Respondents*

Graduate respondents being the highest in number (49%) awarded above average mean score to three factors, viz., F1 (fairness: 3.22), F2 (honesty: 3.94) and F4 (openness: 3.78, Table 4.4.9). Majority of the graduate respondents (94%) found retailers giving due respect to consumers as their valuable clients (3.93) and behaving politely and patiently (3.94) in their dealings with consumers. About the same number of respondents observed retailers giving adequate after sales services to them by repairing the products purchased (3.81) and listening to their other complaints (3.75). About 61% of the total respondents found retailers protecting consumer rights (3.23) and two third of them get fair treatment from retailers while purchasing specialty products in the retail stores (3.34). About 75% of the total respondents got accurate and timely information about the different brands of the product (3.57) and 72% of them experienced no psychological pressure by the retailers for buying the product (3.41). About 55% of the total respondents found retailers charging the same price from all consumers for a product (3.12) and even considering less profitable consumers with humility.

(iv) *Post Graduate Respondents*

Majority of the post graduate respondents (82%) found retailers as respectful and courteous (4.73) in their dealings with all the consumers and considering their complaints (3.49) regarding the product purchased by them. About 78% of them got adequate after sale services (3.68) from retailers of specialty goods and half of them found retailers protecting consumer rights (2.77) and not criticising their competitors (3.34) with consumers while convincing them for purchasing the products.

(C) Religion wise Respondents

ANOVA depicts insignificant differences among consumers belonging to different religious communities (F = 1.505, Sig. = .223). Further, factor wise analysis reveals insignificant mean differences in all the five factors (Table 4.4.8). Majority of the respondents gave similar responses for all the five factors (Table 4.4.9).

(D) Occupation wise Respondents

The occupation of the respondents has been segregated into four categories viz. service business, retired and others. ANOVA reveals insignificant mean differences among different respondents belonging to different occupations (F = 0.913, Sig. = .435). Further factor wise analysis reveals insignificant mean differences in four factors, viz., F1 (fairness: Sig. =.120), F3 (respect & recognition: .238), F4 (responsiveness: .208) and F5 (openness: .108, Table 4.4.8). Most of the respondents accorded same mean values for most of the factors (Table 4.4.9).

4.9 Hypothesis Testing

H$_2$ *Ethical values positively influence customer satisfaction.*

To find out the impact of ethical values on customer satisfaction, Structural Equation Modelling (SEM) has been used. For applying SEM, Exploratory Factor Analysis (EFA) and Confirmatory Factor Analysis (CFA) have already been explained above. The hypothesis is tested separately for different response of customers for three types of goods, viz., Convenience, shopping and specialty.

4.9.1 Testing of Hypothesis in case of Convenience Goods

After EFA and CFA, the final model of SEM has been developed to find out the impact of ethical values on customer satisfaction (Roman, 2003; Thomas et al., 2002). The customer satisfaction has been taken as dependent variable and ethics as an independent variable. The model has been found to be appropriate and fit after keeping one modification between honesty and fairness (CMIN/DF = 1,004 RMR = .023, GFI = .997, AGFI = .987, CFI = 1.000, TLI = 1.000 and RMSEA = .003, Table 4.6). The hypothesis stands accepted as impact is positive and significant (b= .91; p = .000).

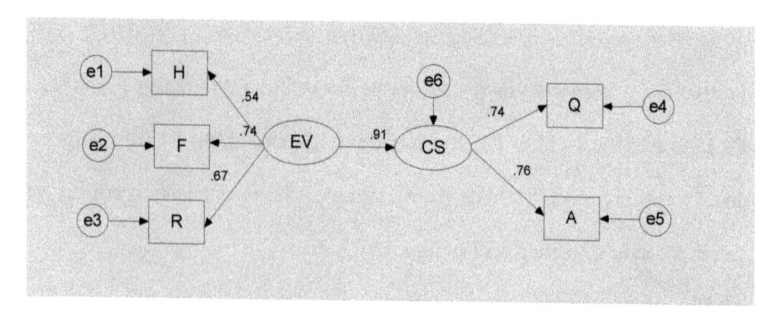

Fig. 4.7 *Structural Model of SEM for Convenience Goods*

Key: EV = *Ethical Values,* H = *Honesty,* F = *Fairness,* R = *Recognition,* CS = *Customer Satisfaction* Q = *Quality and* A= *Assistance*

4.9.3 Testing of Hypothesis in case of Shopping Goods

After EFA and CFA, the final model of SEM has been developed to find out the impact of ethical values on customer satisfaction (Roman, 2003; Thomas et al., 2002). The model has been found to be appropriate and fit after making one modification between fairness and recognition (CMIN/DF = 4.891, RMR = .014, GFI = .988, AGFI =.941, CFI = .985, TLI = .949 and RMSEA = .08, Table 4.7). The hypothesis is accepted as impact is positive and significant (b = .88; p = .000).

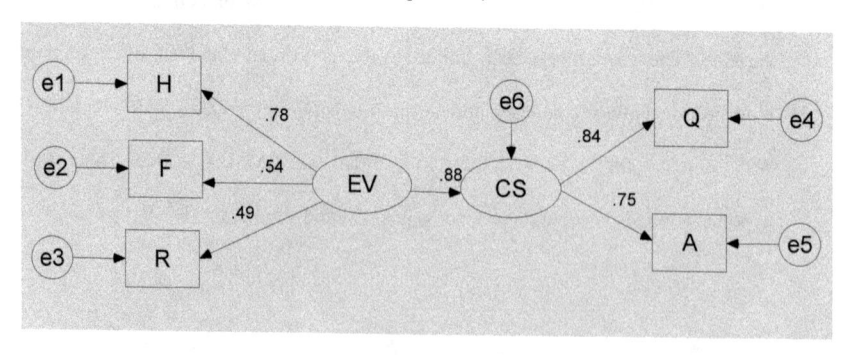

Fig. 4.8 *Structural Model of SEM for Shopping Goods*

Key: EV = *Ethical Values,* H = *Honesty,* F = *Fairness,* R = *Recognition,* CS = *Customer Satisfaction,* Q = *Quality and* A= *Assistance*

4.9.4 Testing Of Hypothesis: Specialty Goods

After EFA and CFA, the final model of SEM has been developed to find out the impact of ethical values on customer satisfaction (Roman, 2003; Thomas et al., 2002). The model has been found to be appropriate and fit after making three modifications between fairness and honesty, fairness and recognition and honesty and quality (CMIN/DF = 5.187, RMR = .011, GFI = .996, AGFI =.978, CFI = .997, TLI = .991 and RMSEA = .039, Table 4.8). The hypothesis stands accepted as impact is positive and significant (b = .85; p = .000).

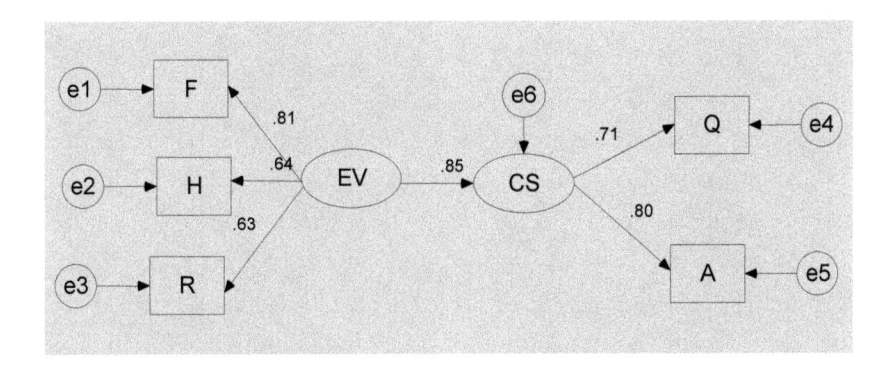

Fig. 4.9 *Structural Model of SEM for Specialty Goods*

Key: *EV = Ethical Values, H = Honesty, F = Fairness, R = Recognition, CS = Customer Satisfaction, Q = Quality and A= Assistance*

4.10 Conclusion

On the whole, the study reveals moderate level of ethical values being observed by the retailers dealing in convenience, shopping and specialty goods. The study found customers getting equal and fair treatment from the retailers and having access to all possible alternatives available in the store. They experienced retailers behaving politely and patiently and have been quite courteous, respectful and helpful. The customers found them satisfied with quality, quantity, packing and brands but dissatisfied from parking facility. Retailers assist customers in buying decisions. Customers perceived educated retailers as more humble, helpful and respectful than their younger counterparts. The ethical values have strong positive and significant impact on the customer satisfaction. This means that, if the retailers behave ethically, it increases customer satisfaction.

References

Davies, Iain A.; Zoe Lee and Ine Ahonkhai (2012), "Do Consumers Care about Ethical Luxury?", *Journal of Business Ethics*, Vol. 106, pp. 37-51

Dornoff, R. J. and C. B. Tankersley (1976), "Do Retailers Practice Social Responsibility", *Journal of Retailing*, Vol. 51, pp. 33–42

Dubinsky, Alan J.; Rajan Nataraajan and Wen-Yeh Huang (2004), "The Influence of Moral Philosophies on Retail Salespeople's Ethical Perceptions", *The Journal of Consumer Affairs*, Vol. 38 (2), pp. 297-317

Dubinsky, A. J. and M. Levy (1985), "Ethics in Retailing Perceptions of Retail Salespeople", *Journal of Academy of Marketing Science,* Vol, 13(1), pp. 1-16

Fassin Yves (2009), "The Stakeholder Model Refined", *Journal of Business Ethics*, Vol. 84, pp. 113-135

Hair, J. F.; William C. Black; Barry J. Babin; Ralph E. Anderson and Ronald L. Tathum (2009), Multivariate Data Analysis, Sixth Ed. Pearson Prentice Publishers, New Delhi.

Jamal, A. and N. Kamal (2003) "Factors Influencing Customer Satisfaction in the Retail Banking Sector in Pakistan", *International Journal of Consumer Marketing*, Vol. 13 (2) pp. 20-52

Kaptein, Muel (2008), Developing a Measure of Unethical Behaviour in the Workplace: A Stakeholder Perspective, *Journal of Management,* Vol. 34 (October), pp. 978-1008

Kenhova, Patrick Van; Kristof De Wulf and Sarah Steenhaut (2003), "The Relationship between Consumers' Unethical Behaviour and Customer Loyalty in a Retail Environment", *Journal of Business Ethics,* Vol. 44, pp.261-278

Kotler, Philip (2005), 'Marketing Management', Eleventh Ed., Pearson Education, Delhi

Kujala, Johanna (2001), "Analysing Moral Issues in Stakeholder Relations", *Business Ethics: A European Review,* Vol. 10, pp. 233-247

Kurt, Gizem and Gungor Hacioglu (2010), "Ethics as a Customer Perceived value Driver in the Context of Online Retailing", *African Journal of Business Management,* Vol. 4 (5), pp. 672-677

Lavorata, Laure and Suzanne Pontier (2005), "The Success of a Retailers' Ethical Policy: Focusing on Local Actions", *The Journal of Academy of Marketing Science Review*, Vol. 2005 (12), pp. 1-9

Lee, Monle; Anurag Pant and Abbas Ali (2010), "Does the Individualist Consume More? The Interplay of Ethics and Beliefs that Governs Consumerism across Cultures" *Journal of Business Ethics*, Vol. 93, pp. 567–581

Lii, Yuan-Shuh and Monle Lee (2012), "Doing Right Leads to Doing Well: When the Type of CSR and Reputation Interact to Affect Consumer Evaluations of the Firm", *Journal of Business Ethics*, Vol. 105, pp. 69-81

Limbu Yam B.; Marco Wolf and Dale L. Lunsford (2011), "Consumers' Perceptions of Online Ethics and its Effects on Satisfaction and Loyalty", *Journal of Research in Interactive Marketing*, Vol. (1), pp. 71-89

Lin, Grace Tyng-Ruu and Jerry Lin (2006), "Ethical Customer Value Creation: Drivers and Barriers", *Journal of Business Ethics*, vol. 67, pp. 93-105

Malhotra, Naresh (2008), 'Marketing Research', An Applied Orientation, Fifth Edition, Prentice Hall of India, New Delhi

Mulki, Jay Prakash and Fernando Jaramillo (2011), "Ethical reputation and value received: customer perceptions", *International Journal of Bank Marketing*, Vol. 29 (5), pp. 358-372

Roman, Sergio and Pedro J. Cuestas (2008), "The Perceptions of Consumers Regarding Online Retailers' Ethics and Their Relationship with Consumers' General Internet Expertise and Word of Mouth: A Preliminary Analysis", *Journal of Business Ethics*, Vol. 83, pp. 641-651

Roman, S. and S. Ruiz (2005), "Relationship Outcomes of Perceived Ethical Sales Behaviour: The Customers' Perspective", *Journal of Business Research*, Vol. 58, pp. 439-445

Roman S. (2003), "The Impact of Ethical Sales Behaviour on Customer Satisfaction, Trust and Loyalty to the Company: An Empirical Study in the Financial Services Industry", *Journal of Marketing Management*, Vol. 19, pp. 915-939

Sarma, Nripendra Narayan (2007), "Ethics in Retailing-Perception of Management and Sales Personnel", *(http:// dspace.iimk.ac.in/bitstream/2259/388/1/61-68.pdf)*, last accessed on March 20, 2012

Sharma R. D. and Bodh Raj Sharma (2011), "Legal Provisions and Ethical Values in Retail Sector: Study of Convenience Goods", *Arash, A Journal of ISMDR*, Vol. 1 (1), January, pp. 1-9

Sharma R. D. and Bodh Raj Sharma (2009), "Ethics in Retailing: Perceptions of Consumers", *Saaransh: Journal of Management*, Vol. 1 (1, July), pp. 43-55

Thomas, James L., Scott J. Vitell, Faye W. Gilbert, Gregory M.. Rose (2002), "The Impact of Ethical Cues on Customer Satisfaction with Service", *Journal of Retailing,* Vol. 78, pp. 167–173

Valenzuela Leslier M.; Jay P. Mulki and Jorge Fernando Jaramillo (2010), "Impact of Customer Orientation, Inducements and Ethics on Loyalty to the Firm: Customers' Perspective" *Journal of Business Ethics*, Vol. 93, pp. 277–291

Whysall, Paul (2000), "Retailing and the Internet: A Review of Ethical Issues", *International Journal of Retail & Distribution Management*, Vol. 28 (11), pp. 481-489

Whysall, Paul (2000), "Addressing Ethical Issues in Retailing: A Stakeholder Perspective", *International Review of Retail, Distribution and Consumer Research,* Vol. 10 (3), July, pp. 305–318

Whysall, Paul (2000), "Stakeholder Mismanagement in Retailing: A British Perspective", *Journal of Business Ethics*, Vol. 23, pp. 19-28

Whysall, Paul (1998), "Ethical Relationship in Retailing: Some Cautionary Tales", *Business Ethics: A European Review*, Vol. 7 (2), pp. 103-110

Table 4.1 - Respondent Profile

Variables	Frequency	Percentage	Variables	Frequency	Percentage
Age:			Occupation:		
Below average	238	51	Service	137	29
Average	11	02	Business	95	20
Above average	221	47	Retired	73	16
Gender:			Others	165	35
Male	281	60	Family type:		
Female	189	40	Nuclear	324	69
Qualification:			Joint	146	31
Matriculate	64	14	Family expenditure:		
Under graduate	61	13	Below average	283	60
Graduate	228	48	Above average	187	40
Post graduate			Family income		
and above	117	25	Below average	355	75
Marital Status:			Above average	115	25
Married	389	83	Purchase decisions:		
Unmarried	81	17	Head of Family	92	20
Religion:			Collective	339	72
Hindu	426	91	Others	39	08
Sikh	37	08			
Others	7	01			

Table 4.2.1 Split Half Reliability and Cronbach Alpha

Group	Before Factor Analysis	After Factor Analysis
Group I (Mean)	3.25	3.28
Group II	3.29	3.31
Cronbach Alpha	0.941	0.932

Table 4.2.2 Factor Analysis regarding Legal Provisions

Rounds	Variance Explained	Items Emerged	No of Factors Extracted	Iterations	No of Items Deleted	KMO	Bartlett.
1	52.78	27	6	6	6	.881	3833.736
2	56.45	21	5	5	-	.873	3184.379

Table 4.2.3 Factor Analysis regarding Ethical Values

Rounds	Variance Explained	Items Emerged	No of Factors Extracted	Iterations	No of Items Deleted	KMO	Bartlett.
1	51.19	24	5	10	2	.879	3234.201
2	52.60	22	5	13	2	.863	2856.327
3	53.07	20	5	8	-	.851	2277.105

Table 4.2.4 Factor Analysis regarding Customer Satisfaction

Rounds	Variance Explained	Items Emerged	No of Factors Extracted	Iterations	No of Items Deleted	KMO	Bartlett.
1	58.49	19	5	7	4	.874	2882.551
2	57.57	15	4	5	2	.841	2164.339
3	63.70	13	4	5	-	.839	1990.804

Table 4.2.5 Factor regarding Analysis Other Issues

Rounds	Variance Explained	Items Emerged	No of Factors Extracted	Iterations	No of Items Deleted	KMO	Bartlett
1	62.40	9	3	4	2	.721	961.269
2	59.44	7	2	3	1	.708	804.218
3	67.11	6	2	3	-	.687	754.991S

Table 4.2.6 Factorial Profile in Convenience Goods

D*	Variables	M	SD	FL	% of VE
LP	**F1 Product quantity**	3.60	0.16		20.112
	Proper weight of product	3.63	0.88	.620	
	Proper records	3.69	0.79	.651	
	Proper packing	3.73	0.77	.706	
	Package contains printed quantity	3.86	0.64	.641	
	Fair advertising	3.39	1.03	.626	
	Accurate information	3.44	1.00	.695	
	Fair sales promotion	3.56	0.91	.666	
	Promise of warranty	3.70	0.79	.629	
	No sale of after expiry date products	3.44	1.05	.534	
	F2 Product quality	3.18	0.30		13.528
	Genuine quality products	3.57	0.94	.680	
	Standardised products	2.99	1.16	.797	
	No adulteration	2.91	1.19	.818	
	Safe Products	3.27	1.08	.825	
	F3 Information	2.76	0.19		7.867
	No unbranded product as superior	2.53	1.08	.555	
	Adequate discount	2.88	1.10	.662	
	After sales dealings	2.67	1.08	.643	
	Actual price as per advertisement	2.94	1.09	.643	
	F4 Pricing norms	3.27	0.09		7.621
	Fair prices	3.33	1.17	.820	
	No price discrimination	3.20	1.21	.808	
	F5 Social norms	2.83	0.54		7.327
	No employment to minors	2.45	1.36	.743	
	No environment pollution	3.21	1.16	.584	
	Grand Mean S D and Variance Explained	3.13	0.34		**56.455**
	F1 Honesty	2.66	0.37		12.856
EV	Truthful, sincere and honest	2.00	1.20	.689	
	Priority to customer's needs	2.48	1.13	.549	
	No excuses for products unavailable in store	2.84	1.10	.565	
	Truth of product features	2.74	1.09	.712	
	Less profitable customers	2.95	1.16	.593	
	No pressure for purchase	2.95	1.22	.604	
	F2 Fairness	3.46	0.23		12.795
	Equal and fair dealings	3.17	1.14	.607	
	Knowledge to salesmen	3.57	0.93	.668	
	Accurate information	3.39	1.02	.620	
	Access to all alternatives	3.70	0.76	.722	
	F3 Respect and Recognition	3.68	0.28		11.737
	After sales dealings	3.25	0.68	.655	
	Recognition as consumer	3.93	0.58	.605	
	Cognizance to complaints	3.56	0.93	.614	
	Politeness and patience	3.88	0.70	.656	
	Courteous and respectful	3.80	0.71	.605	

	F4 Openness	**2.86**	**0.28**		8.126
	Don't disparage competitors	3.05	1.16	.629	
	Don't conceal their limitations	2.66	1.02	.568	
	F5 Responsiveness	**2.68**	**0.17**		7.554
	No false claims	2.82	1.01	.656	
	Products as per customer type	2.50	1.01	.613	
	Assist all customers	2.73	1.06	.766	
	Grand Mean S D and Variance Explained	**3.07**	**0.47**		**53.068**
	F1 Product quality	**3.79**	**0.07**		23.442
CS	Good quality products	3.75	0.73	.745	
	Authentic quantity	3.81	0.71	.818	
	Proper and safe packing	3.83	0.71	.708	
	Desired brands	3.86	0.75	.639	
	Printed price	3.68	0.88	.688	
	F2 Assistance	**3.79**	**0.08**		21.115
	Correct and timely information	3.75	0.89	.582	
	Available at store	3.91	0.73	.734	
	Help in buying decision process	3.79	0.81	.857	
	Provide needed assistance	3.72	3.72	.812	
	F3 Store facilities	**1.49**	**0.04**		10.164
	Proper sitting arrangement	1.51	1.04	.846	
	Proper parking space	1.46	0.97	.747	
	F4 Store location	**3.76**	**0.64**		8.974
	Convenient store location	4.21	0.90	.833	
	No discrimination	3.31	1.05	.515	
	Total Mean S D and Variance Explained	**3.21**	**1.15**		**63.695**
	F1 Education and ethics	**3.75**	**0.20**		33.956
OI	Education contributes to ethics	3.91	0.80	.811	
	Educated retailers abide by norms and regulation	3.53	1.01	.771	
	Educated retailers are humble, helpful and respectful	3.80	0.77	.868	
	F2 Age and ethics	**3.50**	**0.15**		33.157
	Age fosters polite behaviour	3.42	1.10	.776	
	Aged retailers are more honest	3.41	1.09	.867	
	Aged retailers controls unethical behaviour of salesmen	3.67	0.90	.768	
	Total Mean S D and Variance Explained	**3.62**	**0.17**		**67.113**

* D = Dimensions, LP = Legal Provisions, EV = Ethical Values, CS = Customer Satisfaction, M = Mean, S D = Standard Deviation, FL Factor Loadings, VE Variance Explained

Table 4.2.7 Confirmatory Factor Analysis: Convenience Goods

Dimensions	Factors	Total Items	No of Items Deleted	No of Items Retained	Retained Items	Factor Loadings/ Regression Weights	Sig.
Ethics	Honesty	5	2	3	h1	.706	***
					h2	.694	***
					h3	.612	***
	Fairness	4	-	4	f1	.625	***
					f2	.599	***
					f3	.716	***
					f4	.595	***
	Recognition	5	3	2	rc1	.693	***
					rc2	.897	***
CS	Quality	5	-	5	q1	.636	***
					q2	.899	***
					q3	.793	***
					q4	.510	***
					q5	.534	***
	Assistance	4	-	4	a1	.680	***
					a2	.659	***
					a3	.778	***
					a4	.817	***

*** means significance <.05

Table 4.2.8 Demographic Profile wise ANOVA Results in Convenience Goods

Factors	Age wise		Qualification wise		Religion wise		Occupation wise	
	F	Sig.	F	Sig.	F	Sig.	F	Sig.
F1 Honesty	4.498	.012	2.267	.080	1.669	.190	.160	.923
F2 Fairness	5.556	.004	4.612	.003	1.194	.304	1.509	.211
F3 Respect & Recognition	.291	.748	5.012	.002	.517	.596	1.533	.205
F4 Openness	2.210	.111	2.071	.103	1.576	.208	1.419	.237
F5 Responsiveness	.091	.913	.037	.990	.123	.884	1.293	.276
Overall	4.311	.014	3.311	.020	1.689	.186	.736	.531

Table 4.2.9 Demographic Group wise Factorial Mean Values in Convenience Goods

Demographic/ Factors		F1	F2	F3	F4	F5	Overall
Age	BA Age (N=238)	2.56	3.37	3.67	2.79	2.67	3.01
	Average Age (N=11)	2.50	3.18	3.64	2.59	2.64	2.91
	AA Age (N=221)	2.77	3.57	3.70	2.94	2.70	3.14
Qualification	Matriculate (N=64)	2.70	3.59	3.74	3.03	2.69	3.15
	UG (N=61)	2.45	3.51	3.71	2.84	2.70	3.04
	G (N=228)	2.73	3.52	3.74	2.88	2.68	3.11
	PG & Above (N=117)	2.62	3.25	3.53	2.71	2.67	2.96
Religion	Hindu (N=426)	2.64	3.45	3.68	2.84	2.68	3.06
	Sikh (N=37)	2.77	3.58	3.72	2.86	2.74	3.14
	Others (N=07)	3.10	3.75	3.86	3.43	2.67	3.36
Occupation	Service (N=137)	2.66	3.35	3.63	2.79	2.72	3.03
	Business (N=95)	2.67	3.49	3.76	2.75	2.55	3.04
	Retired (N=73)	2.71	3.52	3.73	2.91	2.71	3.11
	Others (N=165)	2.63	3.51	3.67	2.94	2.72	3.09

Table 4.3.1 Split Half Reliability and Cronbach Alpha

	Before Factor Analysis	After Factor Analysis
Group I (Mean)	3.27	3.28
Group II	3.34	3.40
Cronbach Alpha	0.933	0.910

Table 4.3.2 Factor Analysis regarding Legal Provisions

Rounds	Variance Explained	Items Emerged	No of Factors Extracted	Iterations	No of Items Deleted	KMO	Bartlett.
1	58.454	27	8	14	5	.864	3265.897
2	60.031	22	7	9	2	.837	2500.583
3	59.202	20	6	11	1	.839	2369.729
4	59.882	19	6	6	2	.821	2105.143
5	63.415	17	6	6	-	.804	1828.155

Table 4.3.3 Factor Analysis regarding Ethical Values

Rounds	Variance Explained	Items Emerged	No of Factors Extracted	Iterations	No of Items Deleted	KMO	Bartlett.
1	54.299	24	6	8	5	.878	3007.822
2	53.111	19	5	6	1	.834	1969.895
3	54.760	18	5	6	-	.838	1820.745

Table 4.3.4 Factor Analysis regarding Customer Satisfaction

Rounds	Variance Explained	Items Emerged	No of Factors Extracted	Iterations	No of Items Deleted	KMO	Bartlett.
1	60.192	19	5	9	2	.889	3052.805
2	62.193	17	5	6	1	.865	2575.692
3	58.447	16	4	5	-	.872	2521.752

Table 4.3.5 Factor Analysis regarding Other Issues

Rounds	Variance Explained	Items Emerged	No of Factors Extracted	Iterations	No of Items Deleted	KMO	Bartlett
1	62.344	9	3	5	1	.734	966.886
2	68.088	8	3	5	-	.726	913.389

Table 4.3.6 Factorial Profile in Shopping Goods

D	Variables	Mean	SD	FL	% of VE
LP	**F1 Product Quantity**	**3.81**	**0.07**		14.69
	Proper size of product	3.86	0.68	.654	
	Proper records	3.73	0.75	.629	
	Proper packing	3.80	0.75	.736	
	Package contains printed size	3.90	0.64	.727	
	No sale of expired date products	3.75	0.81	.634	
	F2 Product Quality	**3.45**	**0.20**		14.43
	Genuine quality products	3.63	0.82	.607	
	Standardised products	3.17	1.09	.735	
	No adulteration	3.44	0.99	.813	
	Safe Products	3.56	0.90	.805	
	F3 Pricing Norms	**3.01**	**0.11**		9.89
	Fair prices	3.08	1.22	.846	
	No price discrimination	2.93	1.22	.826	
	F4 Social Norms	**2.96**	**0.43**		9.10
	No employment to minors	2.65	1.34	.726	
	No environment pollution	3.26	1.13	.737	
	F5 Information Norms	**2.60**	**0.04**		7.79
	Unbranded products as superior	2.63	1.11	.789	
	Adequate discount	2.57	1.28	.795	
	F6 After Sale Services	**3.29**	**0.28**		7.52
	Repair in warrantee period	3.49	1.03	.834	
	Issue bills on purchase	3.09	1.30	.582	
	Total Mean and Variance Explained	**3.33**	**0.45**		**63.42**
EV	**F1 Honesty**	**3.81**	**0.12**		14.21
	Recognition as consumer	3.92	0.60	.658	
	Knowledge to salesmen	3.63	0.96	.600	
	Access to all varieties	3.78	0.79	.642	
	Politeness and patience	3.91	0.69	.674	
	Courteous	3.80	0.74	.730	
	F2 Fairness	**2.92**	**0.15**		13.62
	Equal and fair dealings	3.13	1.15	.512	
	Truth of product features	2.72	1.11	.500	
	Less profitable customers	2.96	1.14	.681	
	No pressure for purchase	2.84	1.25	.646	
	No preference to some customers	2.97	1.16	.744	
	F3 Respect and Recognition	**2.60**	**0.21**		11.13
	Priority to customer's needs	2.47	1.12	.839	
	Low margin product	2.49	1.06	.794	
	No excuses for unstock products	2.84	1.10	.541	
	F4 Responsiveness	**2.62**	**0.19**		8.53
	No false claims	2.70	0.99	.654	
	Products as per customer needs	2.40	0.97	.571	
	Assist all customers	2.75	1.06	.724	
	F5 Openness	**2.98**	**0.39**		7.27

	After sales dealings	3.25	0.68	.675	
	Don't conceal their limitations	2.70	1.38	.639	
	Total Mean, SD Variance Explained	**2.99**	**0.51**		**54.76**
CS	**F1 Product Quality and Quantity**	**3.85**	**0.13**		20.22
	Good quality products	3.80	0.73	.735	
	Authentic quantity	3.88	0.71	.678	
	Proper and safe packing	3.91	0.69	.665	
	Desired brands	3.99	0.76	.648	
	Printed price	3.61	0.99	.710	
	Supply on delivery date	3.90	0.64	.568	
	F2 Assistance	**3.71**	**0.27**		19.61
	Correct and timely information	3.76	0.92	.620	
	Available at store	3.95	0.72	.712	
	Help in buying decision process	3.82	0.83	.857	
	Provide needed assistance	3.76	0.83	.694	
	Implement suggestions	3.25	1.07	.591	
	F3 Store Services	**3.49**	**0.53**		9.60
	Long queue	3.09	1.08	.695	
	Attractive displays	4.10	0.73	.561	
	No discrimination	3.29	1.05	.611	
	F4 Store Location	**3.46**	**1.00**		9.01
	Convenient store location	4.16	0.80	.643	
	Proper sitting arrangement	2.75	1.45	.691	
	Total Mean, S D Variance Explained	**3.69**	**0.39**		**58.45**
OI	**F1 Education and Ethics**	**3.74**	**0.19**		27.39
	Education contributes to ethics	3.89	0.82	.778	
	Educated retailers abide by norms and regulation	3.52	1.01	.808	
	Educated retailers are humble, helpful and respectful	3.81	0.78	.841	
	F2 Age and Ethics	**3.50**	**0.14**		26.42
	Age fosters polite behaviour	3.43	1.10	.794	
	Aged retailers are more honest	3.41	1.07	.833	
	Aged retailers controls unethical behaviour of salesmen	3.66	0.90	.724	
	F3 Fairness	**2.63**	**0.18**		14.28
	Young retailers do fair practices	2.76	1.15	.662	
	Less educated retailers are fair	2.50	1.01	.783	
	Total Mean, S D Variance Explained	**3.37**	**0.49**		**68.09**

* D = Dimensions, LP = Legal Provisions, EV = Ethical Values, CS = Customer Satisfaction, M = Mean, SD = Standard Deviation, FL Factor Loadings, VE Variance Explained

Table 4.3.7 Confirmatory Factor Analysis: Shopping Goods

D	Factors	Total Items	No of Items Deleted	No of Items Retained	Retained Items	Factor Loadings/ Regression Weights	Sig.
EV	Honesty	5	-	5	h1	.526	***
					h2	.546	***
					h3	.582	***
					h4	.530	***
					h5	.704	***
	Fairness	5	-	5	f1	.507	***
					f2	.667	***
					f3	.638	***
					F4	.536	***
					f5	.561	***
	Recognition	3	-	3	rc1	.593	***
					rc2	.749	***
					rc3	.765	***
CS	Quality	6	-	6	q1	.710	***
					q2	.814	***
					q3	.805	***
					q4	.513	***
					q5	.517	***
					q6	.563	***
	Assistance	5	-	5	a1	.742	***
					a2	.675	***
					a3	.739	***
					a4	.725	***
					a5	.532	***

*** means significance <.05
D = Dimensions, EV = Ethical Values, CS = Customer Satisfaction

Table 4.3.8 Demographic Profile wise ANOVA Results in Shopping Goods

Factors	Age wise		Qualification wise		Religion wise		Occupation wise	
	F	Sig.	F	Sig.	F	Sig.	F	Sig.
F1 Honesty	2.813	.061	4.564	.004	.394	.674	2.284	.078
F2 Fairness	6.273	.002	1.771	.152	1.597	.204	.960	.411
F3 Respect & Recognition	2.518	.082	.516	.672	.476	.622	1.073	.360
F4 Openness	.435	.648	.007	.999	.142	.868	1.352	.257
F5 Responsiveness	.291	.748	4.639	.003	.522	.594	1.147	.330
Overall	4.016	.019	2.366	.070	1.194	.304	.817	.485

Table 4.3.9 Demographic Profile Group Wise Factorial Mean Values in Shopping Goods

Demographic/ Factors		F1	F2	F3	F4	F5	Overall
Age	BA Age (N=238)	3.76	2.82	2.51	2.60	2.96	2.93
	Average Age (N=11)	3.69	2.60	2.67	2.45	2.82	2.85
	AA Age (N=221)	3.87	3.06	2.69	2.63	2.99	3.05
Qualification	Matriculate (N=64)	3.88	3.01	2.60	2.61	3.30	3.08
	UG (N=61)	3.85	2.76	2.55	2.61	2.98	2.95
	G (N=228)	3.85	2.98	2.65	2.62	2.94	3.01
	PG & Above (N=117)	3.66	2.85	2.53	2.61	2.85	2.90
Religion	Hindu (N=426)	3.80	2.91	2.59	2.61	2.97	2.98
	Sikh (N=37)	3.83	3.09	2.65	2.67	2.99	3.04
	Others (N=07)	3.97	3.29	2.91	2.67	3.29	3.22
Occupation	Service (N=137)	3.72	2.83	2.59	2.64	2.91	2.94
	Business (N=95)	3.87	3.00	2.55	2.49	2.97	2.98
	Retired (N=73)	3.88	2.98	2.77	2.69	2.90	3.04
	Others (N=165)	3.82	2.93	2.56	2.63	3.06	3.00

Table 4.4.1 Split Half Reliability and Cronbach's Alpha

Group	Before Factor Analysis	After Factor Analysis
Group I	3.38	3.40
Group II	3.51	3.53
Cronbach's Alpha	0.936	0.924

Table 4.4.2 Factor Analysis of regarding Legal Provisions

Rounds	Variance Explained	Items Emerged	No of Factors Extracted	Iterations	No of Items Deleted	KMO	Bartlett.
1	55.835	27	7	11	8	.882	3543.044
2	54.025	19	5	6	1	.849	2132.683
3	55.243	18	5	6	-	.846	1984.394

Table 4.4.3 Factor Analysis of regarding Ethical Values

Rounds	Variance Explained	Items Emerged	No of Factors Extracted	Iterations	No of Items Deleted	KMO	Bartlett.
1	52.124	24	5	9	3	.891	3366.789
2	56.102	21	5	8	-	.886	2948..051

Table 4.4.4 Factor Analysis of regarding Customer Satisfaction

Rounds	Variance Explained	Items Emerged	No of Factors Extracted	Iterations	No of Items Deleted	KMO	Bartlett.
1	62.892	19	6	7	2	.860	2816.057
2	64.335	17	6	8	2	.829	2198.653
3	57.866	15	4	7	1	.838	2125.280
4	60.987	14	4	6	1	.838	2064.868
5	56.823	13	3	5	-	.836	2026.012

Table 4.4.5 Factor Analysis of regarding Other Issues

Rounds	Variance Explained	Items Emerged	No of Factors Extracted	Iterations	No of Items Deleted	KMO	Bartlett
1	62.830	9	3	4	-	.740	1022.594

Table 4.4.6 Factorial Profile of Specialty Goods

D	Variables	M	SD	FL	% of VE
LP	**F1 Product Quality**	**3.61**	**0.21**		14.804
	Genuine quality products	3.85	0.79	.534	
	Standardised products	3.46	1.08	.741	
	No adulteration	3.66	1.00	.793	
	Safe Products	3.74	0.88	.793	
	No hoarding of gifts	3.33	1.18	.525	
	F2 Product Quantity	**3.77**	**0.29**		12.358
	Proper size of product	3.91	0.73	.619	
	Proper records	3.87	0.75	.549	
	Proper packing	3.96	0.78	.696	
	Package contains specified size	3.34	0.61	.765	
	F3 Promotion	**3.50**	**0.14**		11.943
	Fair advertising	3.34	1.14	.706	
	Accurate information	3.59	1.05	.763	
	Fair sales promotion	3.57	0.99	.760	
	F4 Social Norms	**3.24**	**0.32**		8.575
	No price discrimination	3.35	1.19	.654	
	No employment of minors	2.88	1.38	.652	
	Issue of bills on purchase	3.49	1.18	.710	
	F5 Pricing Norms	**2.72**	**0.09**		7.563
	Adequate discount	2.79	1.08	.621	
	Proper after sales services	2.61	1.01	.668	
	Advertised price	2.75	1.07	.673	
	Total Mean, S D Variance Explained	**3.42**	**0.42**		**55.243**
EV	**F1 Fairness**	**3.13**	**0.20**		17.195
	Equal and fair dealings	3.28	1.18	.618	
	No exploitation of less bargainers	2.91	1.22	.555	
	Accurate information	3.51	0.99	.551	
	Truth of product features	2.90	1.17	.537	
	Less profitable customers	3.12	1.18	.672	
	No pressure for purchase	3.10	1.23	.614	
	No preference to some customers	3.12	1.17	.692	
	Protect consumer rights	3.09	1.13	.622	
	F2 Honesty	**3.89**	**0.12**		13.614
	Recognition as consumer	4.01	0.62	.612	
	Knowledge to salesmen	3.73	0.98	.527	
	Access to all varieties	3.84	0.79	.693	
	Politeness and patience	3.99	0.68	.680	
	Courteous, respectful and honest	3.86	0.75	.712	
	F3 Respect and Recognition	**2.75**	**0.25**		10.713
	Priority to customer's needs	2.59	1.16	.814	
	Low margin product	2.61	1.12	.806	
	No excuses for unstock products	3.04	1.16	.604	
	F4 Responsiveness	**2.63**	**0.17**		7.505
	No false claims	2.72	1.01	.555	
	Products as per customer type	2.43	1.01	.613	

	Assist all customers	2.73	1.06	.775	
	F5 Openness	**3.75**	**0.09**		7.074
	After sales dealings	3.81	0.75	.862	
	Cognizance to complaints	3.68	0.93	.580	
	Total Mean, S D Variance Explained	**3.24**	**0.50**		**56.102**
	F1 Product Quality and Quantity	**4.00**	**0.12**		22.717
CS	Good quality products	3.92	0.77	.683	
	Authentic quantity	4.04	0.70	.800	
	Proper and safe packing	4.08	0.72	.765	
	Desired brands	4.13	0.75	.652	
	Fair and printed price	3.85	0.85	.668	
	F2 Assistance	**3.68**	**0.29**		21.569
	Correct and timely information	3.87	0.94	.663	
	Help in buying decision process	3.92	0.86	.763	
	Provide needed assistance	3.88	0.82	.805	
	No discrimination	3.44	1.09	.595	
	Implement suggestions	3.30	1.10	.689	
	F3 Store Services	**3.84**	**0.61**		12.537
	Convenient store location	4.20	0.77	.600	
	No long queue	3.14	1.08	.606	
	Attractive displays	4.19	0.69	.634	
	Total Mean, S D Variance Explained	**3.83**	**0.34**		**56.823**
	Education and Ethics	**3.76**	**0.20**		25.758
OI	Education contributes to ethics	3.92	0.81	.767	
	Educated retailers abide by norms and regulation	3.54	1.02	.803	
	Educated retailers are humble, helpful and respectful	3.81	0.82	.860	
	Age and Ethics	**3.32**	**0.40**		25.584
	Age fosters polite behaviour	3.40	1.11	.720	
	Aged retailers are more honest	3.44	1.09	.833	
	Young retailers do fair practices	2.75	1.16	.650	
	Aged retailers controls unethical behaviour of salesmen	3.69	0.88	.750	
	F3 Fairness	**2.99**	**0.72**		11.488
	Less educated retailers are fair	2.48	1.02	.605	
	No discrimination by less educated retailers	3.50	0.92	.625	
	Total Mean, S D Variance Explained	**3.39**	**0.48**		**62.830**

* D = Dimensions, LP = Legal Provisions, EV = Ethical Values, CS = Customer Satisfaction, M = Mean, S D = Standard Deviation, FL Factor Loadings, VE Variance Explained

Table 4.4.7 Confirmatory Factor Analysis: Specialty Goods

D	Factors	Total Items	No of Items Deleted	No of Items Retained	Retained Items	Factor Loadings/ Regression Weights	Sig.
EV	Fairness	8	-	8	f1	.587	***
					f2	.610	***
					f3	.581	***
					F4	.638	***
					f5	.671	***
					f6	.587	***
					f7	.591	***
					f8	.632	***
	Honesty	5	-	5	h1	.573	***
					h2	.524	***
					h3	.629	***
					h4	.601	***
					h5	.689	***
	Recognition	3	-	3	rc1	.699	***
					rc2	.810	***
					rc3	.731	***
CS	Quality	6	-	6	q1	.716	***
					q2	.809	***
					q3	.740	***
					q4	.630	***
					q5	.528	***
	Assistance	5	-	5	a1	.733	***
					a2	.753	***
					a3	.802	***
					a4	.535	***

*** means significance <.05
D = Dimensions, EV = Ethical Values, CS = Customer Satisfaction

Table 4.4.8 Demographic Profile wise ANOVA Results in Specialty Goods

Factors	Age wise		Qualification wise		Religion wise		Occupation wise	
	F	Sig.	F	Sig.	F	Sig.	F	Sig.
F1 Honesty	5.981	.003	4.866	.002	1.955	.143	1.953	.120
F2 Fairness	2.310	.100	4.678	.003	1.231	.293	2.871	.036
F3 Respect & Recognition	4.238	.015	1.450	.227	.814	.444	1.415	.238
F4 Openness	.153	.858	.120	.948	.178	.837	1.523	.208
F5 Responsiveness	3.033	.049	3.339	.019	1.120	.327	2.037	.108
Overall	3.867	.022	3.809	.010	1.505	.223	.913	.435

Table 4.4.9 Demographic Profile Group wise Factorial Mean Values in Specialty Goods

Demographic/ Factors		F1	F2	F3	F4	F5	Overall
Age	BA Age (N=238)	3.03	3.84	2.63	2.61	3.77	3.18
	Average Age (N=11)	2.81	3.78	2.64	2.70	3.23	3.03
	AA Age (N=221)	3.26	3.94	2.88	2.64	3.74	3.29
Qualification	Matriculate (N=64)	3.28	3.95	2.78	2.58	3.91	3.30
	UG (N=61)	2.98	3.92	2.63	2.63	3.73	3.18
	G (N=228)	3.22	3.94	2.83	2.64	3.78	3.28
	PG & Above (N=117)	2.95	3.73	2.63	2.63	3.59	3.10
Religion	Hindu (N=426)	3.11	3.87	2.73	2.63	3.73	3.21
	Sikh (N=37)	3.29	3.97	2.84	2.65	3.84	3.32
	Others (N=07)	3.55	4.11	3.14	2.48	4.07	3.47
Occupation	Service (N=137)	2.99	3.78	2.76	2.71	3.63	3.18
	Business (N=95)	3.19	3.93	2.63	2.52	3.83	3.22
	Retired (N=73)	3.17	3.99	2.93	2.65	3.72	3.29
	Others (N=165)	3.19	3.90	2.72	2.60	3.80	3.24

Table 4.5 Result of Various CFA Indices

Goods	C	CMIN	P	CMIN/DF	GFI	AGFI	CFI	TLI	RMR	RMSEA
CG	E	41.100	.022	1.644	.981	.966	.985	.979	.030	.03
	CS	108.569	.000	4.720	.956	.914	.950	.922	.032	.08
ShG	E	144.751	.000	2.373	.956	.935	.943	.927	.048	.05
	CS	170.387	.000	4.156	.938	.901	.935	.913	.035	.08
SpG	E	283.124	.000	2.831	.929	.904	.920	.905	.05	.06
	CS	96.388	.000	3.856	.960	.927	.954	.934	.03	.07

*C= Construct, CS=Customer Satisfaction, E= Ethics

Table 4.6 Final SEM Model for Convenience Goods

Rounds	CMIN	P	CMIN/DF	GFI	AGFI	CFI	TLI	RMR	RMSEA
1	32.662	.000	8.166	.971	.892	.959	.897	.023	..124
2	3.012	.390	1.004	.997	.987	1.000	1.000	.004	.003

Table 4.7 SEM Model for Shopping Goods

Rounds	CMIN	P	CMIN/DF	GFI	AGFI	CFI	TLI	RMR	RMSEA
1	77.874	.000	19.468	.940	.773	.902	.755	.052	.198
2	28.972	.000	4.891	.988	.941	.985	.948	.014	.08

Table 4.8 SEM Model for Specialty Goods

Rounds	CMIN	P	CMIN/DF	GFI	AGFI	CFI	TLI	RMR	RMSEA
1	76.833	.000	19.208	.936	.760	.909	.773	.032	.197
2	62.224	.000	15.556	.949	.810	.927	.819	.028	.176
3	30.180	.000	7.545	.973	.899	.967	.918	.014	.118
4	5.187	.159	1.729	.996	.978	.997	.991	.011	.039

Table 4.9 Validity and Reliability

Nature of Goods	Constructs	Convergent Validity (AVE)	Construct Reliability (CR)	Cronbach's Alpha
Convenience	Ethics	0.59	0.70	.804
	Customer Satisfaction	0.67	0.92	.857
Shopping	Ethics	0.62	0.96	.808
	Customer Satisfaction	0.76	0.93	.864
Specialty	Ethics	0.60	0.85	.868
	Customer Satisfaction	0.65	0.90	.843

CHAPTER 5

ETHICAL RETAIL PRACTICES: PERCEPTIONS OF RETAILERS

5.1. Background

The present chapter examines the perceptions of retailers about the nature and extent of ethical practices in the forms of their dealings with different stakeholders such as, customers, wholesalers, manufacturers, salesmen and regulatory bodies. It also portrays the effect of their demographic background like age and education on the ethical retail practices while dealing with these stakeholders.

As already stated, retailing is one of the pillars of Indian economy. The Indian retail industry is one of the biggest industries with a turnover of around $450-500 billion. With 12 million outlets, India has the largest retail outlet density in the world and being the fifth most attractive emerging retail market (Bajaj et al., 2007). However, the retail sector in India is highly fragmented and unorganised as organised retail in the country is still at a very nascent stage. Organised retailing refers to trading activities undertaken by retailers registered for sales tax, VAT, and income tax These include the corporate-backed hypermarkets and retail chains, and also the privately owned large retail businesses like shopping malls. Unorganised retailing, on the other hand, comprises of the traditional forms of low-cost retailing stores such as the local provisional (kiryana) shops and general stores. However, in the last few years, the process of change started with traditional markets making way for new formats such as departmental stores, supermarkets and specialty stores in the process. Western-style malls appear in metros and other big cities, introducing the Indian consumer to a shopping experience of global standards. This potential of the Indian retail market is making the corporate houses like Reliance, Tata's, ITC and Bombay Dyeing, along with real estate companies venture into retail business. As retailing is emerging market in India, and Jammu, being the city of temples, is not far behind, as it is also witnessing the stupendous growth and opportunities in retailing. There are several conventional family run, 'mom and pop shops', dealing in all kinds of consumer goods including convenience, shopping and specialty goods. Though the organised retail sector is in preliminary stage with the opening of Vishal marts in Jammu city, as most of the retail stores yet come under unorganised ones. In fact, these stores have taken up 98% of the J&K retail market. The growth of retail market in J&K is mainly due to the change in the lifestyle, tastes and preferences of the consumers which brought an innovative change in their shopping attitude and consumption patterns. New generation of consumers has preference towards luxury goods, which due to the strong increase in their discretionary income and changing demographic patterns and life styles. Presently the customers are earning more hefty pay- packages a large number of working women, western influences and more disposable income have opened a lot of opportunities in the retail market of J&K.

Ethics plays a very significant role in retailing (Sharma and Sharma, 2011, 2009; Kurt and Hacioglu, 2010; Sarma, 2007; Dubinsky et al., 2004; Whysall, 2000; Abratt et al., 1999; Whysall, 1995 and Dubinsky and Levy, 1983) This is because the retailers being last in the distribution chain and associated with different stakeholders like consumers, employees, suppliers, financers, government agencies, media and community at large (Fassin, 2009; Kaptein, 2008; Berman and Evans, 2007; Kujala 2001; Whysall, 2000, 1998), who are directly or indirectly associated with them. The retailers need to possess some ethical virtues for managing better retail business (Levy and Dubinsky, 1983). In fact, the retailers have responsibilities towards each stakeholder in their retail business (Fernando, 2009; Kaptein, 2008; Napal, 2003; Kujala, 2001) and are required to fulfill stakeholders' expectations in an ethical manner. Retailers need to observe ethical standards in their decision making, particularly while confronting situations not covered under law (Sarma, 2007; Lavorata and Pontier, 2005 and Dubinsky et al., 2004). If the retailers deal with different stakeholders in an ethical manner, it definitely increases their turnover, profitability, and image of the retail stores as well as the suppliers. On the contrary, unethical retail practices lead to customer dissatisfaction, switching to other stores, less sales, profit and bad image of the retail stores. It is thus, necessary to study their dealings in terms of their relations with different stakeholders (Fassin, 2009) for formulating an appropriate strategic action plan emerges so that retailing practices are further improved, maintained and monitored for sustainable and long term profits within framework of ethical values.

5. 2. Data Collection

The data for the present study have been obtained from both secondary and primary sources. The secondary data were available in the various journals such as *Journal of Academy of Marketing Science, Journal of Business Ethics, Journal of Marketing, Journal of Retailing*, books and the internet. The primary data were collected from 200 retailers from Gandhi Nagar, a posh colony in Jammu city. In total, there were about 250 retailers in Gandhi Nagar dealing in different kinds of products like garments, grocery, stationery, utensil etc. All of them were approached for obtaining the relevant data, but out of them, 200 retailers responded with a response rate of 80%.

5.3. Generation of Scale Items

The primary data were collected through a specifically developed schedule (Annexure II) on the basis of the available literature (Kaptein, 2008; Sarma, 2007; Lavorata and Pontier, 2005; Dubinsky et al., 2004; Kujala, 2001 and Whysall, 2000) and discussions with experts in the related fields of study. It comprised of 14 items of general nature and 52 items based on 5 point Likert scale (5 <-----> 1) ranging from strongly agree (5) to strongly disagree (1) (Malhotra, 2008, p. 274). The schedule consisted of seven dimensions pertaining to the ethical responsibilities of retailers towards consumers (17 items), employees (5 items), suppliers (10 items), competitors (5 items), government (5 items), financers (5 items) and community (5 items).

5.4. Profile of Respondents

The final response from 200 retailers has been examined on the basis of their demographic backgrounds. The demographic and some general information comprised of age, qualification, experience, type of retail store, number of employees and their performance in terms of sales and profit. The age of the respondents has been catagorised into three groups, viz., below average, average and above average age retailers. The average age of the respondents came to be as 40 years through arithmetic mean. About 55% of the total respondents are having below average age and about 57% of them having graduation and above qualification and majority of these retailers (81%) have less than three employees. The respondents have different kinds of stores like garments (24%), general stores (19%), electronics (12%), provisional stores (10%) and others (35%). The average monthly sales of the respondents came to be ₹ 5,00,000 and mainstream of the respondents (81%) have below average sales per month. The average profit per month found to be ₹ 50,000 and majority of the respondents (80%) have below average profit per month because these retail outlets are small and they have a lot of competition among themselves in the area. About half of the respondents have one to ten years of experience of retail business and about 47% of them have membership with retail associations like Federation of Retailers' Association (Table 5.1).

5.5. Reliability and Validity

To check the reliability, Cronbach Alpha and split half values have been worked out (Malhotra, 2008, p. 285) twice i. e. before and after factor analysis by dividing the respondents into two equal halves. The data were found reliable before the factor analysis as mean values of both groups (Group I = 4.08 and Group II = 4.06) were almost similar. Similarly, after factor analysis, the data have proved quite satisfactory in terms of split half reliability as mean obtained from both the groups of respondents were satisfactory (Group I = 4.16 and Group II = 4.17). Moreover, Cronbach Alpha values also proved reliable before and after factor analysis as it came to be .768 and .807 (Table 5.2). The Content validity has been duly assessed by reviewing the literature and discussions with the experts and researchers working on similar topics. Construct validity, which measures the extent to which a single scale measures the same construct, has been examined through factor analysis on the basis of Principal component analysis carried on all items in each scale to determine whether or not they load on a single scale. An Eigen value equal to one is taken as criterion for significance of a factor. The Eigen values of all the factors were greater than one, indicating strong construct validity (Table 5.4). The Convergent validity has been determined through correlation of variables with the construct (Malhotra, 2008, p. 286) and in most of the cases the correlation coefficients were above .5. In addition to this, Discriminant validity has also been proved as the correlation coefficients between constructs were less than .3 (Table 5.15).

5.6. Factor Analysis

The technique of factor analysis has been used through Statistical Package for Social Sciences (SPSS, 17 Version) with Principal component analysis along with varimax rotation for summarisation of the total data into minimum meaningful factors. The items having factor loading less than 0.5 and Eigen value less than 1 were ignored for the subsequent analysis (Hair et al., 2009). As stated earlier, the schedule comprised of 52 items (14 of general information) and after applying factor analysis 31 items got emerged into 10 factors with 70.39% variance explained. The ten factors are F1 (Financers), F2 (Employees), F3 (Legal Regulations), F4 (Customers), F5 (Taxation), F6 (Competitors), F7 (Community), F8 (Suppliers), F9 (Product Quality), F10 (Services). Each factor is discussed in detail as under:-

Factor 1 (*Financers*): Retailers procure funds either from banks and other financial institutions for setting up their retail stores and purchasing the merchandise. They are liable to the financers in terms of interest, accurate information, co-operation and the return of principal amount on the date of maturity. This factor composed of five items, viz., 'cooperate with financers', 'information to financers', 'interest at agreed rate', 'loan on maturity date', 'respect to financers'. The mean score of this factor (3.84) indicates above average ethical values being observed by retailers in relation with financers. The mean values of the items under this factor range from 3.79 to 3.94. About 68% of the total retailers were found to be ethical while dealing with their financers as they give due respect (3.80) and needed information to them (3.79). About the same number of respondents found paying interest on loans taken by them for the establishment and reconstruction of their retail stores at agreed rate (3.83) and also returning the loan on the maturity date (3.79).

Factor 2 (*Employees*): This factor has five items, viz., 'treating all employees equally', 'handling employees' complaints', 'paying for overtime work', 'helping employees when needed' and 'protecting employee rights'. The overall mean of the factor (4.02) with 11.34% variance explained, indicates retailers as ethical in dealing with their employees (salesmen). The mean values of the items under this factor range from 3.87 to 4.30. Majority of the retailers (85%) were found treating their employees equally without any biasness. The employees want equality and justice in terms of workload and remuneration, the absence of which leads to annoyance and jealousy towards peers and the owner (4.30). About the same number of respondents were handling employees' complaints immediately and helping employees when required so that they can work with customers without any dilemma (3.97). About 86% of the retailers shared that employees getting extra money for overtime work (4.00) everyday and for working on holidays (Sunday) and employee rights as employee also being protected to a large extent (3.95).

Factor 3 (*Legal Regulations*): This factor contains four items, viz., 'needed information to suppliers', rules of fair play with competitors', following legal rules and regulations' and 'protecting the environment'. The overall factorial mean on five point Likert scale is 4.47. The factor loadings and mean values of items under this factor range from .795 to .662 and 4.61 to 4.88 respectively (Table 5.4) Majority of the respondents (99%) were found providing the information to the suppliers/wholesalers (4.74) and about 97% of them expressed their compliance to legal norms frames by the government (4.74). About the same number of respondents shared that they act fairly with their competitors and never do any harm to them by negative word of mouth (4.61).

Factor 4 (*Customers*): Retailers are in direct link as front line managers with customers and their dealings with them, are ethical resulting to sustainable consumer satisfaction, loyalty and better business performance. This factor encompasses four items, viz., 'needed information to consumers', 'treating all consumers equally', 'helping customers in making choices' and 'truthfulness with customers'. The overall mean of this factor (4.18) depicts retailers' ethical dealings with customers as they supply timely information regarding the different brands of products available in their retail stores. Majority of the respondents found providing the needed information to the customers about the products (4.18) and at the same time helping them in purchasing decisions (4.17). Customers seek information from retailers about many aspects and also need some help in making choice for the product. About 98% of them found treating all customers equally irrespective of their gender, age, caste, religion and income (4.22).

Factor 5 (*Taxation*): Various types of taxes are levied by the government for generating the public revenue from individuals and business firms. The retailers too are required to fill up the tax return and pay the taxes honestly on time. This factor consists of two items, viz., 'filling the tax return on time' and 'paying the actual rate of tax'. The factor has mean score of 4.13 with 6.23% of variance explained and Eigen value of 1.91. The commonalities of both items were found to be .92 and .93, much higher than standard value of 0.50. About 85% of the total respondents are filling the tax return on time (4.24) and paying the actual rate of tax (4.01, Table 5.4).

Factor 6 (*Competitors*): The retail sector has been becoming more competitive day by day due to the change in structure and size of retail stores from traditional family run stores to departmental stores, multiple shops, companies' franchises of garments such as Allen Cooper, Yougal Sons, Priknit, Outlaw etc. In fact, the organised retailing like shopping malls has been in evolutionary stage in Jammu city and retailers having less competition from the big retail players like Wal Mart, Reliance etc. This factor has three items, namely, 'never criticise competitor', 'not hiring the employees of competitors' and 'respecting competitors'. Majority of the retailers are giving due respect to their competitors (4.12) and not berating their competitors with customers (4.04). Moreover, they do not hire the employees of competitors (4.06) by offering them higher salary and other benefits like accommodation and transportation facilities just with intention to destabilise the competitors.

Factor 7 (*Child Labour*): Besides other stakeholders, the retailers have also ethical responsibilities towards community. This factor constitutes two items, viz., 'no child labour', and 'respect to children and women employees'. The factorial mean is 4.43

with 5.36% of variance explained. The commonalities of both items are above .50 (.83 and .84) and Eigen value is also greater than one (1.35). Majority (99%) of the total respondents do not have child labour in their retail stores (4.38). As it is illegal and unethical to employ the children below the age of 14 years and they are being charged with heavy fine and imprisonment, if they employ the children under the age of 14 years. In addition to this, retailers also give due respect to the women employees (4.47).

Factor 8 (*Suppliers*): Retailers purchase the merchandise from wholesalers and sometimes even from manufacturers. But it was found during the survey that in Jammu city most of the retailers buy their merchandise from wholesalers only. Retailers' relations with their suppliers are based upon cooperation, trust, commitment, and promise keeping. The retailers need to be ethical in their dealings with suppliers. This factor consists of items like, 'helping suppliers as and when needed' and 'fair in dealings with suppliers'. About 95% of the total respondents were found fair in dealing with their suppliers (4.11) as they furnish the needed information to suppliers about consumers' demands of different brands of products and also assist them by making immediate cash payments for the products purchased by them (Table, 5.4)).

Factor 9 (*Product Quality*): The present customer expects quality products at reasonable price. He also wants products to be safe, unadulterated and hygienic. This factor encompasses two items, viz., 'no adulteration of goods', and 'return of outdated products'. The factorial mean score (3.02) indicates just nominal satisfaction about adulteration from viewpoint of retailers as most of the products are packed by the suppliers and retailer's job is to sell them. This can be possible in case of food items which are packed by retailers like pulses, rice etc. To supplement this, about 81% of the total respondents do not sell outdated products to customers because it tarnishes the image of their retail store and they do return the outdated products to their suppliers (3.98).

Factor 10 (*Services*): Retailers, particularly dealing in specialty products like electronic goods, give after sales services to consumers for making them comfortable and familiar with the retail store. Two items, viz., 'supplying demanded goods' and repairing/ replacing the products during the period of warrantee / guarantee', constitute the last factor. The factorial mean (4.41) with 3.52% variance explained and Eigen value (1.02), indicate retailers in Jammu city providing the demanded goods to the customers with adequate after sale services. About 98% of the respondents provide variety of products of different brands (4.75) and thus, fulfill the demands of the customers. Moreover, about the same percentage of respondents dealing in specialty products give after sales services to the customers (4.08) as it helps them in attracting new customers (Table 5.4) and retaining the existing ones.

To sum up, the above average overall mean score (4.14) with standard deviation (.37) accorded by the retailers found them as ethical in their dealings with different stakeholders such as financers, employees, customers, suppliers, competitors, government.

5.7. Demographic Group wise Analysis

The data so collected have further been analysed through ANOVA, for finding out the mean differences about the ethical retail practices of respondents' profile including age, qualification, experience and type of store. ANOVA divulges the differences in mean scores of respondents belonging to different demographic categories. Each one of which has been examined as under:-

5.7.1. Age Wise Analysis

As already stated, respondents have been classified into three categories, viz., below average, average and above average retailers. The average age of respondents came to be as 40 years. Out of the total respondents, more than half (55%) belong to below average age group To find out the mean differences among different age groups regarding ethical values in retail practices, Univariate analysis of variance has been applied. On the whole, ANOVA reveals insignificant mean differences among the respondents belonging to different age groups (F=2.673, Sig. = .072) regarding ethical retail practices. Further, when it is applied factor wise, to examine the significant mean difference in different age groups regarding individual factors constituting the overall construct of ethical retail practices. No significant mean difference has been found in nine factors out of ten factors, viz., F1 (Financers: Sig. = .196), F2 (Employees: .233), F3 (Legal regulation: .549) F4 (Customers: .973), F5 (Taxation: .267) F6 (Competitors: .267), F7 (No child labour: .324), F8 (Suppliers: .502), F10 (Services: .822). Only one factor (F9) has significant difference (Product quality: .008, Table 5.5).

5.7.2. Qualification wise Respondents

To find out the effect of qualification on the ethical retail practices, respondents have been grouped into, matriculate (23%), undergraduate (20%), graduate & above (57%) qualification groups. ANOVA indicates significant mean differences in the responses of retailers belonging to different educational backgrounds (F=11.674, Sig. = .000). When it has been applied on individual factors, it exhibits significance difference merely in two factors i.e. F2 (Employees: .000) and F5 (Taxation: .000). The rest of the factors have insignificant differences, viz., F1 (Financers: Sig. =.700), F3 (Legal regulation: .655) F4 (Customers: .143), F6 (Competitors: .671), F7 (No child labour: .123), F8 (Suppliers: .329), F9 (Product quality: .965) and F10 (Services: .688). Post hoc through

LSD test indicates significant differences in the response of matriculate and graduate respondents but insignificant difference between undergraduate and graduate respondents. The mean values of three age groups range from 4.02 to 4.21. Retailers having graduation or above qualification are more ethical (4.21) followed by undergraduate (4.16) and matriculate (4.02) respondents (Table 5.6). It means that education affects the ethical retail practices as it creates the retailers more knowledge oriented and refines their attitude, behaviour and dealings with different stakeholders.

5.7.3. Experience wise Respondents

On the basis of experience, respondents have been classified into four groups, viz., respondents having experience upto 10 years, 11 to 20 years, 21 to 30 years and finally above 30 years of experience as retailers. Majority of the respondents have experience upto 10 years. For exploring the mean differences among different experienced groups of retailers regarding ethical retail practices, Univariate Analysis of Variance has been used. ANOVA portrays insignificant mean differences among the respondents belonging to different experience groups (F=2.176, Sig. = .092) regarding the ethical retail practices. Further, individual factor wise analysis also reveals insignificant mean differences in nine factors out of ten factors, viz., F1 (Financers: Sig. =.768), F2 (Employees: .168), F3 (Legal regulation: .467) F4 (Customers: .217), F5 (Taxation: .108) F6 (Competitors: .578), F7 (Community: .188), F9 (Product quality: .806) and F10 (Services: .089). Only one factor (F8) has significant mean difference (Suppliers: .000; Table 5.5). Most of the respondents accorded same mean values for most of the factors.

5.7.4. Type of Stores wise Respondents

The respondents have also been classified into five categories on the basis of type of retail stores, viz., garments (24%), general store (19%), electronics (12%), provisional (10%) and others (35%). ANOVA divulges insignificant mean differences among the retailers having different kinds of stores (F = 1.426 Sig. = .227) Further, individual factor wise analysis also discloses no significant mean differences in eight factors, viz. F1 (Sig. =.539), F3 (.169) F4 (.780), F6 (.950), F7 (.729), F8 (.468), F9 (.801) and F10 (.894). Barely two factors viz. F2 (.005) and F5 (.011) have significant mean difference regarding the perceptions of ethical retail practices among retailers with different type of stores Table 5.5).

5.8 Hypotheses Testing

H 1 *There is wide ranging difference of opinion with regard to ethical retail practices among different stakeholders.*

The present study examines the perceptions of different stakeholders in retailing viz. customers, retailers, wholesalers, manufacturers and regulatory bodies. Each stakeholder differs in his perception about ethical retail practices. It is thus, necessary to test the significant mean differences in their perceptions about ethical retail practices. To test the first hypothesis, ANOVA has been applied. ANOVA depicts significant mean differences in the perceptions of different of stakeholders about ethical retail practices (F= 34.315, Sig. = .000, Table 5.9). Thus, the first hypothesis stands accepted.

H 3 (a) *There is significant mean difference in the ethical retail practices of younger and senior in age retailers.*

To test this hypothesis, the respondents were divided into two groups, i. e., below 40 years and above 40 years of age. This has been done as per the guidelines available in the existing literature relating to the subject. Deshpande, (1997) considered respondents below 40 years of age as younger and above 40 years as senior in age. Moreover, average age was calculated as per the age of all respondents. For testing this hypothesis, independent t-test has been applied. The results of t test portray significant mean difference between the younger and senior in age retailers (t = 2.312, Sig. = .02, Table 5.11). The hypothesis is thus, accepted.

H 3 (b) *Highly educated retailers are more ethical than their less educated counterparts.*

To find out the effect of qualification on the ethical retail practices, respondents have been classified as matriculate (23%), undergraduate (20%), graduate and above (57%) qualification groups. ANOVA indicates significant mean differences in the responses of retailers belonging to different educational backgrounds (F=11.674, Sig. = .000, Table 5.12). Thus, the hypothesis is accepted. It means as level of education increases, the retailers become more ethical because education enhances knowledge, wisdom and modifies the behaviour.

H 4 *The regulatory bodies differ in their perceptions about ethical retail practices.*

For finding out the difference in the perceptions of different department regarding ethical retail practices, ANOVA has been used. ANOVA depicts significant mean difference in the response of different regulatory agencies (F= 5.792, Sig. = .001, Table 5.13). Hence, the hypothesis is accepted.

H 5 *Moderate level ethical values are followed by retailers.*

For testing this hypothesis, one sample t test has been applied. Since the data has been based on five point Likert scale and to test this hypothesis a test value is required and thus, 3 being the average, has been fixed as test value representing hypothetical population mean. The one sample t test reveals significant difference between the actual mean and test value or hypothetical population mean (t = 50.87 Sig. = .000, Table 5.14). Thus, the hypothesis is rejected.

5.9 Conclusion

On the whole, retailers are ethical in their dealings with their stakeholders. The retailers argue that they try their best to fulfill the expectations of various stakeholders in ethical manner as they pay interest on loans on time, fill the tax returns, focus on quality and standardised products and get their weight measures annually checked by the Weights and Measures Department. However, they do not make much effort for training their salesmen about ethical issues. In fact, no code of ethics has been framed by any concerned quarter that can guide them for better ethical retail practices. No doubt, some of the retailers having membership with different retail associations but the efforts of these retail associations are very nominal in guiding these retailers. The retailers' associations should frame an ethical code of conduct on the lines of American Marketing Associations so that better ethical practices can be maintained in the retail sector.

References

Abratt, Russell; M. Bendixen and K. Drop (1999), "Ethical Perceptions of South African Retailers: Management and Salespersonnel", *International Journal of Retail and Distribution Management*, Vol. 27, No.2, pp. 91-105

Bajaj, Cretan, Rajneesh Tulip and Niche V. Srivastava (2007), Retail Management, Seventh Edition, Oxford University Press, New Delhi, pp. 9, 10

Berman, Berry and Joel R. Evans (2007), Retail Management, Tenth Edition, Prentice Hall of India Pvt Ltd, New Delhi, pp. 44

Deshpande, Satish P. (1997), "Managers Perception of Proper Ethical Conduct: The Affect of Sex, Age and Level of Education", *Journal of Business Ethics*, Vol. 16, pp.79-85

Dubinsky, Alan J., Rajan Nataraajan and Wen-Yeh Huang (2004), "The Influence of Moral Philosophies on Retail Salespeople's Ethical Perceptions", *The Journal of Consumer Affairs*, Vol. 38 (2), pp. 297-317

Dubinksy, A. J. and M. Levy (1985), "Ethics in Retailing: Perceptions of Retail Salespeople", *Journal of the Academy of Marketing Sciences*, Vol. 13, pp. 1–16.

Fassin Yves (2009), "The Stakeholder Model Refined", *Journal of Business Ethics*, Vol. 84, pp. 113-135

Fernando, A. C. (2009), Business Ethics, An Indian Perspective, First Impression, Dorling Kindersley, Pearson Education, New Delhi, pp. 4, 5, 6

Hair, J. F.; William C. Black; Barry J. Babin; Ralph E. Anderson and Ronald L. Tathum (2009), Multivariate Data Analysis, Sixth Edition. Pearson Prentice Publishers, New Delhi

Kaptein, Muel (2008), "Developing a Measure of Unethical Behaviour in the Workplace: A Stakeholder Perspective", *Journal of Management*, Vol. 34 (October), pp. 978-1008.

Kujala, Johanna (2001), "Analysing Moral Issues in Stakeholder Relations", *Business Ethics: A European Review*, Vol. 10, pp. 233-247

Kurt, Gizem and Gungor Hacioglu (2010), "Ethics as a Customer Perceived value Driver in the Context of Online Retailing", *African Journal of Business Management*, Vol. 4(5), pp. 672-677

Lavorata, Laure and Suzanne Pontier (2005), "The Success of a Retailers' Ethical Policy: Focusing on Local Actions", *The Journal of Academy of Marketing Science Review*, Vol. 2005 (12), pp. 1-9.

Levy, M. and A. J. Dubinsky (1983), "Identifying and Addressing Retail Salespeople's Ethical Problems', *Journal of Retailing,* Vol. 59, pp. 46–66

Malhotra, Naresh (2008), 'Marketing Research', An Applied Orientation, Fifth Edition, Prentice Hall of India, New Delhi

Napal, Geetanee (2003), Ethical Decision Making in Business: Focus on Mauritius, *Business Ethics: A European Review*, Vol. 12 (1), pp. 54-63

Sarma, Nripendra Narayan (2007), "Ethics in Retailing-Perception of Management and Sales Personnel", *(http:// dspace.iimk.ac.in/bitstream/2259/388/1/61-68.pdf),* last accessed on March 20, 2012

Sharma R. D. and Bodh Raj Sharma (2011), "Legal Provisions and Ethical Values in Retail Sector: Study of Convenience Goods", *Arash, A Journal of ISMDR,* Vol. 1, No. 1, (January), pp. 1-9

-- (2009), "Ethics in Retailing: Perceptions of Consumers", *Saaransh RKJ Journal of Management*, Vol. 1, No. 1, (July), pp. 43-55

Whysall, Paul (2000), "Addressing Ethical Issues in Retailing: A Stakeholder Perspective", *International Review of Retail, Distribution and Consumer Research,* Vol. 10 (3), July, pp. 305–318

---------------- (2000), "Stakeholder Mismanagement in Retailing: A British Perspective", *Journal of Business Ethics*, Vol. 23, pp. 19-28

---------------- (1998), "Ethical Relationship in Retailing: Some Cautionary Tales", *Business Ethics: A European Review*, Vol. 7 (2), pp. 103-110

---------------- (1995), "Ethics in Retailing", *Business Ethics: A European Review*, Vol. 4 (3), pp. 150-156

Table 5.1 Demographic Profile of Retailers

Variables	Frequency	Percentage	Variables	Frequency	Percentage
Age:			**Sales**		
Below average	109	55	Below Average	137	81
Average	10	05	Average	06	03
Above average	81	40	Above Average	27	16
Qualification:			**Profit**		
Matriculate	47	23	Below Average	134	80
Under graduate	40	20	Average	14	08
Graduate and above	113	57	Above Average	21	12
Type of Stores			**Experience**		
			0-10	103	52
Garments	47	24	11-20	49	25
General Store	39	19	21-30	35	17
Electronic	25	12	Above 30	13	06
Provisional Store	20	10	**Membership of Retailers' Federations**		
Others	69	35			
Employees					
Below 3	161	81	Yes	93	47
Above 3	39	19	No	107	53

Table 5.2 Split Half Reliability

Groups	Before Factor Analysis	After Factor Analysis
Group I (Mean)	4.08	4.16
Group II	4.06	4.17
Cronbach's Alpha	0.768	0.807

Table 5.3 Process of Data Reduction

Rounds	Variance Explained	Items Emerged	No of Factors Extracted	Iterations	No of Items Deleted	KMO	Bartlett
1	68.849	51	17	21	13	.681	2175.19
2	69.754	38	13	13	5	.687	1743.36
3	73.396	33	12	09	2	.705	1644.86
4	70.386	31	10	09	-	.716	1605.57

Table 5.4 Factorial Profile of Ethical Retail Practices

Variables	M*	SD	FL	C	EV	VE	CA
F1 Financers	**3.83**	**.06**			**5.150**	**13.772**	**.948**
Cooperate with financers	3.94	.76	.852	.762			
Information to financers	3.79	.60	.905	.838			
Interest at agreed rate	3.83	.68	.918	.860			
Loan on maturity date	3.79	.62	.934	.885			
Respect to financers	3.80	.64	.926	.875			
F2 Employees	**4.02**	**.16**			**3.348**	**11.342**	**.858**
Treating all employees equally	4.30	.71	.676	.685			
Handling employees' complaints	3.97	.51	.839	.752			
Paying for overtime work	3.87	.69	.708	.560			
Helping employees when needed	4.00	.53	.888	.840			
Protecting employees' rights	3.95	.47	.917	.879			
F3 Legal Regulations	**4.74**	**.11**			**2.674**	**8.425**	**.735**
Needed information to suppliers	4.74	.46	.795	.674			
Rules of fair play with competitors	4.61	.50	.663	.562			
Follow legal rules and regulations	4.74	.50	.762	.637			
Protect the environment	4.88	.33	.762	.549			
F4 Customers	**4.18**	**.03**			**2.579**	**7.564**	**.739**
Needed information to consumers	4.18	.42	.688	.617			
Treating all consumers equally	4.22	.53	.747	.641			
Helping in choice making	4.17	.39	.724	.691			
Truth with consumers	4.15	.43	.727	.594			
F5 Taxation	**4.13**	**.16**			**1.906**	**6.227**	**.937**
Filling the tax return on time	4.24	1.30	.939	.915			
Paying the actual rates of tax	4.01	1.14	.921	.930			
F6 Competitors	**4.07**	**.04**			**1.489**	**5.585**	**.600**
Never criticising competitor	4.04	.51	.643	.574			
Hiring the employees of competitors	4.06	.44	.726	.646			
Respecting competitors	4.12	.34	.742	.644			
F7 No Child Labour	**4.43**	**.06**			**1.350**	**5.363**	**.755**
No child labour	4.38	.55	.832	.778			
Respecting children and women	4.47	.51	.841	.781			
F8 Suppliers	**4.14**	**.35**			**1.172**	**4.341**	**.601**
Help suppliers as and when needed	4.16	.46	.726	.630			
Fair in dealings with supplier	4.11	.31	.788	.720			
F9 Product Quality	**3.50**	**.68**			**1.134**	**4.252**	**.515**
No adulteration of goods	3.02	.79	.682	.550			
Return expiry dated products	3.98	.80	.619	.491			
F10 Services	**4.41**	**.47**			**1.017**	**3.516**	**.511**
Supplying demanded goods	4.75	.47	.603	.644			
Repair / replace the products	4.08	.80	.678	.616			
Grand Mean, S D and VE	**4.14**	**.37**				**70.386**	

* M= Mean, SD= Standard Deviation, FL= Factor Loadings, C= Commonalities, EV=Eigen values and VE= Variance Explained and CA = Cronbach's Alpha

Table 5.5 Demographic Profile wise ANOVA Results

Factors	Age wise		Qualification wise		Experience		Store Type	
	F	Sig.	F	Sig.	F	Sig.	F	Sig.
F1	1.651	.196	.358	.700	.388	.768	.783	.539
F2	1.470	.233	8.898	.000	1.709	.168	3.849	.005
F3	.602	.549	.424	.656	.852	.467	1.627	.169
F4	.027	.973	1.963	.143	1.495	.217	.439	.780
F5	1.331	.267	19.053	.000	2.052	.108	3.345	.011
F6	1.331	.267	.400	.671	.659	.578	.178	.950
F7	1.132	.324	2.115	.123	1.610	.188	.510	.729
F8	.692	.502	1.118	.329	6.447	.000	.894	.468
F9	4.960	.008	.036	.965	.327	.806	.410	.801
F10	.196	.822	.404	.668	2.203	.089	.275	.894
Overall	2.673	.072	11.674	.000	2.176	.092	1.426	.227

Table 5.6 Age and Qualification wise Factorial Mean Values

Factors	Age			Qualification		
	BA N=109	A N=10	AA N=81	M N=47	UG N=40	G & PG 113
F1	3.85	4.24	3.74	3.78	3.91	3.80
F2	4.09	3.91	3.96	3.72	4.05	4.13
F3	4.76	4.73	4.71	4.73	4.70	4.76
F4	4.17	4.20	4.18	4.12	4.13	4.22
F5	4.23	3.70	4.03	3.28	4.24	4.43
F6	4.10	4.10	4.03	4.08	4.03	4.09
F7	4.46	4.50	4.36	4.32	4.39	4.48
F8	4.11	4.10	4.17	4.18	4.16	4.11
F9	3.55	3.95	3.38	3.48	3.51	3.50
F10	4..43	4.40	4.39	4.37	4.39	4.44
Overall	4.19	4.18	4.11	4.03	4.16	4.21

* BA= Below Average, A= Average, AA= Above Average, M= Matriculate, UG=Undergraduate, G= Graduate and PG= Post Graduate

Table 5.7 Experience wise Factorial Mean Values

Factors	Experience (Years)			
	0-10 N=103	11-20 N=49	21-30 N=35	30 Above N=13
F1	3.86	3.74	3.80	3.96
F2	4.04	4.13	3.90	3.80
F3	4.76	4.72	4.68	4.83
F4	4.21	4.14	4.09	4.25
F5	4.00	4.48	3.97	4.12
F6	4.10	4.07	4.01	4.08
F7	4.48	4.43	4.27	4.42
F8	4.10	4.17	4.06	4.46
F9	3.50	3.53	3.51	3.35
F10	4.41	4.53	4.30	4.27
Overall	4.16	4.21	4.08	4.18

Table 5.8 Type of Retail Store wise Factorial Mean Values

Factors	Type of Retail Store				
	Garments N=47	General N=39	Electronics N=25	Provisional N=20	Others N=69
F1	3.71	3.80	4.04	3.90	3.81
F2	4.13	3.77	4.20	3.83	4.06
F3	4.68	4.77	4.69	4.66	4.81
F4	4.21	4.12	4.20	4.19	4.17
F5	4.35	3.72	4.46	3.60	4.22
F6	4.09	4.09	4.08	4.05	4.05
F7	4.44	4.44	4.30	4.43	4.46
F8	4.14	4.21	4.16	4.08	4.10
F9	3.45	3.60	3.50	3.45	3.49
F10	4.40	4.40	4.34	4.43	4.45
Overall	4.18	4.11	4.20	4.08	4.18

Table 5.9 Difference in the Perceptions of Stakeholders (ANOVA)

Source of Variation	Sum of Squares	Degree of Freedom	Mean Square	F	Sig.
Between Groups	103.36	4	25.840	34.315	.000
Within Groups	603.92	802	0.753		
Total	707.28	806			

Table 5.10 Perceptions of Stakeholders about Ethical Retail Practices

Stakeholders	N	Mean	SD
Customers	470	3.24	1.04
Retailers	200	4.06	.29
Wholesalers	70	3.81	.80
Manufacturers	32	3.75	.67
Regulatory Bodies	35	3.51	.82

Table 5.11 Age and Ethical Retail Practices (Independent t- test)

Age	N	Mean	Standard Deviation	F	Sig.	t value	Sig.
Younger	119	4.19	0.23	.252	.616	2.312	.022
Senior in Age	81	4.11	0.24				

Table 5.12 Qualification and Ethical Retail Practices (ANOVA)

Source of Variation	Sum of Squares	Degree of Freedom	Mean Square	F	Sig.
Between Groups	1.135	2	.568	11.674	.000
Within Groups	9.578	197	.049		
Total	10.713	199			

Table 5.13 Difference in the Perceptions of Regulatory Bodies (ANOVA)

Source of Variation	Sum of Squares	Degree of Freedom	Mean Square	F	Sig.
Between Groups	4.379	4	1.095	5.792	.001
Within Groups	5.670	30	.189		
Total	10.049	34			

Table 5.14 Ethical Retail Practices (One sample t- test)

	N	Mean	Standard Deviation	Mean Difference	t- value	Sig.
Retailing Ethics	200	4.06	0.30	1.06	50.87	.000

Table 5.15 Discriminant Validity

Factors	F1	F2	F3	F4	F5	F6	F7	F8	F9	F10
F1	1									
F2	.161	1								
F3	.082	.217**	1							
F4	.165	.104	.097	1						
F5	.083	.318**	-.069	.135	1					
F6	.075	.037	.112	.063	.180*	1				
F7	.182*	.106	.241**	.281**	.054	.141*	1			
F8	.138	-.008	-.023	.185**	.053	.151*	.067	1		
F9	.228*	-.028	.126	-.076	.027	.079	.134	-.031	1	
F10	-.013	-.028	-.002	.137	.059	.078	.118	.064	.058	1

** Correlation is significant at the 0.01 level (2-tailed)

* Correlation is significant at the 0.05 level (2-tailed)

CHAPTER 6

ETHICAL RETAIL PRACTICES: PERCEPTIONS OF WHOLESALERS

6.1 Background

One area that has been less focused by the researchers in the marketing ethics is suppliers' perspective of ethical issues in retailing operations (Arbuthnot, 1997). Retailers mostly purchase merchandise from wholesalers for reselling the same to the ultimate consumers (Lusch and Vargo, 1998). Wholesalers and retailers, being the two important types of middlemen, form significant a part of the distribution chain in the marketing of products (Mallen, 1996) by acting as an intermediary link between the manufacturers and the consumers. They specialise in providing a wide range of services to both the producers as well as the consumers by reducing the amount of efforts required by the manufacturer in distributing his product to the final consumers and providing a vast market coverage to his products (Fassin, 2009). They increase the efficiency of exchange and lead to reduction in total cost of distribution of products by providing immediate delivery of goods to the consumers at places convenient and accessible to them (Hunt and Nevin, 1974). Along with this, they provide after sale services and handle consumer grievances and on the same time acting as a communication channel by furnishing information about the products to the consumers on one hand, and the consumer feedback to the producers on the other hand (Fernando, 2009, p. 5; Kaptein, 2008 and Whysall, 1998).

A Wholesaler operates between the producers (from whom they purchase goods) and the retailers (to whom they sell goods). Wholesaler refers to any individual or business firm selling goods in relatively large quantities to buyers (retailers) other than the ultimate consumers. In addition, they assist retailers in advertising and promoting the products and provide financial assistance as well by selling goods on credit and thus, helping retailers to operate with small working capital (Arbuthnot, 1997). A wholesaler, being the ware-house keeper (Wilkinson, 1979) protects the retailer from the risk of loss arising from holding large stocks of the product (Sarma, 2007 and Whysall, 2000).

Rapid changes in media, transport and communications technology have made the world economy more interconnected now than in any previous period of history (Humphreys et al., 2001). Businesses and industries increasingly find themselves facing external pressure to improve their ethical track record. An interesting feature of the rise of consumer activism has increased scrutiny of business activities and thus, retailers being in final touch with their suppliers and consumers, required to behave ethically in their dealings with them. Ethical practices with suppliers build long term relationship and loyalty with strong commitment and firm faith. The relationships between retailers and wholesalers has, historically, been characterised by hard negotiations with each party pursuing their respective interests. In the fast paced and extremely competitive consumer goods market, retailers and wholesalers are increasingly recognising that the development and maintenance of sound relationship (Fynes and Voss, 2002) and cooperation (Gill and Allerheiligen, 1996) in channels of distribution is in their own best interests of business (Napal, 2003).

6.2 Data Collection

The data have been obtained from both secondary and primary sources. The former have been acquired from books, journals and the internet and the latter through a specifically designed schedule based on five point Likert scale (5<----->1). The responses were obtained from the wholesalers referred by retailers while gathering information from them. On the whole, a list of 100 wholesalers operating in different parts of Jammu city, supplying merchandise to the retailers in Gandhi Nagar area of Jammu city and retailers in other areas was framed. But the present study, being exploratory, comparative and chain type, requires the selection of those wholesalers from whom the retailers under reference buy merchandise so that a whole picture of ethical values of retailers in their dealings with wholesalers can be drawn.

6.3 Data Collection Form

As already stated, a schedule was developed specifically for the study after needed review of literature and in consultation with the experts on the subject (Kaptein, 2008; Sarma, 2007; Lavorata and Pontier, 2005 Dubinsky et al., 2004; Kujala, 2001; Whysall, 2000 and Whysall, 1998). The schedule comprised of 9 items of general information and 35 other items based on five point Likert scale ranging from 5 to 1, where 5 means strongly agree and 1 means strongly disagree (5<.....>1). The general information includes the age, qualification, experience, monthly sales and profit of the wholesalers selected as respondents. The other items represent the ethical values of retailers in their dealings with their wholesalers as their contact with wholesalers influence their conduct with ultimate markets also.

6.4 Profile of Respondents

The final survey was conducted on 100 wholesalers who supply goods to the retailers serving in Gandhi Nagar colony of Jammu city. Out of 100 wholesalers, 70 of them furnished the required information. The demographic and some general information includes the age, qualification, experience, type of products, number of employees and their performance in terms of sales and profit. The age of the respondents has been catagorised into three heads viz. below average, average and above average. The average age of the respondents came to be as 44 years and about half (49%) of them having below average age. About 63% of total respondents found to be as graduate and above graduate. About one third of the respondents are having less than 10 years of experience as wholesaler and about 76% of them have less than five employees. About one third of the respondents found to be suppliers of grocery items to the retailers. The monthly sale of the respondents ranges from Rs 30,000 to Rs 1 crore and profit ranges from Rs 10,000 to Rs 10 lakhs (Table 6.1).

6.5 Reliability and Validity

Reliability is an assessment of degree of consistency between multiple measurements of a construct (Hair et al., 2009, p. 161). To check the reliability, Cronbach Alpha and split half values have been worked out (Malhotra, 2008, p. 285) twice i.e. before and after factor analysis by dividing the respondents into two equal halves. The data were found reliable before the factor analysis as mean values of both groups (Group I= 3.30 and Group II = 3.55) are almost similar. Similarly, after factor analysis, the data proved quite satisfactory in terms of split half reliability as mean values obtained from both halves of respondents are quite satisfactory (Group I= 3.24 and Group II= 3.56). Moreover, Cronbach Alpha values also proved reliable before and after factor analysis as it came to be 0.923 and 0.888 respectively i.e. above 0.7 (Table 6.2). Validity (the extent to which a scale or set of measures accurately represent the concept of interest) assessed in terms of content, convergent discriminant analysis (Hair et al., 2009, p. 161). The Content validity has been worked out by reviewing the literature and discussions with the experts and researchers working on similar topic. Convergent validity assesses the degree to which two measures of the same concept are correlated and it was found to be as satisfactory (Malhotra, 2008, p. 286) as the correlations between items were significant and their values were > 0.5. Moreover, commonalities of all the items were also above 0.5, indicating convergent validity (Table 6.4). Discriminant validity is the degree to which two conceptually similar concepts are distinct. For proving this type of validity, the correlation between two constructs should be low, demonstrating one construct being different from the other constructs (Hair et al., 2009, p. 162). Discriminate validity has also been proved as the correlations between most of the constructs were < 0.3 (Table 6.12).

6.6 Data Reduction

The technique of factor analysis has been used for data reduction through Statistical Package for Social Sciences (SPSS, 17 Version) with Principal Component Analysis along with varimax rotation. Factor analysis examines the underlying patterns or relationship for condensing the total data into minimum meaningful factors (Hair et al 2009, p. 128). The items having factor loadings less than 0.5 and Eigen value less than 1 were ignored for the subsequent analysis. With application of factor analysis, the data converged into five factors with 68.44% of variance explained (Table 6.3), viz., F1 (Fairness), F2 (Billing), F3 (Long term relations), F4 (Pricing), F5 (Expiry dated products).

6.7 Factorial Findings

Factor 1 (*Fairness*): Retailers purchase merchandise from wholesalers and their dealing with them is of great significance for long term sustainability. Fairness of retailers with wholesalers ensures easy and timely availability of products. This factor comprised of ten items, viz., 'trust the retailers', 'commitment of retailers', 'satisfied with retailers, 'help when required', 'fair business practices', 'humbleness', 'sincerity', 'straightforward', 'keep promises', 'no deception'. The overall factorial mean (3.61) ranging from 3.44 to 3.76 indicates moderate level of ethical values being practiced by retailers in their dealings with wholesalers. About 80% of the total respondents found retailers trustful (3.66) and committed (3.64) and about 70% of them were satisfied (Table 6.4) in dealings with retailers. (3.50). Majority (81%) of the respondents experienced retailers as humble (3.70), straightforward (3.49) and sincere (3.76) because retailers, now a days, are well aware that if they do fair dealings with their wholesalers, they enjoy more co-operation and assistance from wholesalers

Factor 2 (*Billing*): Retailers purchase merchandise from wholesalers, mostly on credit basis and are required to make payments within the stipulated period agreed upon. This factor made up of three items, viz., 'payments of bills on time', 'exact amount as agreed', 'terms and conditions'. The factor loadings range from 0.863 to 0.602. About half of the respondents found retailers delaying the payments in the stipulated time period and making payments quite late on one excuses or another (2.96). The respondents found retailers unethical in terms of making payments on time which creates serious problems for the wholesalers who have to make prompt payments to the manufacturers and sometimes even advance payments for getting the regular supply of goods. About the same percentage of respondents (53%) experienced retailers paying the exact amount as agreed during credit sales (3.11) as they know if they do not make exact payments, they may not get merchandise in future on regular basis.

Factor 3 (*Long Term Relations*): The retailers are supposed to build long term relations with wholesalers for better dealings like regular and timely supply of goods, less transportation costs, reimbursement of promotion expenses. This factor is comprised of three items viz. 'not criticising other retailers', 'loyalty' and 'not shifting to other wholesalers'. The overall mean of this factor (3.04) with 9.19% of variance explained indicates moderate level of focus on building long term relations with wholesalers. The Eigen value of this factor is 1.72 and factor loadings range from 0.626 to 0.760 and commonalities of all items found to be above threshold value of 0.5. About 74% of the total respondents found retailers loyal (3.51) only if they are given more commission and credit facilities but in case of cash sales and less margins they shift to other wholesalers (2.61). About half of the respondents found retailers sometimes criticising (3.00) their competitors with them to gain more importance in the eyes of the suppliers.

Factor 4 (*Pricing*): This factor has three items viz. 'excuse for keeping of stock', 'printed price' and 'promotional expenses'. Wholesalers sometimes put the products into smaller packs and they fix the price of these smaller packs and instruct the retailers to charge the printed price. About 56% of the total respondents found retailers charging printed price (3.41) and about two third of them experienced retailers sometimes making lame excuses for keeping more merchandise in the retail store (2.70). About 55% of the total respondents experienced retailers not asking for reimbursement of promotional expenses (3.30) because in Jammu retailers are less promotion oriented, particularly dealing in convenience goods.

Factor 5 (*Expiry Dated Products*): This factor is made up of 'return of expiry dated products' and 'adequate profits'. One of the most important issues between the wholesaler and a retailer is expiry dated products, as some goods become outdated in the retail outlets. The reason may be less demand, change in consumer's taste and preferences, availability of product substitutes in the market etc. It is unethical not only but crime on the part of retailers to sell the outdated products to ultimate consumers. In fact, the wholesalers have made provisions for the retailers to return the outdated products as soon as possible, so that they can either be recycled or disposed off by the manufacturers because passing on outdated products prove to be risky, unhygienic and unsafe for the consumers as well as all this tarnishes the image of the manufacturers and middlemen in the eyes of the consumers.

Thus, wholesales find retailers ethical in many aspects like their dealings, pricing, promotion but found them unethical in terms of billing as they delay the payments sometimes for many months causing a serious problem for the wholesalers who are in return are liable to manufacturers.

6.8 Demographic Group wise Analysis

The data so collected from wholesalers have further been analysed through ANOVA for finding out the effect of respondents profile including age, qualification, experience and type of store on the perceptions of wholesalers about ethical values in retail practices. ANOVA gives the differences in mean scores of ethical values on the part of the respondents belonging to different demographic categories. Each one of which has been examined as under:-

6.8.1 Age wise Analysis

As already mentioned, respondents have been classified into three categories viz. below average, average and above average wholesalers. The average age of respondents came to be 44 years through arithmetic mean. Out of the total respondents, about 49% belong to below average age group, about 48% have above average age and only 03% fall in the average age group. To find out the mean differences among different age groups regarding ethical retail practices, Univariate analysis of variance has been applied. On the whole, ANOVA reveals insignificant mean differences of ethical values in retail practices among the respondents belonging to different age groups ($F=0.845$, Sig. = 0.169, Table 6.5). When further applied factor wise, to examine the significant mean difference in different age groups regarding individual factors constituting the overall construct of ethical retail practices, insignificant mean differences have been found in all the five factors, viz., F1 (Fairness: Sig. = .420), F2 (Billing: .860) F3 (Long term Relations: .431), F4 (Pricing: .642), F5 (Expiry dated products: .769, Table 6.5). All the respondents accorded similar mean scores to all the factors (Table 6.6).

6.8.2 Qualification wise Respondents

To find out the effect of qualification on the ethical retail practices, respondents have been grouped into matriculate (20%), undergraduate (17%), graduate & above (63%) qualification groups (Table 6.1). ANOVA indicates insignificant mean differences in the responses of wholesalers belonging to different educational backgrounds (F=1.353, Sig. = .265, Table 6.7). When it is applied factor wise, to examine the significant mean difference in different qualification groups regarding individual factors constituting the overall construct of ethical retail practices, insignificant mean differences have been found in four factors out of the total five factors, viz., F1 (Fairness: Sig. =.602), F2 (Billing: .364) F4 (Pricing: .939), F5 (Expiry dated products: .707) but F3 (Long term Relations: .026) has significant mean difference (Table 6.5). It was found that graduate and post graduate respondents perceived retailers as less loyal (2.88) as compared to their matriculate (3.05) and undergraduate (3.64) counterparts because highly educated wholesalers are stricter regarding timely payments of bills (Table 6.6).

6.8.3 Experience wise Respondents

On the basis of experience, respondents have been classified into four groups, viz. respondents having experience 0 to 10 years (32%), 11 to 20 years (24%), 21 to 30 years (21%) and finally above 30 years (23%) of experience as a wholesaler. For exploring the mean differences among different experienced groups of wholesalers regarding ethical retail practices, Univariate analysis of variance has been performed. On overall basis ANOVA portrays insignificant mean differences regarding the ethical retail practices among the respondents belonging to different experience groups, (F=.1.080, Sig. = .364) (Table 6.5). Further, factor wise analysis also reveals insignificant mean differences in all the five factors F1 (Fairness: Sig. =.769), F2 (Billing: .659) F3 (Long term Relations: .417), F4 (Pricing: .597), F5 (Expiry dated products: .170). Most of the respondents accorded same mean values for most of the factors (Table 6.8) and thus, most of the factors on the whole, have same mean values (Table 6.9).

6.8.4 Type of Product wise Respondents

The respondents have also been classified into four categories on the basis of type of products they deal with, such as grocery (30%), garments (17%), medicine (10%), others (43%). ANOVA reveals insignificant mean differences among the wholesalers dealing in different kinds of products (F= 1.914 Sig. = .136) Further, factor wise analysis also discloses insignificant mean differences in four out of five factors viz. F1 (Fairness: Sig. =..156), F2 (Billing: .853) F3 (Long term Relations: .735) and F5 (Expiry dated products: .080, Table 6.5), while only one factor has significance mean difference i.e. F4 (Pricing: .005, Table 6.10). The wholesalers dealing in garments considered retailers more unethical in terms of pricing (F4) Most of the respondents accorded same mean values for the rest of the factors (Table 6.11).

Hence, all the above demographic variables viz. age, qualification, experience and types of products have insignificant mean difference in the perceptions of wholesalers regarding the ethical retailing practices.

Conclusion

On the whole, wholesalers viewed retailers unethical in terms of making payments on time which creates serious problems for the wholesalers who have to make prompt payments to the manufacturers and sometimes even advance payments for getting the regular supply of goods. In addition to this, wholesalers found retailers loyal only if they are given more commission and credit facilities but in case of cash sales and less margins retailers shift to other wholesalers.

References

Arbuthnot, Jeanette Jaussaud (1997), "Identifying Ethical Problems Confronting Small Retail Buyers During the Merchandise Buying Process, *Journal of Business Ethics*, Vol. 16, pp. 745-755

Dubinsky, Alan .J, Rajan Nataraajan and Wen-Yeh Huang (2004), "The Influence of Moral Philosophies on Retail Salespeople's Ethical Perceptions", *The Journal of Consumer Affairs*, Vol. 38 (2), pp. 297-317

Fassin Yves (2009), "The Stakeholder Model Refined", *Journal of Business Ethics*, Vol. 84, pp. 113-135

Fernando, A. C. (2009), Business Ethics, An Indian Perspective, First Impression, Dorling Kindersley, Pearson Education, New Delhi

Fynes, Brians and Chris Voss (2002), "The Moderating Effect of Buyer- Supplier Relationships on Quality Practices and Performance", *International Journal of Operations & Production Management,* Vol. 22, No. 6, pp. pp. 589-613

Gill, Lynn E. and Robert P. Allerheiligen (1996), "Cooperation in Channels of Distribution: Physical Distribution Leads the Way", *International Journal of Physical Distribution and Logistics Management,* Vol. 26, No. 5, pp. 49-63

Hair, J. F; William C. Black; Barry J. Babin; Ralph E. Anderson and Ronald L. Tathum (2009), Multivariate Data Analysis, Sixth Edition. Pearson Prentice Publishers, New Delhi

Humphreys, P. K.; W. K. Shiu and F. T. S. Chan (2001), "Collaborative Buyer-Supplier Relationship in Hong Kong Manufacturing Firms", *Supply Chain Management: An International Journal,* Vol. 6, No. 4, pp. 152-162

Hunt, S. and J. R.. Nevin (1974), "Power in a Channel of Distribution: Sources and Consequences," *Journal of Marketing Research*, Vol. 11, pp. 186-193

Kaptein, Muel (2008), "Developing a Measure of Unethical Behaviour in the Workplace: A Stakeholder Perspective", *Journal of Management,* Vol. 34 (October), pp. 978-1008

Kujala, Johanna (2001), "Analysing Moral Issues in Stakeholder Relations", *Business Ethics: A European Review,* Vol. 10, pp. 233-247

Lavorata, Laure and Suzanne Pontier (2005), "The Success of a Retailers' Ethical Policy: Focusing on Local Actions", *The Journal of Academy of Marketing Science Review*, Vol. 2005 (12), pp. 1-9

Lusch, Robert F. and Stephen L. Vargo (1998), "Multiplex Retailers versus Wholesalers", *International Journal of Physical Distribution and Logistics Management,* Vol. 28, No. 8, pp. 581-598

Mallen, Bruce (1996), "Selecting Channels of Distribution: A Multi-stage Process", *International Journal of Physical Distribution and Logistics Management,* Vol. 26, No. 5, pp. 5-21

Malhotra, Naresh (2008), 'Marketing Research', An Applied Orientation, Fifth Edition, Prentice Hall of India, New Delhi

Napal, Geetanee (2003), Ethical Decision Making in Business: Focus on Mauritius, *Business Ethics: A European Review*, Vol. 12 (1), pp. 54-63

Sarma, Nripendra Narayan (2007), "Ethics in Retailing-Perception of Management and Sales Personnel", *(http:// dspace.iimk.ac.in/bitstream/2259/388/1/61-68.pdf),* last accessed on January, 25, 2012

Whysall, Paul (2000), "Stakeholder Mismanagement in Retailing: A British Perspective", *Journal of Business Ethics*, Vol. 23, pp. 19-28

-------------- (1998), "Ethical Relationship in Retailing: Some Cautionary Tales", *Business Ethics: A European Review,* Vol. 7 (2), pp. 103-110

Wilkinson, L F (1979), "Power and Satisfaction in Channels of Distribution" *Journal of Retailing*, Vol. 55, pp. 79-94

Table 6.1 Demographic Profile of Wholesalers

Variables	Frequency	Percentage	Variables	Frequency	Percentage
Age:			**Experience**		
Below average	34	49	0-10	22	31
Average	02	03	11-20	17	24
Above average	34	48	21-30	15	22
Qualification:			Above 30	16	23
Matriculate	14	20	**Religion**		
Under graduate	12	17	Hindu	69	98
Graduate and above	44	63	Sikh	01	02
Type of Products			**Sales**		
Grocery	21	30	Median: Rs 6,00,000		
Garments	12	17	Range (99,70,000)		
Medicines	07	10	Minimum: Rs 30,000		
Others	30	43	Maximum: Rs 1,00,00,000		
Employees			**Profit**		
0-5	53	76	Median Rs 50,000		
6-10	09	13	Range (Rs 9,90,000)		
11-15	02	03	Minimum: Rs 10,000		
Above 15	06	08	Maximum: Rs 10,00,000		

Table 6.2 Split Half Reliability

Groups	Before Factor Analysis	After Factor Analysis
Group I (Mean)	3.30	3.24
Group II	3.55	3.56
Cronbach's Alpha	0.923	0.888

Table 6.3 Factor Analysis

Rounds	Variance Explained	Items Emerged	No of Factors Extracted	Iterations	No of Items Deleted	KMO	Bartlett
1	70.71	34	9	10	8	.774	1483.23
2	69.80	26	7	7	2	.808	1042.10
3	67.99	24	6	8	2	.809	946.70
4	71.39	22	6	7	1	.811	893.08
5	68.44	21	5	6	-	.825	866.15

Table 6.4 Factorial Profile of Ethical Retail Practices: Wholesalers' Perspective

Variables	M	SD	FL	C	EV	VE	CA
F1 Fairness	**3.61**	**0.12**			8.04	31.80	0.93
Trust the retailers	3.66	1.01	.844	.813			
Commitment of retailers	3.64	0.92	.853	.810			
Satisfied with retailers	3.50	1.06	.806	.732			
Help when required	3.73	0.83	.740	.630			
Fair business practices	3.71	0.82	.804	.729			
Humbleness	3.70	0.84	.802	.736			
Sincerity	3.76	0.81	.838	.795			
Straightforward	3.49	1.00	.647	.500			
Keep promises	3.46	1.05	.770	.726			
No deception	3.44	0.97	.560	.557			
F2 Fair Billing	**3.17**	**0.25**			1.91	11.62	0.81
Payments of bills on time	2.96	1.30	.863	.816			
Exact amount as agreed	3.11	1.16	.868	.795			
Terms and conditions	3.44	0.96	.602	.595			
F3 Long Term Relations	**3.04**	**0.45**			1.72	9.19	0.61
Not criticising competitors	3.00	1.36	.760	.654			
loyalty	3.51	0.97	.631	.696			
Not shifting to wholesalers	2.61	1.15	.626	.500			
F4 Pricing and Promotion	**3.14**	**0.38**			1.49	8.33	0.64
No excuse for inventory	2.70	1.13	.618	.506			
Printed price	3.41	0.96	.797	.689			
Promotional expenses	3.30	1.24	.678	.543			
F5 Expiry Dated Products	**3.40**	**0.05**			1.23	7.50	0.60
Adequate margins	3.43	1.21	.802	.768			
Return of expiry dated products	3.36	1.01	.808	.808			
Grand M, SD, VE and CA	**3.38**	**0.33**				68.44	0.88

* M = Mean, SD = Standard Deviation, FL = Factor Loadings, C = Commonalities, EV = Eigen values, VE = Variance Explained and CA = Cronbach Alpha

Table 6.5 ANOVA (Age wise)

Factors	Source of Variation	Sum of Squares	Df.	Mean Square	F	Sig.
Age*F1	Between Groups	.972	2	.486	.880	.420
	Within Groups	37.003	67	.552		
	Total	37.975	69			
Age*F2	Between Groups	.296	2	.148	.151	.860
	Within Groups	65.647	67	.980		
	Total	65.943	69			
Age*F3	Between Groups	1.313	2	.656	.853	.431
	Within Groups	51.559	67	.770		
	Total	52.871	69			
Age*F4	Between Groups	.355	2	.177	.446	.642
	Within Groups	26.644	67	.398		
	Total	26.998	69			
Age*F5	Between Groups	.468	2	.234	.264	.769
	Within Groups	59.478	67	.888		
	Total	59.946	69			
Age*Overall	Between Groups	.092	2	.046	.169	.845
	Within Groups	18.247	67	.272		
	Total	18.339	69			

Table 6.6 Age and Qualification wise Factorial Mean Values

Factors	Age			Qualification		
	BA N=34	A N=02	AA N=34	M N=14	UG N=12	G & PG 44
F1	3.49	3.55	3.73	3.69	3.76	3.54
F2	3.24	3.00	3.12	3.33	3.44	3.05
F3	2.90	3.17	3.18	3.05	3.64	2.88
F4	3.07	3.33	3.20	3.14	3.19	3.12
F5	3.47	3.50	3.31	3.21	3.38	3.45
Overall	3.23	3.31	3.31	3.29	3.48	3.21

* BA = Below Average, A = Average, AA = Above Average, M = Matriculate, UG = Undergraduate, G = Graduate and PG = Post Graduate

Table 6.7 ANOVA (Qualification Wise)

Factors	Source of Variation	Sum of Squares	Df.	Mean Square	F	Sig.
Qualification*F1	Between Groups	.570	2	.285	.511	.602
	Within Groups	37.405	67	.558		
	Total	37.975	69			
Qualification*F2	Between Groups	1.960	2	.980	1.026	.364
	Within Groups	63.983	67	.955		
	Total	65.943	69			
Qualification*F3	Between Groups	5.448	2	2.724	3.848	.026
	Within Groups	47.424	67	.708		
	Total	52.871	69			
Qualification*F4	Between Groups	.051	2	.025	.063	.939
	Within Groups	26.947	67	.402		
	Total	26.998	69			
Qualification*F5	Between Groups	.618	2	.309	.349	.707
	Within Groups	59.329	67	.886		
	Total	59.946	69			
Qualification*Overall	Between Groups	.712	2	.356	1.353	.265
	Within Groups	17.627	67	.263		
	Total	18.339	69			

Table 6.8 ANOVA (Experience wise)

Factors	Source of Variation	Sum of Squares	Df.	Mean Square	F	Sig.
Experience*F1	Between Groups	.642	3	.214	.379	.769
	Within Groups	37.332	66	.566		
	Total	37.975	69			
Experience*F2	Between Groups	1.567	3	.522	.536	.659
	Within Groups	64.375	66	.975		
	Total	65.943	69			
Experience*F3	Between Groups	2.208	3	.736	.959	.417
	Within Groups	50.663	66	.768		
	Total	52.871	69			
Experience*F4	Between Groups	.753	3	.251	.631	.597
	Within Groups	26.245	66	.398		
	Total	26.998	69			
Experience*F5	Between Groups	4.359	3	1.453	1.725	.170
	Within Groups	55.587	66	.842		
	Total	59.946	69			
Experience*Overall	Between Groups	.858	3	.286	1.080	.364
	Within Groups	17.481	66	.265		
	Total	18.339	69			

Table 6.9 Experience Wise Factorial Mean Values

Factors	Experience (Years)			
	0-10 N=22	11-20 N=17	21-30 N=15	30 Above N=16
F1	3.67	3.51	3.51	3.73
F2	3.33	3.02	3.00	3.27
F3	2.83	3.10	3.00	3.31
F4	3.03	3.14	3.11	3.31
F5	3.64	3.26	3.00	3.56
Overall	3.30	3.21	3.12	3.44

Table 6.10 ANOVA (Product wise)

Factors	Source of Variation	Sum of Squares	Df.	Mean Square	F	Sig.
Type of product*F1	Between Groups	2.873	3	.958	1.801	.156
	Within Groups	35.102	66	.532		
	Total	37.975	69			
Type of product *F2	Between Groups	.772	3	.257	.261	.853
	Within Groups	65.170	66	.987		
	Total	65.943	69			
Type of product *F3	Between Groups	1.005	3	.335	.426	.735
	Within Groups	51.866	66	.786		
	Total	52.871	69			
Type of product *F4	Between Groups	4.780	3	1.593	4.733	.005
	Within Groups	22.218	66	.337		
	Total	26.998	69			
Type of product *F5	Between Groups	5.801	3	1.934	2.357	.080
	Within Groups	54.145	66	.820		
	Total	59.946	69			
Type of product *Overall	Between Groups	1.468	3	.489	1.914	.136
	Within Groups	16.872	66	.256		
	Total	18.339	69			

Table 6.11 Type of Product Wise Factorial Mean Values

Factors	Type of Products			
	Grocery N=21	Garments N=12	Medicines N=07	Others N=30
F1	3.74	3.47	3.07	3.70
F2	3.22	3.00	3.00	3.24
F3	3.22	3.00	2.90	2.97
F4	3.46	2.97	2.57	3.11
F5	3.64	2.92	3.86	3.30
Overall	3.46	3.07	3.08	3.26

Table 6.12 Discriminant Validity

Factors	F1	F2	F3	F4	F5
F1	1				
F2	.498**	1			
F3	.456**	.183	1		
F4	.369**	.132	.313**	1	
F5	.150	.132	-.009	.171	1

** Correlation is significant at the 0.01 level (2-tailed).

CHAPTER 7

ETHICAL RETAIL PRACTICES: PERCEPTIONS OF MANUFACTURERS

7.1 Background

The retailers and manufacturers need to work in collaboration for their mutual interest as well as for the consumers they serve. Through such collaboration, retailers and manufacturers become more responsible in adjusting product assortment, promotion efforts and effective pre and post sales services. Improved shelf arrangements build stronger consumer loyalty for stores that carry the right assortment of always-available goods, and for brands that provide the right offers in the right stores (Fynes and Voss, 2002; Humphreys et al.., 2001 and Gill and Allerheiligen, 1996). As goods pass through several hands before they reach consumer, sometimes manufacturers sell directly or through the retailers without involving other middlemen (Wilson, 1995, Ganesan, 1993). The producers sell goods to retailers who in turn sell to the ultimate consumers (Weitz and Jap, 1995) and this channel is more suitable under the conditions when goods are of perishable nature and cater to the needs of local market such as milk, bread and other food items and when the retailers are big in size of their business and buy in bulk but sell in smaller units directly to the consumers. The producers usually sell directly to retailers through their salesmen who take orders from retailers and immediate delivery of products is made to them at their retail outlets. For the manufacturer, it is beneficial as it reduces the cost of distribution (Arbuthnot, 1997 and Weitz and Sandy, 1995) by eliminating wholesalers. On the other hand, there are no ordering and transportation costs to the retailers (Murry and Heidy, 1998 and Dwyer et al., 1987). It is an obligation on the part of retailers to behave ethically in their dealings with manufacturers (Whysall, 1998). They seem to be ethical when they behave fairly, honestly, sincerely and in a sense of truthfulness and responsiveness (Whysall, 1995) which in turn fosters parties' trust, commitment, loyalty and image of the manufacturer's products along with retail outlets (Kujala, 2001; Whysall, 2000 Mallen, 1996 and Walters, 1989).

7.2 Data Collection

The data have been obtained from both secondary and primary sources. The secondary data have been acquired from books, journals and the internet. The primary data through a specifically developed schedule, based upon some demographic and other items representing the ethical values of retailers in their dealings with manufacturers structured on five point Likert scale (5< --- >1). The data were obtained from the manufacturers referred by the retailers from whom these retailers procure their merchandise. On the whole, a list of 40 manufacturers functioning in different parts of Jammu city, supplying goods to the retailers under consideration and other retailers also. As the present study being exploratory, comparative and chain type, requires the selection of those manufacturers from whom the retailers under reference buy merchandise so that the whole picture of ethical values of retailers in their dealings with manufactures can be drawn.

7.3 Data Collection Form

For collecting primary data from manufacturers, a schedule was developed specifically for the study under reference by reviewing the needed literature (Kujala, 2001; Whysall, 2000, 1998 and 1995) and discussion with the experts on the subject. The schedule comprised of, 9 items of general information and 37 other items based on five point Likert scale ranging from 5 to 1, where 5 means strongly agree and 1 means strongly disagree (5<.....>1). The demographic and general information comprised of the age, qualification, experience, type of business, number of employees, monthly sales and profit of the manufacturers, being selected as respondent. All other items represented the ethical values of retailers in their dealings with manufacturers.

7.4 Profile of Respondents

The final survey was conducted on 40 manufacturers who supply goods directly to the retailers serving in Gandhi Nagar colony of Jammu city. Out of 40 manufacturers, 32 of them furnished the required information. As mentioned above, the demographic and some general information include the age, qualification, experience, type of products, number of employees and their performance in terms of sales and profit. The age of the respondents has been catagorised into three heads viz. below average, average and above average. The average age of the respondents came to be 45 years through arithmetic mean and more than half (56%) of the respondents have age less than 45 years. About 76% of total respondents were graduate and above graduate. About 47% of the respondents possess less than 10 years of experience as a manufacturer and about 31% of the respondents employ more than 30 workers. Manufacturers were also catagorised according to product produced as milk (6%), Oil (9%), Steel (16%) and others (69%). The monthly sale of the respondents ranges from Rs 20,00,000 to Rs 1 crore and profit ranges from Rs 30,000 to Rs 30 lakhs (Table 7.1).

7.5 Reliability and Validity

To check the reliability, i. e., degree of consistency between multiple measurements of a construct, (Hair et al., 2009, p. 161), Split half and Cronbach Alpha have been worked out (Malhotra, 2008, p. 285) by dividing the respondents into two equal halves. The data found to be reliable as mean values of both halves were quite satisfactory (Group I = 3.64 and Group II = 3.32). Moreover, Cronbach Alpha values also proved reliable as it came to be 0.923 which have been above 0.7 (Table 7.2). Similarly, Validity (the extent to which a scale or set of measures accurately represent the concept under review) can be assessed in terms of content, convergent, discriminant measures (Hair et al, 2009, p. 161). The Content validity has been worked out by reviewing the literature and discussions with the experts and researchers working on similar topics. Convergent validity (the degree to which two measures of the same concept are correlated) was found to be satisfactory (Malhotra, 2008, p. 286) as the correlations between items were significant and their values have been > 0.5. Moreover, commonalities of all the items came above 0.5, indicating convergent validity. Discriminant validity is the degree to which two conceptually similar concepts are distinct. For proving this type of validity, the correlation between two constructs should be low, demonstrating that one construct is sufficiently different from the other similar constructs (Hair et al., 2009, p. 162). Discriminate validity has been proved as the correlations between most of the constructs were < 0.3 (Table 7.9).

7.6 Data Reduction

The technique of factor analysis has been used through Statistical Package for Social Sciences (SPSS, 17 Version) with Principal component analysis along with varimax rotation. Factor analysis examines the underlying patterns or relationship for condensing the total data into minimum meaningful factors (Hair et al., 2009, p. 128). The items having factor loading less than 0.5 and Eigen value less than 1 were ignored for the subsequent analysis (Hair et al., 1995). With application of factor analysis, the data converged into six factors with 77.47% of variance explained (Table 7.3). The six factors are F1 (Fairness), F2 (Billing), F3 (Out dated products), F4 (Gifts), F5 (Pricing) and F6 (Mutual interest). The factor wise analysis is as under:-

Factor 1 (*Fairness*): Few retailers purchase merchandise directly from manufacturers, as the salesmen of the manufacturers take orders from retailers and delivery is made to the retailers at their stores. This factor comprised of items such as, 'responsible', 'satisfied from retailers', 'sincere', 'respectful', 'helpful', 'space to products in retail store', 'no deception', 'commitment', 'honest', 'loyal', 'long term relations', 'humble', 'straight forward', 'fair business practices', 'keeping of promises' and 'trustful'. The overall factorial mean value (3.60) indicates moderate level of ethical values being practiced by retailers in dealings with manufacturers. Majority (91%) of the total respondents found satisfied (3.76) with retailers as they get due respect (3.72) and felt them honest (3.74) in their dealings with them. About 80% of them found retailers responsible (3.63), humble (3.69) and loyal (3.59) and provide needed space to manufacturers' products in their retail outlets (3.75). Further, retailers develop long term relations with manufacturers (3.59) which help them in terms of more margins and other assistance like reimbursement of promotion and transportation costs (Murry and Haidy, 1998). Moreover, about 70% of the respondents find retailers doing fair business as they keep their promises (3.47), remain straightforward (3.52), committed and do not deceive (3.53). However, the mean values are not so high indicating retailers being not highly ethical (Table 7.4).

Factor 2 (*Billing*): Retailers purchase merchandise from manufacturers mostly on credit basis and are required to make payments within the stipulated period as agreed upon. This factor comprised of three items, viz. 'payments of bills on time', 'exact amount as agreed', 'no irritation for billing'. The factor loadings range from 0.950 to 0.526. About 60% of the total respondents found retailers delaying the payments in the stipulated time period and make payments quite late on one excuse or another to them (2.81). They viewed retailers as unethical in terms of making payments on time, which creates serious problems for the manufacturers who have to make prompt payments to the suppliers and sometimes even advance payments for getting the regular supply of goods. About the same percentage of respondents (59%) experienced retailers paying less amount as agreed upon (2.81) on the promise that they would make the payment as and when they get from customers to whom they have sold goods on credit.

Factor 3 (*Out Dated Products*): This factor comprised of items, 'out dated products' and 'supply of required information' with factor loadings of .838 and .823 respectively. One of the most important issues between the manufacturer and a retailer is regarding out dated products as some goods become out dated in the retail outlets due to less demand, change in consumer's taste and preferences, product substitutes in the market. It is unethical on the part of retailers to sell the outdated products to ultimate consumers. The manufacturers, in fact, have made provisions for the retailers to return the out dated products as soon as possible so that they can either be recycled or disposed off by the manufacturers because passing on out dated products prove to be unsafe, unhygienic and risky for the consumers as well as these products tarnish the image of the manufacturers and retailers in the eyes of the consumers and public at large. About half of the respondents found retailers returning the goods (3.44) within the period allowed by the manufacturers.

Factor 4 (*Gifts*): This factor has two items, viz., 'printed price' and 'excessive gifts'. Manufacturers fix the price of the products and instruct the retailers to charge the printed price. About 75% of the total respondents found retailers charging printed price (3.47) and about the same percentage of respondents experienced retailers not demanding excessive gifts for keeping more merchandise in the retail store (3.38). In fact, manufacturers offer gifts at their own will as they feel it necessary for business relationship and keeping into consideration the needs of the retailers.

Factor 5 (*Pricing*): This factor has two variables, viz., 'not pressurising for setting high prices' and 'no threat for keeping other manufacturers' products'. It is unethical on the part of the retailers to pressurise the manufacturers for setting the higher price for enjoying good margin. For more margins retailers do communicate to the manufacturers that if adequate margin is not available, they will shift to other manufacturers. However, the present study reveals retailers not pressurising manufacturers for setting higher prices of the product and in Jammu retailers do not have such dictating position over the manufacturers regarding price fixation (3.97).

Factor 6 (*Mutual Interest*): This factor has two items, viz., 'mutual interest', and 'adequate margins' with factor loadings of .826 and .656 respectively (Table 7.4) along with 6.15% of variance explained. The retailer - manufacturer relations can become strong if both see mutual interest of each other and retailers get adequate margin for selling the manufacturers' products. About 69% of the total respondents experienced retailers not focusing on mutual interest as they see their own interest first and thereafter interest of manufacturers (2.53). About 81% of the total respondents agreed to have given adequate margins to the retailers for selling their products (3.59).

Thus, manufacturers viewed retailers ethical in many aspects like their fair dealings, pricing, etc. but at the same time find retailers unethical in terms of billing as they delay the payments sometimes for many months causing a serious problems for the manufacturers for payments to suppliers.

7.7 Demographic Group wise Analysis

The data so obtained from manufacturers have further been analysed through ANOVA for finding out the effect of different factors like age, qualification, experience and type of product on the perceptions of manufacturers about ethical retail practices. ANOVA depicts the differences in mean scores of ethical values on the part of respondents belonging to different demographic categories. Each one of these groups has been discussed as under:-

7.7.1 Age wise Analysis

On the basis of age, respondents have been classified into three categories, viz. below average, average and above average. The average age of respondents is 45 years. Out of the total respondents, more than half (56%) have below average age. About 35% have above average age and only 9% fall in the average age group. To find out the mean differences among different age groups regarding ethical retail practices, Univariate Analysis of Variance has been applied. On the whole, ANOVA reveals insignificant mean differences of ethical retail practices among the respondents belonging to different age groups (F=0.643, Sig. = 0.533, Table 7.5). Further, in different age groups regarding individual factors constituting the overall construct of ethical retail practices, insignificant mean differences have been found in all the six factors, viz., F1 (Fairness: Sig. =.633), F2 (Billing: .743), F3 (Out dated products: .318), F4 (Gifts: .208), F5 (Pricing: .657) and F6 (Mutual Interest: .819, Table 7.5).

7.7.2 Qualification wise Respondents

To find out the effect of qualification on the ethical retail practices, respondents have been grouped into matriculate (09%), undergraduate (15%), graduate & above (76%) qualification groups (Table 7.1). ANOVA portrays insignificant mean differences in the responses of manufacturers having different educational backgrounds (F= .223, Sig. = .801). Further, to examine the significant mean difference in different qualification groups regarding individual factors constituting the overall construct of ethical retail practices, insignificant mean differences have been found in all the six factors, viz., F1 (Fairness: Sig. =.286), F2 (Billing: .496), F3 (Outdated Products: = .994), F4 (Gifts: .887), F5 (Pricing: .358) and F6 (Mutual interest: .801, Table 7.6).

7.7.3 Experience wise Respondents

On the basis of experience, respondents have been classified into four groups, viz., respondents having experience up to 10 years (47%), 11 to 20 years (25%), 21 to 30 years (19%) and finally above 30 years (09%) experience as a manufacturer. For exploring the mean differences among different experienced groups of manufacturers regarding ethical retail practices, Univariate Analysis of Variance has been applied. On overall basis, ANOVA portrays insignificant mean differences regarding the ethical retail practices among the respondents belonging to different experience groups (F=.532, Sig. = .664). Further, factor wise analysis also reveals insignificant mean differences in all the six factors, viz., F1 (Fairness: Sig. =.616), F2 (Billing: .584), F3 (Out dated Products: = .448), F4 (Gifts: .145), F5 (Pricing: .708) and F6 (Mutual Interest: .637, Table 7.7).

7.7.4 Type of Product wise Respondents

The respondents have also been classified into four categories on the basis of type of products they deal in such as milk (6%), oil (9%), Steel (16%), others (69%). ANOVA portrays insignificant mean differences among the manufacturers dealing in different kinds of products (F= .203 Sig. = .893) Further, when it was applied on individual factor wise, it discloses insignificant mean differences in five out of six factors, viz., F1 (Fairness: Sig. =.771), F2 (Billing: .498), F3 (Out dated Products: = .464), F4 (Gifts: .105), and F6 (Mutual Interest: .180, Table 7.8) and only one factor i. e., F5 (Pricing: .044) has significance mean difference which indicates that manufacturers dealing in oil (4.17) and steel (4.20) found retailers more ethical than their other counterparts (3.47) regarding pricing issues.

On the whole, manufacturers observed retailers under reference as ethical to some extent but considered retailers unethical in terms of the payment of bills on time and exact amount. Retailers having such dealings with the manufacturers ultimately influence their transactions with the ultimate market.

References

Arbuthnot, Jeanette Jaussaud (1997), "Identifying Ethical Problems Confronting Small Retail Buyers During the Merchandise Buying Process, *Journal of Business Ethics*, Vol. 16, pp. 745-755

Dwyer, Robert H.; Schurr H. Paul and Oh Sejo (1987), "Developing Buyer-Seller Relationships", *Journal of Marketing*, Vol. 52, pp. 21-34.

Fynes, Brians and Chris Voss (2002), "The Moderating Effect of Buyer - Supplier Relationships on Quality Practices and Performance", *International Journal of Operations & Production Management*, Vol. 22, No. 6, pp. 589-613

Ganesan, Shankar (1993), "Negotiation Strategies and the Nature of Channel Relationships", *Journal of Marketing Research*, Vol. 30, pp. 183-203.

Gill, Lynn E. and Robert P. Allerheiligen (1996), "Cooperation in Channels of Distribution: Physical Distribution Leads the Way", *International Journal of Physical Distribution and Logistics Management*, Vol. 26 (5), pp. 49-63

Hair, J. F.; William C. Black; Barry J. Babin; Ralph E. Anderson and Ronald L. Tathum (2009), 'Multivariate Data Analysis', Sixth Ed. Pearson Prentice Publishers, New Delhi

Humphreys, P. K.; W. K. Shiu and F. T. S. Chan (2001), "Collaborative Buyer-Supplier Relationship in Hong Kong Manufacturing Firms", *Supply Chain Management: An International Journal*, Vol. 6, No. 4, pp. 152-162

Kujala, Johanna (2001), "Analysing Moral Issues in Stakeholder Relations", *Business Ethics: A European Review*, Vol. 10, pp. 233-247

Mallen, Bruce (1996), "Selecting Channels of Distribution: A Multi-stage Process", *International Journal of Physical Distribution and Logistics Management*, Vol. 26 (5), pp. 5-21

Malhotra, Naresh (2008), 'Marketing Research', An Applied Orientation, Fifth Edition, Prentice Hall of India, New Delhi

Murry, John P. Jr. and Jan B. Heidy (1998), "Managing Promotion Program Participation within Manufacturer-Retailer Relationships", *Journal of Marketing*, Vol. 62, pp. 58-68

Walters, Rockney G. (1989), "An Empirical Investigation into Retailer Response to Manufacturer Trade Promotions," *Journal of Retailing*, Vol. 65 (2), pp. 253-272

Weitz, Barton A. and Jap Sandy (1995), "Relationship Marketing and Distribution Channels," Journal *of the Academy of Marketing Science*, Vol. 23 (4), pp. 305-320

Whysall, Paul (2000), "Stakeholder Mismanagement in Retailing: A British Perspective", *Journal of Business Ethics*, Vol. 23, pp. 19-28

---------------- (1998), "Ethical Relationship in Retailing: Some Cautionary Tales", *Business Ethics: A European Review*, Vol. 7, pp. 103-110

---------------- (1995), "Ethics in Retailing", *Business Ethics: A European Review*, Vol. 4 (3), pp. 150-156

Wilson, David T. (1995), "An Integrated Model of Buyer-Seller Relationships", *Journal of the Academy of Marketing Science*, Vol. 23 (4), pp. 335-345

Table 7.1 Demographic Profile of Manufacturers

Variables	Frequ-ency	Perce-Ntage	Variables	Frequ-Ency	Perce-ntage
Age:			**Experience**		
Below average	18	56	0-10	15	47
Average	03	09	11-20	08	25
Above average	11	35	21-30	06	19
Qualification:			Above 30	03	09
Matriculate	03	09	**Sales**		
Under graduate	05	15	Median: Rs 60,00,000		
Graduate and above	24	76	Range (79,80,000)		
			Minimum: Rs 20,00,000		
Type of Products			Maximum: Rs 1,00,00,000		
Milk	02	06	**Profit**		
Oil	03	09	Median Rs 10,00,00		
Steel	05	16	Range (Rs 29,70,000		
Others	22	69	Minimum: Rs 30,000		
Employees			Maximum: Rs 30,00,000		
0-10	13	40			
11-20	05	16			
21-30	04	13			
Above 30	10	31			

Table 7.2 Split Half Reliability

Groups	Mean & Alpha
Group I (Mean)	3.64
Group II	3.32
Cronbach's Alpha	0.920

Table 7.3 Factor Analysis

Rounds	Variance Explained	Items Emerged	No of Factors Extracted	Iterations	No of Items Deleted	KMO	Bartlett
1	81.95	36	9	22	1	-	-
2	82.90	35	9	17	4	-	-
3	80.44	31	8	10	1	-	-
4	78.19	30	7	08	2	-	-
5	79.68	28	7	10	1	.552	944.39
6	77.47	27	6	09	-	.578	930.33

Table 7.4 Factorial Profile of Ethical Retail Practices: Manufacturers' Perspective

Variables	M	SD	FL	C	EV	VE	CA
F1 Fairness	**3.60**	**0.10**			12.13	41.27	.966
Responsible	3.63	1.01	0.945	.952			
Satisfied from retailers	3.76	0.81	0.911	.925			
Sincere	3.59	0.98	0.878	.892			
Respectful	3.72	0.89	0.856	.925			
Helpful	3.50	0.80	0.829	.840			
Space to products	3.75	0.80	0.826	.898			
No deception	3.53	0.76	0.825	.736			
Committed	3.58	0.87	0.823	.767			
Honest	3.74	0.79	0.797	.795			
Loyal	3.59	0.98	0.795	.803			
Long term relations	3.59	1.07	0.791	.775			
Humble	3.69	0.90	0.783	.664			
Straight forward	3.52	0.90	0.769	.728			
Fair business practices	3.53	0.94	0.706	.602			
Keeping of promises	3.47	0.92	0.697	.698			
Trustful	3.44	1.27	0.643	.643			
F2 Billing	**2.93**	**0.20**			2.28	10.22	.832
Payments of bills on time	2.81	1.47	0.950	.928			
Exact amount as agreed	2.81	1.53	0.942	.934			
Not Irritable for billing	3.16	1.22	0.526	.692			
F3 Out Dated Products	**3.69**	**0.35**			1.979	7.07	.500
Outdated products	3.44	0.91	0.838	.781			
Information	3.94	0.44	0.823	.762			
F4 Gifts	**3.43**	**0.06**			1.694	6.59	.655
Printed price	3.47	0.98	0.739	.743			
Excessive gifts	3.38	1.21	0.715	.692			
F5 Pricing	**3.60**	**0.53**			1.527	6.17	.527
Not forcing for high prices	3.97	1.06	0.804	.685			
No threat for other products	3.22	1.07	0.658	.674			
F6 Common Interest	**3.06**	**0.75**			1.301	6.15	.512
Mutual interest	2.53	0.98	0.825	.774			
Adequate margins	3.59	1.10	0.656	.692			
Grand M, SD ,VE and CA	**3.48**	**0.33**				77.47	.920

* M= Mean, SD= Standard Deviation, FL= Factor Loadings, C= Commonalities, EV=Eigen values, VE= Variance Explained and CA= Cronbach's Alpha

Table 7.5 ANOVA (Age wise)

Factors	Source of Variation	Sum of Squares	Df.	Mean Square	F	Sig.
Age*F1	Between Groups	.547	2	.274	.464	.633
	Within Groups	17.091	29	.589		
	Total	17.638	31			
Age*F2	Between Groups	.940	2	.470	.300	.743
	Within Groups	45.445	29	1.567		
	Total	46.385	31			
Age*F3	Between Groups	.370	2	.185	1.191	.318
	Within Groups	4.505	29	.155		
	Total	4.875	31			
Age*F4	Between Groups	2.883	2	1.441	1.661	.208
	Within Groups	25.172	29	.868		
	Total	28.055	31			
Age*F5	Between Groups	.634	2	.317	.426	.657
	Within Groups	21.585	29	.744		
	Total	22.219	31			
Age*F6	Between Groups	.299	2	.150	.201	.819
	Within Groups	21.576	29	.744		
	Total	21.875	31			
Age*Overall	Between Groups	.265	2	.133	.643	.533
	Within Groups	5.986	29	.206		
	Total	6.252	31			

Table 7.6 ANOVA (Qualification Wise)

Factors	Source of Variation	Sum of Squares	Df.	Mean Square	F	Sig.
Qualification*F1	Between Groups	1.458	2	.729	1.307	.286
	Within Groups	16.179	29	.558		
	Total	17.638	31			
Qualification*F2	Between Groups	2.190	2	1.095	.719	.496
	Within Groups	44.195	29	1.524		
	Total	46.385	31			
Qualification*F3	Between Groups	.002	2	.001	.006	.994
	Within Groups	4.873	29	.168		
	Total	4.875	31			
Qualification*F4	Between Groups	.232	2	.116	.121	.887
	Within Groups	27.823	29	.959		
	Total	28.055	31			
Qualification*F5	Between Groups	1.519	2	.759	1.064	.358
	Within Groups	20.700	29	.714		
	Total	22.219	31			
Qualification*F6	Between Groups	.269	2	.134	.180	.836
	Within Groups	21.606	29	.745		
	Total	21.875	31			
Qualification*Overall	Between Groups	.095	2	.047	.223	.801
	Within Groups	6.157	29	.212		
	Total	6.252	31			

Table 7.7 ANOVA (Experience wise)

Factors	Source of Variation	Sum of Squares	Df.	Mean Square	F	Sig.
Experience*F1	Between Groups	1.078	3	.359	.608	.616
	Within Groups	16.560	28	.591		
	Total	17.638	31			
Experience*F2	Between Groups	3.059	3	1.020	.659	.584
	Within Groups	43.326	28	1.547		
	Total	46.385	31			
Experience*F3	Between Groups	.433	3	.144	.911	.448
	Within Groups	4.442	28	.159		
	Total	4.875	31			
Experience*F4	Between Groups	4.846	3	1.615	1.949	.145
	Within Groups	23.208	28	.829		
	Total	28.055	31			
Experience*F5	Between Groups	1.058	3	.353	.467	.708
	Within Groups	21.160	28	.756		
	Total	22.219	31			
Experience*F6	Between Groups	1.267	3	.422	.574	.637
	Within Groups	20.608	28	.736		
	Total	21.875	31			
Experience*Overall	Between Groups	.337	3	.112	.532	.664
	Within Groups	5.914	28	.211		
	Total	6.252	31			

Table 7.8 ANOVA (Product wise)

Factors	Source of Variation	Sum of Squares	Df.	Mean Square	F	Sig.
Type of product*F1	Between Groups	.684	3	.228	.376	.771
	Within Groups	16.954	28	.605		
	Total	17.638	31			
Type of product *F2	Between Groups	3.711	3	1.237	.812	.498
	Within Groups	42.675	28	1.524		
	Total	46.385	31			
Type of product *F3	Between Groups	.420	3	.140	.879	.464
	Within Groups	4.455	28	.159		
	Total	4.875	31			
Type of product *F4	Between Groups	5.433	3	1.811	2.242	.105
	Within Groups	22.621	28	.808		
	Total	28.055	31			
Type of product *F5	Between Groups	5.513	3	1.838	3.080	.044
	Within Groups	16.705	28	.597		
	Total	22.219	31			
Type of product *F5	Between Groups	3.454	3	1.151	1.750	.180
	Within Groups	18.421	28	.658		
	Total	21.875	31			
Type of product *Overall	Between Groups	.133	3	.044	.203	.893
	Within Groups	6.119	28	.219		
	Total	6.252	31			

Table 7.9 Discriminant Validity

Factors	F1	F2	F3	F4	F5	F6
F1	1					
F2	.385*	1				
F3	-.080	-.015	1			
F4	.461**	.235	.083	1		
F5	.095	.100	.162	-.031	1	
F6	.269	.010	-.230	.097	.026	1

*. Correlation is significant at the 0.05 level (2-tailed).
**. Correlation is significant at the 0.01 level (2-tailed).

CHAPTER 8

ETHICAL RETAIL PRACTICES: PERCEPTIONS OF REGULATORY BODIES

8.1 Background

A regulatory body is a public authority/government department/a voluntary organisation, responsible for exercising needed authority over some areas of human activity in a regulatory/supervisory capacity. Regulatory bodies take care of administrative legal and regulative activities (codifying and enforcing rules and regulations and imposing supervision for the benefit of the public at large). The existence of independent regulatory agencies is justified by the complexity of certain regulatory and supervisory tasks that require expertise, the need for rapid implementation of public authority in certain sectors, and the drawbacks of political interferences. Regulatory agencies are usually a part of the executing branch of the government. They have statutory authority to perform their functions with oversight from the legislative branch. Regulatory bodies are commonly set up to enforce standards and safety and to oversee use of public goods and regulate business. There are different regulatory bodies for regulating the retailing sector such as Food and Supply Department, Taxation Department, Labour and Employment Department, Weights and Metrology Department and Retailers' Associations as self regulating agencies. The Food and Supply Department ensures the quality and safety of products of retail stores through sampling methods and Taxation Department collects the taxes from retailers and controls tax evasion and avoidance. Labour and Employment Department is concerned with issues of child labour, fair pay, working conditions and Weight and Metrology Department evaluates the measures of weights used by the retailers. Retailers have framed their associations for their own welfare and better support from regulating agencies and these associations guide their members from time to time and make them aware about the new trends in retail sector by organising seminars and workshops etc. (Botero et al., 2004).

As already stated, the retailers are expected to behave in ethical manner with all the stakeholders including these regulatory bodies (Whysall, 1995). They are considered ethical when they are honest, fair, responsible and truthful in their dealings with all concerned (Whysall, 2000; Fredrich, 1993). They are supposed to furnish all the needed information and documents authentically and without any delay. In fact, it is the moral obligation on the part of retailers to fully cooperate with these regulatory bodies so that they can regulate the retail sector for the benefit of all the stakeholders involved in it particularly the consumers (Kujala, 2001; Clarkson, 1995; Carroll, 1991). The present study, thus, examines the perceptions of five regulatory bodies namely Food and Supply Department, Taxation Department, Labour and Employment Department, Weights and Metrology Department and Retailers' Associations regarding ethical retail practices (Sharma and Sharma, 2011 and 2011).

8.2 Data Collection

The data for the present study have been obtained from both secondary and primary sources. The secondary data were taken from journals, books and the internet. The primary data have been gathered through a specifically self developed schedule. The responses were obtained from the regulatory bodies referred by retailers under consideration of the present study during survey. The retailers were asked to name the regulatory bodies that regulate their retailing practices so that a whole picture of ethical values of retailers under reference in their dealings with various regulatory bodies can be examined empirically.

8.3 Data Collection Form

A schedule was developed specifically for the study after needed review of literature and in consultation with the experts on the subject (Fassin, 2009; Kaptein, 2008; Lavorata and Pontier, 2005; Kujala, 2001 and Whysall, 1995). The schedule comprised of 45 items in total based on five point Likert scale ranging from 5 to 1, where 5 means strongly agree and 1 means strongly disagree (5<.....>1). Out of the total, 16 items represent ethical values applicable to all the regulatory bodies while 29 items cover legal provisions viz. 6 items relating to Taxation Department, 8 items relating to Food and Supply Department, 5 items to Labour Department and 10 items relating to Retailers' Associations.

8.4 Profile of Respondents

The final data obtained from different regulatory bodies in Jammu city such as Food and Supply Department, Taxation Department, Labour and Employment Department, Weights and Metrology Department and Retailers' Associations. The officials of the regulatory bodies, who visited the retail stores and having experience of retailers' dealings and practices, were contacted. The final response was available from a total of 35 respondents i.e. Food and Supply Department (35%), Taxation Department (26%), Labour and Employment Department (14%), Weights and Metrology Department (11%) and Retailers' Associations (14%, Table 8.1). The respondents belonging to Food and Supply, Labour and employment, Weights and Metrology visit retail stores on monthly basis while Taxation Department officials visit quarterly. A large number of retailers have membership of retailers' association and these associations charge annual subscription fee from their members for carrying out their activities. The retailers associations particularly of provisional stores (kiryana) also prepares a price list which each member has to follow and these lists are displayed at the retail stores so that it always remain visible to the consumers.

8.5 Reliability and Validity

Reliability, an assessment of degree of consistency between multiple variables of a construct (Hair et al., 2009, p. 161) was checked through Split half values and Cronbach Alpha (Malhotra, 2008, p. 285), by dividing the respondents into two equal halves. The data were proved satisfactory in terms of split half reliability as mean values obtained from both the halves were quite satisfactory (Group I = 3.28 and Group II = 3.42). Moreover, Cronbach Alpha value also proved reliable which came to be 0.797, being above the minimum threshold of 0.7 (Table 8.2). Validity, the extent to which a scale or set of measures accurately represent the concept of interest was assessed in terms of content, convergent and discriminant analysis (Hair et al., 2009, p. 161). The Content validity has been worked out by reviewing the concerned literature and discussions with the experts on similar topic. Convergent validity, the degree to which two measures of the same concept are correlated, was found to be satisfactory (Malhotra, 2008, p. 286), as the correlations between items were significant and their values found to be > 0.5. Further, communalities of all the items were also above 0.5 (Table 8.4), indicating convergent validity. Discriminant validity, the degree to which two constructs are different, proves if there is no correlation between two constructs. It demonstrates one construct as sufficiently different from the other constructs (Hair et al., 2009, p. 162). Discriminate validity has also been proved as the correlations between most of the constructs were < 0.3 (Table 8.8).

8.6 Perceptions of Regulatory Bodies regarding Ethical Values

As stated above, the variables relating to ethical values are common for all regulatory bodies and thus, factor analysis was applied on these items to converge them into factors. While items relating to legal provisions were specific to each regulatory body and number of respondents was low. Therefore, factor analysis has not been applied on them. For data purification of ethical values, the technique of factor analysis has been used through Statistical Package for Social Sciences (SPSS, 17 Version) with Principal component analysis along with varimax rotation. Factor analysis examines the underlying patterns or relationship for condensing the total data into minimum meaningful factors (Hair et al., 2009, p. 128). The items having factor loading less than 0.5 and Eigen value less than 1 were not considered for the subsequent analysis. With application of factor analysis, the data converged into three factors with 67.09% of variance explained (Table 8.3). The three factors are F1 (Cooperation), F2 (Honesty), F3 (Fairness). The status of each factor is discussed in detail as under:-

Factor 1 (*Cooperation*): Retailers have ethical obligation to cooperate with the regulatory bodies by providing them the required information. This factor is made up of items like, 'respect', 'cooperation', 'no criticism of competitors', 'authentic information', 'follow instructions' and 'needed information'. The overall factorial mean value (3.65) indicates retailers' cooperating with regulatory bodies. The Eigen value of this factor is 4.191 with 27.76 percent of variance explained. The factor loadings range from .824 to .635 and commonalities fall between .688 and .663. Majority of the respondents (88%) found retailers giving due respect (4.23) to them as they visit their retail stores and about 91% of them experienced full cooperation (4.20) from retailers. About 75% of the total respondents experienced retailers furnishing the needed information (3.80) which is authentic to some extent (3.74). While about 77% of them observed retailers criticising their competitors with regulatory authorities just to shift their attention to other retailers (2.29).

Factor 2 (*Honesty*): This factor comprised of variables such as, 'responsible', 'follow legal norms', 'honest' and 'truthful'. The overall factorial mean value (3.07) indicates retailers as moderately honest with regulatory bodies. The Eigen value of this factor is 2.451 with 25.94 percent of variance explained. The factor loadings range from .899 to .587 and commonalities fall between .841 and .501. About 74% of the total respondents found retailers responsible (3.06), honest (3.09), follower of legal norms (3.20) and less truthful (2.94). As these mean scores are not so high, indicating retailers moderately ethical in their dealings with regulatory bodies.

Factor 3 (*Fairness*): This factor has two items, viz., 'no corruption for unfair practices' and 'disclosing all the facts'. The factorial mean arrived at 3.00 with Eigen value of 1.408 with 13.39 percent of variance explained. About half of the respondents found retailers not offering money for doing unfair practices (3.40) as they were afraid of corruption. However, 60% of the total respondents found retailers sometimes hiding some facts (2.60) about the retail business.

8.7 Perceptions of Regulatory Bodies regarding Legal Provisions

The present study makes an attempt to segregate ethical and legal practices in retailing as ethics covers law in its domain. There are some actions of retailers which are illegal and unethical. Retailers are bound to do retail business by following law and order. Thus, the perception of regulatory bodies about legal norms observed in retailing is as under:-

8.7.1 Taxation Department

Retailers are required to maintain proper books of accounts and disclose their actual sales and profit to the taxation authorities (Yetmar and Eastman, 2000). They are also required to fill the tax return on time and pay the actual rate of tax. In fact, it is illegal on the part of retailers to evade tax (Kujala, 2001; Whysall, 2000, 1995; Cowell, 1988).

They should not evade tax by manipulating the books of accounts by disclosing less sales and profit (Reckers and Roark, 1994). About 44% of the total respondents found retailers not making books of accounts properly (2.78) and about 80% of them observed retailers not disclosing actual sales (1.89) and profit (1.56). Two third of the total respondents experienced retailers filling the tax return on time but at the same time they found retailers evading tax (2.44) to some extent by manipulating some facts about the sales and profit.

8.7.2 Food and Supply Department

Food and Supply Department scrutinises the quality and safety standard of the products sold by the retailers. They deal with adulteration of the products, products safety, packaging, outdated products etc. About 55% of the total respondents found products sold by retailers as safe and hygienic (3.27) but there is little adulteration in some products by few retailers, particularly those who themselves pack eatable products. About 73% of them found packages as good (3.82) and quantity as accurate (3.36) as mentioned on the pack. About 72% of the respondents observed retailers less likely able to sell the out dated products as consumers are more conscious than before and suppliers take back the outdated products for either recycling or disposing off the products within an agreed period of time.

8.7.3 Labour and Employment Department

The sole responsibility of this department is to regulate the employees' wages, working conditions, child labour etc. Majority (80%) of the respondents observed retailers not employing child labour (3.80) and giving reasonable salary to the employees (3.60). The respondents also found retailers not harassing the employees at store (3.40) as employees are well aware about their rights and can protect themselves from the exploitation by retailers.

8.7.4 Retailers' Associations

Retailers have framed their associations for their security and protection. Retailers' associations work for creating the right environment for the growth and development of the retail practices. These bodies encourage, develop, facilitate and support retailers to become modern and adopt best practices that give delight to customers. These associations take annual membership fee and guide their members regarding various issues of common interest from time to time. They conduct meetings, seminars, workshops and circulate price list among members. Majority of the respondents (80%) viewed retailers paying membership fee (3.80), following the price list (4.00), attending meetings (3.60), selling standardised products (4.00) and not practicing price discrimination (3.20). Most of the associations, guide their members regarding fair retail practices (4.40). They warn those who do unfair retail practices but their membership is not cancelled (1.80) by them. The Retailers' associations have not yet prepared a code of ethics (1.20) but they agreed to formulate code of ethical practices and implement it soon and circulate to all members like the price list.

8.8 Agency wise Differences (ANOVA)

For finding out the mean differences in the perceptions of different agencies regarding ethical retail practices, ANOVA was used. ANOVA depicts significant mean differences in the perceptions of different regulatory departments about ethical retail practices (F= 5.792, Sig. = .001, Table 8.6). Further, post hoc analysis has been applied. The post hoc analysis shows significant difference in the response of Labour and Employment Department and Taxation Department. The respondents belonging to Labour and Employment Department accorded the highest mean score (3.64) followed by Food and Supply Department (3.46), Retailers Association (3.31) and Taxation (3.04, Table 8.7).

Conclusion

On the whole, the regulatory bodies observed retailers ethical and legal to some extent as the mean values are moderate. Retailers are more unethical from the viewpoint of taxation authorities as they evade tax by disclosing less sales and profit. Retailers' association should become more active and conscious about the retail practices and terminate the membership of those doing unfair and illegal practices and keep them disassociated and isolated for such a crime. They should adopt ethical code and train the members for more ethical retail practices.

References

Botero, Juan, Simeon Djankov, Rafael La Porta, Florencio Lopez-de-Silanes and Andrei Shleifer (2004), "The Regulation of Labour," *Quarterly Journal of Economics*, Vol. 118, pp. 1339-1382

Carroll, A. B. (1991), "The Pyramid of Corporate Social Responsibility: Toward the Moral Management of Organisational Stakeholders", *Business Horizons*, Vol. 34, pp. 39–48

Clarkson, M. B. E. (1995), "A Stakeholder Framework for Analyzing and Evaluating Corporate Social Performance", *Academy of Management Review*, Vol. 20, pp. 92–117

Cowell, F., & J. Gordon (1988), "Unwillingness to Pay: Tax Evasion and Public Goods Provision", *Journal of Public Economics*, Vol. 36, pp. 305–321

Fassin, Yves (2009), "The Stakeholder Model Refined", *Journal of Business Ethics*, Vol. 84, pp. 113-135.

Fredrich J. P. (1993), "The Ethical Behaviour of Retail Managers", *Journal of Business Ethics*, Vol. 12, pp. 207-218

Hair, J. F.; William C. Black; Barry J. Babin; Ralph E. Anderson and Ronald L. Tathum (2009), Multivariate Data Analysis, Sixth Edition, Pearson Prentice Publishers, New Delhi

Kaptein, Muel (2008), "Developing a Measure of Unethical Behaviour in the Workplace: A Stakeholder Perspective", *Journal of Management*, Vol. 34 (October), pp. 978-1008

Kujala, Johanna (2001), "Analysing Moral Issues in Stakeholder Relations", *Business Ethics: A European Review*, Vol. 10, pp. 233-247

Lavorata, Laure and Suzanne Pontier (2005), "The Success of a Retailers' Ethical Policy: Focusing on Local Actions", *The Journal of Academy of Marketing Science Review*, Vol. 2005 (12), pp. 1-9

Malhotra, Naresh (2008), 'Marketing Research', An Applied Orientation, Fifth Edition, Prentice Hall of India, New Delhi

Reckers, P., D. Sanders and S. Roark (1994), "The Influence of Ethical Attitudes on Taxpayer Compliance", *Journal of National Tax* Vol. 47(4), pp. 825–836

Sharma R. D. and Bodh Raj Sharma (2011), "Legal Provisions and Ethical Values in Retail Sector: Study of Convenience Goods", *Arash, A Journal of ISMDR*, Vol. 1, No. 1, (January), pp. 1-9

-- (2009), "Ethics in Retailing: Perceptions of Consumers", *Saaransh RKJ Journal of Management*, Vol. 1, No. 1, (July), pp. 43-55

Whysall, Paul (2000), "Stakeholder Mismanagement in Retailing: A British Perspective", *Journal of Business Ethics*, Vol. 23, pp. 19-28

----------------- (1995), "Ethics in Retailing", *Business Ethics: A European Review*, Vol. 4 (3), pp. 150-156

Yetmar, S and K Eastman (2000), "Tax Practitioners' Ethical Sensitivity: A Model and Empirical Examination', *Journal of Business Ethics,* Vol. 26, pp. 271–288.

Table 8.1 Respondent Profile

Regulatory Body	Frequency	Percentage
Food and Supply Department	12	35
Taxation Department	09	26
Labour and Employment	05	14
Weight and Metrology	04	11
Retailers' Associations	05	14
Total	**35**	**100**

Table 8.2 Split Half Reliability

Group	Mean and Alpha Values
Group I	3.28
Group II	3.42
Cronbach's Alpha	0.797

Table 8.3 Factor Analysis

Rounds	Variance Explained	Items Emerged	No of Factors Extracted	Iterations	No of Items Deleted	KMO	Bartlett
1	72.48	15	04	06	02	.589	326.71
2	74.78	13	04	06	01	.641	247.67
3	67.09	12	03	05	-	.641	214.54

Table 8.4 Factorial Profile of Ethical Retail Practices

Variables	M	SD	FL	C	EV	VE
F1 Cooperation	**3.65**	**0.71**			4.191	27.76
Respect	4.23	0.88	.824	.688		
Cooperation	4.20	0.68	.777	.621		
No criticism of competitors	2.29	0.83	.720	.578		
Authentic Information	3.74	0.82	.708	.625		
Follow instructions	3.63	0.94	.689	.617		
Needed information	3.80	0.72	.635	.563		
F2 Honesty	**3.07**	**0.11**			2.451	25.94
Responsible	3.06	0.87	.899	.837		
Follow legal norms	3.20	0.90	.885	.841		
Honest	3.09	0.92	.864	.814		
Truthful	2.94	1.08	.587	.501		
F3 Fairness	**3.00**	**0.57**			1.408	13.39
No corruption for unfair practices	3.40	1.24	.867	.773		
Disclosing all the facts	2.60	1.29	.642	.675		
Grand Mean, S D, VE and CA	**3.35**	**0.60**				67.08

* M= Mean; SD= Standard Deviation; FL= Factor Loadings; C= Commonalities; EV=Eigen values and VE= Variance Explained

Table 8.5 Perceptions about Legal Provisions

Variables	Mean	Std Dev
Taxation Department (N=09)	**2.54**	**0.71**
Retailers maintain proper books of accounts	2.78	1.09
They show actual sales	1.89	0.78
They disclose actual profit	1.56	0.73
The fill the tax return on time	3.22	0.97
They pay the tax on prescribed rates	3.33	1.00
They evade tax	2.44	1.13
Food and Supply Department (N=12)	**3.36**	**0.31**
Retailers do not adulterate the products	2.91	1.14
The products are safe and hygienic	3.27	1.01
Packages are good	3.82	1.08
The quantity is authentic	3.36	1.03
The quality of products is genuine	3.45	0.93
They do not sell outdated products	3.67	1.05
They have accurate measures of weight	3.00	0.77
They charge the printed price	3.36	0.81
Labour Department (N=05)	**3.44**	**0.26**
They do not employ minors in their stores	3.80	1.10
They close their shops on the last Sunday	3.20	0.45
They give reasonable salary to the employees	3.60	1.14
Employees are not harassed at retail store	3.40	0.89
Retailers are doing fair retailing practices	3.20	0.84
Retailers Association (N=05)	**3.22**	**1.02**
Your members follow price list	4.00	1.00
They give you needed information	3.80	0.84
They pay the membership fee	3.40	1.52
They attend the meetings called by you	3.60	1.14
They sell standardised products	4.00	0.71
They do not practice price discrimination	3.20	0.84
Their promotion is not deceptive	2.80	0.45
You guide them for fair retail practices	4.40	0.55
You cancel membership of those who do unfair practices	1.80	0.45
You have developed a code of ethics for your members	1.20	0.45
Overall Mean and Standard Deviation	**3.15**	**0.75**

Table 8.6 ANOVA (Agency wise)

Factors	Source of Variation	Sum of Squares	Df.	Mean Square	F	Sig.
F1	Between Groups	2.380	4	.595	4.661	.005
	Within Groups	3.830	30	.128		
	Total	6.210	34			
F2	Between Groups	10.633	4	2.658	8.126	.000
	Within Groups	9.814	30	.327		
	Total	20.446	34			
F3	Between Groups	16.074	4	4.018	4.935	.004
	Within Groups	24.426	30	.814		
	Total	40.500	34			
Age*Overall	Between Groups	4.379	4	1.095	5.792	.001
	Within Groups	5.670	30	.189		
	Total	10.049	34			

Table 8.7 Agency wise Factorial Mean Values

Factors	Agencies				
	Food and Supply N=12	Taxation N=09	Labour and Employment N=05	Weight and Measures N=04	Retailers' Association N=05
F1	3.80	3.22	3.93	3.75	3.67
F2	3.17	2.83	3.20	1.94	4.05
F3	3.42	3.06	3.80	1.63	2.20
Overall	3.46	3.04	3.64	2.44	3.31

Table 8.8 Discriminant Validity

Factors	Cooperation	Honesty	Fairness
Cooperation	1		
Honesty	.270	1	
Fairness	-.026	.313	1

CHAPTER 9
MAJOR FINDINGS AND STRATEGIC ACTION PLAN

The chapter summarises the major findings emerging from the study and suggests accordingly strategic action plan for strengthening the ethical values in retailing practices.

9.1 Major Findings

The present research study examines empirically the perceptions of several stakeholders such as customers, retailers, wholesalers, manufacturers and regulatory bodies. The data collected from different stakeholders have been analysed separately and thus, the major findings emerging from this study are summarised separately for each stakeholder as under:-

9.1.1 Perceptions of Customers

The perceptions of customers about ethical retail practices have been studied separately for convenience, shopping and specialty goods. It is as under:-

(A) Convenience Goods

- Customers perceive retailers dealing in convenience goods as moderate in ethical values (M = 3.07).
- Customers get equal and fair treatment from the retailers (3.17) and have access to all alternatives available in the store (3.70).
- Retailers behave politely and patiently (3.88) and quite courteous, respectful and helpful (3.80).
- Customers are satisfied with quality (3.75), product quantity (3.81); product packing and desired brands (3.86).
- Retailers assist customers in buying decisions (3.79).

- Customers are dissatisfied from parking facility available around the market (1.46).
- Customers observe educated retailers as more humble, helpful and respectful (3.80).

(B) Shopping Goods

- The overall mean score (2.99) reflects moderate level ethical value system observed by the retailers dealing in shopping goods.
- Customers experience retailers quite courteous (3.80), giving them due recognition (3.92), and dealing with them politely and patiently (3.91).
- Customers get equal and fair treatment from the retailers (3.13).
- Retailers sometimes make lame excuses for the products which are not in stock (2.84) for retaining the existing customers.
- The customers are satisfied with quality (3.80), price (3.61), packing (3.91) and brands of products (3.99) available from the retailers.
- Customers find retailers giving correct and timely information (3.76), assisting them in buying decisions (3.82) and implementing their suggestions (3.25) for better retail practices.
- Customers are highly satisfied with displays (4.10) and experience no price discrimination (3.29) in case of shopping goods. In fact, retailers charge fixed and printed price.

(C) Specialty Goods

- The overall mean score of ethical values came to be as 3.24, reflecting moderate level of ethical values being practiced by the retailers who deal in these goods.
- Customers experience equal and fair treatment from the retailers (3.28) with accurate and timely information (3.51) as when sought.

- Customers find retailers giving needed importance to less profitable customers, not pressurising them for purchase, giving no preference to specific customers of higher and regular business and protecting consumer rights to some extent.
- Customers experience retailers as courteous and respectful (3.86); giving due recognition to them (4.01) as customer and behaving politely and patiently (3.99).
- Customers observe retailers providing them adequate after sale services (3.81) and giving due consideration to their complaints (3.68).
- Customers were satisfied with quality (3.92), highly satisfied with packages (4.08) and availability of desired brands (4.13).
- Retailers furnish correct and timely information (3.87) and help in buying decisions (3.92) by providing the needed help (3.88) as and when required.
- About two third of respondents observe retailers not discriminating against them (3.44) and implementing their suggestions (3.23) for better retail practices.

9.1.2 Perceptions of Retailers

- Retailers are ethical in their dealings with their financers as they give due respect (3.80) and the needed information to them (3.79), pay interest on loans taken by them for the establishment of retail stores at agreed rate (3.83) and also returning the principal amount on maturity (3.79) without carrying any problem in this regards.
- Retailers treat their employees fairly and equally; handle employees' complaints immediately and help employees as and when required so that they could work without any problem (3.97).
- Retailers maintain their compliance to legal norms framed by the government (4.74) for regulating the retail market.

- Retailers are quite good in treating all customers fairly and equally irrespective of gender, age, caste, religion and income (4.22).
- Retailers claim of filling the tax return on time (4.24) and paying the actual amount of tax (4.01).
- Majority of the retailers selected as respondents express due respect to their competitors (4.12) and not criticising their competitors with customers for doing business with them (4.04). Moreover, they do not hire the employees of competitors (4.06) by offering them higher salary and other benefits just with intention to destablise the competitors.
- Most of the retailers do not have child labour in their retail stores (4.38). They understand that it is illegal and unethical to employ the children below the age of 14 years and they are charged with heavy fine and imprisonment if they employ the children under the age of 14 years.

9.1.3 Perceptions of Wholesalers

- Majority of the wholesalers find retailers as trustful (3.66), committed (3.64), humble (3.70), straightforward (3.49) and sincere (3.76).
- Majority of the respondents experience retailers delaying the payments in the stipulated time period and making payments quite late on one or other excuses (2.96). This creates serious problems for the wholesalers who have to make prompt payments to the manufacturers and sometimes even advance payments for getting the regular supply of goods.
- Wholesalers find retailers loyal (3.51) if they are given more commission and credit facilities but in case of cash sales and less margins they shift to other wholesalers (2.61).

- About half of the wholesalers, do find retailers sometimes criticising their competitors with them.
- Retailers make lame excuses for keeping more merchandise in the retail store (2.70).
- Retailers do not ask for reimbursement of promotional expenses (3.30) because in Jammu retailers are less promotion oriented, particularly who deal in convenience goods.
- Retailers return the out dated products to the wholesalers within the agreed period of time.

9.1.4 Perceptions of Manufacturers

- Manufacturers are satisfied (3.76) with retailers and focused experienced them as respectful (3.72), honest (3.74), providing needed space to their products in their retail outlets (3.75).
- They perceive retailers as responsible (3.63), humble (3.69) and developing long term relations with them (3.59).
- About 60% of the total respondents find retailers delaying the payments in the stipulated time period by making payments quite late (2.81) and paying less amounts as agreed upon (2.81).
- About half of the respondents observe retailers returning the goods (3.44) to them within the period allowed by them.

9.1.5 Perceptions of Regulatory Bodies

- Majority of the respondents find retailers giving due respect (4.23). They get full cooperation (4.20) from retailers during their visits to the retail stores.

- Retailers furnish the needed information (3.80) which is authentic and adequate (3.74). However, retailers do criticise their competitors with regulatory authorities just to shift their attention to other retailers (2.29).
- About 74% of the total respondents observe retailers responsible (3.06), honest (3.09), follower of legal norms (3.20) but less truthful (2.94) to them.
- About half of the respondents experience retailers not offering money for doing unfair practices (3.40). In fact, retailers understand that corruption is not good.
- About 60% of the total respondents find retailers sometimes hiding some facts (2.60) about the retail business.
- Retailers do not make proper books of accounts (2.78), disclose actual sales (1.89) and profit (1.56).
- Two third of the total respondents view retailers filling the tax return on time but they do evade tax (2.44) to some extent.
- About 55% of the total respondents find products sold by retailers as safe and hygienic (3.27) while little adulteration in some products by a few retailers, particularly those who themselves pack eatable products.
- About 73% of them view packages as good (3.82) and quantity is accurate (3.36) as mentioned on the pack.
- About 72% of the respondents find retailers less likely able to sell the out dated products as consumers are more conscious than before and suppliers take back the out dated products for either recycling or disposing off the products within an agreed period of time.
- The respondents experience retailers not employing child labour (3.80) and giving reasonable salary to the employees (3.60). The respondents also find retailers not harassing the employees at store (3.40). In fact, employees are also

well aware about their rights and can protect themselves from the exploitation by retailers.

- Retailers' Associations view retailers paying membership fee (3.80), following the price list (4.00), attending meetings (3.60), selling standardised products (4.00) and do not practice price discrimination (3.20).
- Retailers' Associations have not yet prepared any code of ethics (1.20) for its members

9.2 Perceptual Gap of Ethical Values between Retailers and Customers

The perceptual gap has been measured to examine the discrepancy in the opinions of retailers and their customers towards ethical values in retailing practices. To test the significant mean differences, independent t test has been used. The results of t test exhibit significant mean differences between retailers and customers about ethical retail practices (Table 9.1). Retailers accorded higher mean scores to most of the items and thus, claim themselves as more ethical in their dealings with customers. While, the mean scores allotted by their customers to similar items proved retailers as less ethical. Retailers however, assigned less mean scores to items like 'truthfulness', 'no adulteration', and 'no preference to some customers'. Retailers argued that it is very difficult to speak truth in present retail business because of lot of competition and complexity of retail business. They further, stated that adulteration is done by the suppliers and manufacturers as they sell already packed products. While, customers found retailers unethical in terms of adulteration, accurate and timely information about product usage, preference to existing customers and issuance of bills for product purchased by customers. They focus on more sales and high profit margins than customer satisfaction and truthfulness. On the whole customers found retailers moderately ethical as compared to retailers who claimed themselves as highly ethical in their retail practices with customers (Table 9.1).

9.3 Perceptual Gap of Ethical Values among Retailers, Wholesalers and Manufacturers

For determining the perceptual gap in terms of perceptions of retailers, wholesalers and manufacturers, ANOVA has been applied. ANOVA depicts significant mean differences among the three groups in all the items representing ethical retail practices. The retailers, by according higher mean scores for most of the items, claimed themselves as highly ethical in their dealings with suppliers. While, the mean scores allotted by the wholesalers and manufacturers to the same items have been less than retailers. Wholesalers viewed retailers more ethical than manufacturers as they assigned higher mean scores to most of the items except mutual interest and expiry dated products. The reason being that the manufacturers take expiry dated products from retailers with least hesitation either for recycling or for disposing off, while the wholesalers have to send the expiry dated products to their manufacturers (Table 9.2).

9.4 Perceptual Gap of Ethical Values between Retailers and Regulatory Bodies

The perceptual gap between customers and regulatory bodies about ethical retail practices has been examined through independent t test. The results of t test indicate significant mean differences in the opinion of retailers and regulatory bodies about ethical retail practices (Table 9.3). Retailers, by according higher mean scores to most of the items, believe themselves ethical in their dealings with regulatory authorities. On the other hand, regulatory bodies assigned less mean scores to all the items than retailers, indicating retailers as less ethical than what retailers claimed of themselves. The regulatory bodies found little adulteration (2.91) by retailers who do packing of goods themselves. The regulatory authorities also found retailers criticising their competitors with them, just to divert their attention. They also found retailers evading taxes (2.44) by manipulating sales and profits (Table 9.3).

9.5 Strategic Action Plan

The present study provides a strategic action plan for strengthening the abidance of legal norms by retailers and ensuring ethical retail practices on the basis of the data obtained from different stakeholders in retailing. The data have been analysed and inferences have drawn with the purpose of identifying the issues areas in retail which require immediate attention of all the covered. The findings lead to the formulation of strategic action plan for better consumer oriented and ethical values among retailers so that expectations of all stakeholders can be fulfilled in legal and ethical manner (Sharma and Sharma 2011, 2009; Kaptein, 2008, Sarma, 2007; Lavorata and Pontier, 2005; Dubinsky et al., 2004; Kujala, 2001 and Whysall, 2000 and 1998). In fact, if retailers are ethical they get more sales, high profit margins, more market share with strong image of the retail stores. In addition to this, consumers will feel satisfied and become loyal to the retail outlets from which they purchase goods (Abratt et al., 1999). Thus, the following strategic action plan is suggested:-

> ➤ *__Need for High Ethical Values__*: The mean scores of different stakeholders about ethical retail practices i.e. customers (3.07), retailers (4.14), wholesalers (3.38), manufacturers (3.48) and regulatory bodies (3.35), indicate retailers moderately ethical, as the mean values in this regard are not so high. Retailers need to be highly ethical in their dealings with different stakeholders. Retailers should make every effort to make sure that their retail practices meet the expectations of all the stakeholders in an ethical manner. The regulatory bodies, consumer organisations and government agencies should become more active while regulating the retailing practices.

- ➤ **_Truthfulness_**: The retailers were found to be less truthful. They should try to speak truth with the stakeholders, as truthfulness pays in the long run in terms of customers' trust on retailers, customer satisfaction and loyalty to the retail stores in the long run.

- ➤ **_Fair Sales Promotion_**: Customers found retailers dealing in shopping goods, particularly apparel, offering high discounts by enhancing the price of the same product (2.57). Sales promotion if fairly done is good for raising sales in the short period. Thus, it is suggested that the promotion about offered products should not be deceptive.

- ➤ **_Regular and effective vigilance over the illegal retail practices_**: The regulatory bodies should be active to reduce illegal and unethical retail practices. Those responsible for illegal activities should be punished and the same should be publicised, so that it proves to be deterrent to others also. The loopholes in the existing laws coming in the way of fair retailing transactions need to be plugged immediately. The Food Safety and Standards Act, 2006 (FSSA) has been implemented all over India including J&K. All retailers need to understand its provisions.

- ➤ **_Protection of Consumer and Employee Rights_**: Concerned agencies are required to make the retailers aware of consumers and employee rights and consequences, if the same are violated. Moreover, consumers and employees ought to be sensitised about their own rights. Consumer organisations should play their role significantly by awakening the general public and protecting consumers.

- ➤ **_Code of Ethics_**: Most of the big business houses or their associations have framed code of ethics for guiding their members. The present study finds that retailers' associations have not yet prepared the ethical code for their members (M = 1.20) In fact, retailers' associations are formed to protect the interest of their members, yet they can not ignore the unethical retail practices by their members. Retailers' associations need to evolve a code of ethics for their own members for strengthening ethical retail practices much more effectively by these associations on the lines of American Marketing Association.

- ➤ *__Payment of bills to Suppliers__*: The suppliers in retailing viz., wholesalers and manufacturers complained that retailers do not make payments on time and of exact amount. The wholesalers have been facing a serious problem of payment of bills by the retailers as they have to make immediate payments to manufacturers. The retailers should make payments on time and of exact amount to the wholesalers and manufacturers so that they can meet their obligations to their suppliers and ensure the regular supply of goods in the market.

- ➤ *__Long term relations with suppliers__*: Wholesalers opined that retailers are loyal only if they give them credit for longer period, otherwise they shift to other wholesalers. The retailers should build long term relations with their suppliers who may assist them financially or in some other forms of gifts and services.

- ➤ *__Proper Books of Accounts__*: Retailers do not prepare proper books of accounts, particularly who deal in convenience goods (2.78). They should prepare proper books of accounts in prescribed format and get audited by the charted accountant so that authentic information can be furnished to the regulatory bodies.

- ➤ *__Issuance of Bills to Customers__*: Retailers dealing in convenience goods do not issue the bills for goods purchased by the consumers. Retailers, however, argued that customers resist in taking bills, but it seems to be a lame excuse for not issuing bills. They should issue bills to the customers like other retailers dealing in shopping and specialty goods who even not allow their customers to leave the retail store without bills.

- ***Payment of Taxes***: Taxation authorities shared that retailers do not disclose actual sales (1.89) and profits (2.56) to them. They manipulate the figures of sales and profit very tactfully to evade tax (2.44). But it is unethical on the part of retailers to do so because the non payment of tax not only illegal and unethical but also causes serious problems of socio economic development of the society. The taxation authorities should identify those retailers who evade taxes and, with the help of media, publicise their names. The retailers' associations should develop a feeling of civic consciousness among their members that payment of taxes contributes to the national exchequer as public revenue and comes back to them in the form of public expenditure for the welfare of all.

- ***Awareness Programmes***: Retailers' associations and other regulatory bodies should conduct more seminars, workshops and ethical awareness programmes to make retailers more ethical. In fact the retailers and their sales people need to undergo some orientation training programmes to understand customer focused retail business and ethical operations for their own long term and sustainable benefits and also for the benefit of the society as a whole.

- ***Supply of Standardised and Branded Products***: Quality is more important than quick profits. Retailers should focus on qualitative goods as the present customer is not price conscious but quality conscious. Retailers dealing in convenience goods, quite often are found unethical in terms of selling low standard (2.99), and adulterated (2.91) products, and also claming unbranded products as superior (2.53). The retailers should keep standardised products, protect the consumer rights and supply safe, hygienic and risk free products.

> *__Parking Facility__*: The customers found dissatisfied with parking facilities near the retail outlets. It is surprising that in this age of planned shopping markets, the customers do not have adequate parking facility. In fact, it is the joint responsibility of both the administration and the retailers.

On the whole, the present study suggests for the retailers to inculcate high ethical values in their retail practices in their dealings with different stakeholders. These ethical values shall help them in terms of more sales, high profits, customer satisfaction, loyalty and reputation of the retail stores. **Lord Buddha says,** *"A businessman should be like a honey bee that sucks the honey but does not harm the flower."* In the same sense, retailers should earn his livelihood in the society but without squeezing or doing any harm to the stakeholders. **Lord Krishna also says in Bhagavad Gita,** *"A wise and ethical person by performing his prescribed duties (Dharma), gets success and enjoys this life and thereafter.* Thus, the retailers should take help from scriptures for inculcating higher ethical values in their retailing practices so that all the stakeholders in retailing can be satisfied in an ethical manner.

References

Abratt, Russell; M. Bendixen and K. Drop (1999), "Ethical Perceptions of South African Retailers: Management and Salespersonnel", *International Journal of Retail and Distribution Management*, Vol. 27, No.2, pp. 91-105

Dubinsky, Alan J.; Rajan Nataraajan and Wen-Yeh Huang (2004), "The Influence of Moral Philosophies on Retail Salespeople's Ethical Perceptions", *The Journal of Consumer Affairs*, Vol. 38, No. 2, pp. 297-317.

Kaptein, Muel (2008), "Developing a Measure of Unethical Behavior in the Workplace: A Stakeholder Perspective", *Journal of Management*, Vol. 34, No. 5, (October), pp. 978-1008

Kujala, Johanna (2001), "Analysing Moral Issues in Stakeholder Relations", *Business Ethics: A European Review*, Vol. 10, pp. 233-247

Lavorata, Laure and Suzanne Pontier (2005), "The Success of a Retailers' Ethical Policy: Focusing on Local Actions", *The Journal of Academy of Marketing Science Review*, Vol. 2005, No.12, pp. 1-9

Sarma, Nripendra Narayan (2007), "Ethics in Retailing-perception of management and sales personnel", *(http:// dspace.iimk.ac.in/bitstream/2259/388/1/61-68.pdf)*, last accessed on March 20, 2012

Sharma R. D. and Bodh Raj Sharma (2011), "Legal Provisions and Ethical Values in Retail Sector: Study of Convenience Goods", *Arash, A Journal of ISMDR*, Vol. 1, No. 1, (January), pp. 1-9

-- (2009), "Ethics in Retailing: Perceptions of Consumers", *Saaransh RKJ Journal of Management*, Vol. 1, No. 1, (July), pp. 43-55

Whysall, Paul (2000), "Stakeholder Mismanagement in Retailing: A British Perspective", *Journal of Business Ethics*, Vol. 23, pp. 19-28

---------------- (1998), "Ethical Relationship in Retailing: Some Cautionary Tales", *Business Ethics: A European Review*, Vol. 7 (2), pp. 103-110

Table 9.1 Perceptual Gap of Ethical Values between Retailers and Customers

Items	R	C	MD	t Value	Sig.
Demanded goods	4.75	3.86	0.89	15.546	.000
No adulteration	3.02	2.91	0.11	1.112	.267
Safe packing	4.71	3.73	0.98	16.528	.000
Inform about product usage	4.33	2.74	1.59	19.510	.000
Repair/ replace products	4.08	3.52	0.56	6.827	.000
Printed price	4.05	3.68	0.37	4.954	.000
Proper rate of VAT	4.18	3.66	0.52	7.234	.000
Fair advertising	4.16	3.39	0.77	8.737	.000
No preference to some customers	2.60	2.96	0-.36	-3.705	.000
Issue of bills	4.24	2.56	1.67	15.401	.000
Provide needed information	4.18	3.44	0.74	10.102	.000
Equal treatment to customers	4.22	3.17	1.05	12.386	.000
Help in choice making	4.17	3.79	0.38	6.179	.000
Focus on customer satisfaction	4.15	2.48	1.67	20.290	.000
Truthfulness	2.37	2.00	0.37	3.921	.000
Protection of consumer rights	4.12	3.04	1.07	13.241	.000
Ethical in dealing with customers	4.05	3.24	0.81	10.797	.000

* R= Retailers, C= Customers, MD= Mean Difference

Table 9.2 Perceptual Gap of Ethical Values among Retailers, Wholesalers and Manufacturers

Items	R	W	M	F Value	Sig.
Information	4.74	3.97	3.94	89.834	.000
Truthfulness	4.13	3.19	3.13	49.727	.000
Payment of bills on time	4.32	2.96	2.78	88.304	.000
Follow terms and conditions	4.09	3.44	3.34	23.287	.000
Long term relations	4.29	3.81	3.50	20.754	.000
Respect	4.33	3.89	3.72	23.106	.000
Assistance	4.16	3.73	3.72	23.106	.000
Mutual Interest	4.21	2.36	2.53	203.170	.000
Expiry dated products	3.98	3.36	3.44	16.353	.000
Fair dealings with suppliers	4.11	3.81	3.75	13.065	.000

* R= Retailers, W= Wholesalers, M= Manufacturers

Table 9.3 Perceptual Gap of Ethical Values between Retailers and Regulatory Bodies

Items	R	RB	MD	t Value	Sig.
No adulteration	3.02	2.91	0.11	.424	.672
Proper packing	4.71	3.82	0.89	5.379	.000
Printed Price	4.05	3.36	0.69	2.415	.017
Expiry dated products	3.98	3.67	0.31	1.437	.152
No criticism of competitors	4.04	2.29	1.75	16.896	.000
Follow legal rules and regulations	4.74	3.20	1.54	14.616	.000
Supply needed information	4.09	3.80	0.29	3.614	.000
Corruption	4.03	3.40	0.63	2.906	.004
Fill tax returns on time	4.24	3.22	1.02	2.324	.021
Tax evasion	4.00	2.44	1.56	4.031	.000
Employ minors	4.38	3.80	0.58	2.248	.026
Ethical with Regulatory bodies	4.06	3.51	0.55	7.186	.000

* R= Retailers, RB= Regulatory Bodies, MD= Mean Difference

Bibliography

- Abratt, Russell; M. Bendixen and K. Drop (1999), "Ethical Perceptions of South African Retailers: Management and Salespersonnel", *International Journal of Retail and Distribution Management*, Vol. 27, No.2, pp. 91-105
- Abratt, Russell and Neale Penman (2002), "Understanding Factors Affecting Salespeople's Perceptions of Ethical Behaviour in South Africa", *Journal of Business Ethics*, Vol. 35, pp. 269-280
- Ardichvili, Alexandre; Douglas Jondle; Brenda Kowske; Edgard Cornachione; Jessica Li and Thomas Thakadipuram (2012), "Ethical Cultures in Large Business Organisations in Brazil, Russia, India, and China", *Journal of Business Ethics*, Vol. 105, pp. 415-528
- Bone, Paula Fitzgerald and Robert John Corey (2000), "Packaging Ethics: Perceptual Difference among Packaging Professionals, Brand Managers and Ethically-Interested Consumers", *Journal of Business Ethics*, Vol. 24, pp. 199-213
- Burns David J. and John T. Brady (1996), "Retail Ethics as Appraised by Future Business Personnel in Malaysia and United States", *The Journal of Consumer Affairs*, Vol. 30, No. 1, pp. 195-217
- Casali, Gian Luca (2011), "Developing a Multidimensional Scale for Ethical Decision Making", *Journal of Business Ethics*, Vol. 104, pp. 485-497
- Cole C. Barbara and Dennie L. Smith (1996), "Perceptions of Business Ethics: Students versus Business People", *Journal of Business Ethics*, Vol. 15, pp. 889-896
- Crawford, C. Marle (1970), "Attitudes of Marketing Executives towards Ethics in Marketing Research', *Journal of Marketing*, Vol. 34, pp. 46-52.
- Davies, Iain A.; Zoe Lee and Ine Ahonkhai (2012), "Do Consumers Care about Ethical-Luxury?", *Journal of Business Ethics*, Vol. 106, pp. 37-51
- Dawson, Leslie M. (1997), "Ethical Differences between Men and Women in the Sales Profession", *Journal of Business Ethics*, Vol. 16, pp. 1143-1152
- Deshpande, S. P.; Jacob Joseph and V. V. Maximov (2000), "Perceptions of Proper Ethical Conduct of Male and Female Russian Managers", *Journal of Business Ethics*, Vol. 24, pp. 179-183

- Deshpande, S. P. (1997), "Managers Perception of Proper Ethical Conduct: The Affect of Sex, Age and Level of Education", *Journal of Business Ethics,* Vol. 16, pp. 79-85
- Desplaces, D. E.; D. E. Melcher, L. L. Beauvais, and S. M. Bosco (2007) "The Impact of Business Education on Moral Judgment Competence: An Empirical Study", *Journal of Business Ethics,* Vol. 74 (1), pp. 73-87
- Dominguez, Luis Rodriguez; Isabel Gallego-Alvarez and Isabel Maria Garcia-Sanchez (2009), "Corporate Governance and Codes of Ethics", *Journal of Business Ethics,* Vol. 90, pp. 187–202
- Dornoff, R. J. and C. B. Tankersley (1976), "Do Retailers Practice Social Responsibility", *Journal of Retailing,* Vol. 51 (Winter), pp. 33–42
- Dornoff, R. J. and C. B. Tankersley (1975), "Perceptual Differences in Market Transactions: A Source of Consumer Frustration", *Journal of Consumer Affair,* Vol. 9, pp. 97–103
- Dubinsky, Alan J.; Rajan Nataraajan and Wen-Yeh Huang (2004), "The Influence of Moral Philosophies on Retail Salespeople's Ethical Perceptions", *The Journal of Consumer Affairs,* Vol. 38, No. 2, pp. 297-317
- Dubinsky, A. J. and M. Levy (1985), "Ethics in Retailing Perceptions of Retail Salespeople", *Journal of Academy of Marketing Science,* Vol, 13 (1), pp. 1-16
- Ergeneli, Azize and Semra Ankan (2000), "Gender Difference in Ethical Perceptions of Salespeople: An Empirical Examination in Turkey", *Journal of Business Ethics,* Vol. 40, pp. 247-260
- Fassin Yves (2009), "The Stakeholder Model Refined", *Journal of Business Ethics,* Vol. 84, pp. 113-135
- Ferrell, O. C. and K. Mark Weaver (1978), "Ethical Beliefs of Marketing Managers", *Journal of Marketing,* Vol. 42, July, pp. 69-73
- File, K. M. and R. A. Prince (1992), "Positive Word of Mouth: Customer Satisfaction and Buyer Behaviour", *International Journal of Bank Marketing,* Vol. 10, No. 1, pp. 25-29
- Freyne, P. (2009), "Are Ethics Back in Business?", *Journal of Business & Finance,* Vol. 15, pp. 46–47
- Goodman, Charles S. and Merle C. Crawford (1974), "Young Executives: A Source of New Ethics?", *Journal of Personnel,* Vol. 53, pp. 180-187

- Grant, R. M. and M. Visconti (2006), "The Strategic Background to Corporate Accounting Scandals", *Long Range Planning*, Vol. 39, pp. 361-383
- Higgins, Eleanor O. and Bairbre Kelleher (2005), "Comparative Perspective on the Ethical Orientations of Human Resources, Marketing and Finance Functional Managers", *Journal of Business Ethics*, Vol. 56, pp. 275-288
- Honeycutt, Jr. Earl D.; Myron Glassman; M T Zugelder and Kiran Karande (2001), "Determinants of Ethical Behaviour: A Study of Autosalespeople", *Journal of Business Ethics*, Vol. 32, pp. 69-79
- Izraeli, D. (1988), "Ethical Beliefs and Behaviour among Managers: A Cross Cultural Perspective", *Journal of Business Ethics*, Vol. 7, pp. 263-271
- Jones, T. M. (1991), "Ethical Decision Making by Individuals in Organizations: An Issue-Contingent Model", *Academy of Management Review* Vol. 16, pp. 366-395
- Kaptein, Muel (2008), "Developing a Measure of Unethical Behaviour in the Workplace: A Stakeholder Perspective", *Journal Of Management*, Vol. 34, No. 5, October, 2008, pp. 978-1008
- Kidwell, J. M.; R. E. Stevens and A. L. Bethke (1987), "Differences in the Ethical Perceptions Between Male and Female Managers: Myth or Reality", *Journal of Business Ethics*, Vol. 6, pp. 489-493
- Kohli, A. K. and B. J. Jaworski (1990), "Market Orientation: the Construct, Research Propositions, and Managerial Implications", *Journal of Marketing*, Vol. 54, April, pp. 20-35.
- Kujala, Johanna (2001), "Analysing Moral Issues in Stakeholder Relations", *Business Ethics: A European Review*, Vol. 10, pp. 233-247
- Kurt, Gizem and Gungor Hacioglu (2010), "Ethics as a Customer Perceived Value Driver in the Context of Online Retailing", *African Journal of Business Management*, Vol. 4 (5), pp. 672-677
- Lam, Kit-Chun and Guicheng Shi (2008), "Factors Affecting Ethical Attitudes in Mainland China and Hong Kong", *Journal of Business Ethics*, Vol. 77, pp. 463-479
- Lau, Cubie L. L. (2010), "A Step Forward: Ethics Education Matters!", *Journal of Business Ethics*, Vol. 93, pp. 565-584

- Lavorata, Laure and Suzanne Pontier (2005), "The Success of a Retailers' Ethical Policy: Focusing on Local Actions", *The Journal of Academy of Marketing Science Review*, Vol. 2005, No.12, pp. 1-9
- Lee, Monle; Anurag Pant and Abbas Ali (2010), "Does the Individualist Consume More? The Interplay of Ethics and Beliefs that Governs Consumerism across Cultures" *Journal of Business Ethics*, Vol. 93, pp. 567–581
- Levy, M. and A. J. Dubinsky (1983), "Identifying and Addressing Retail Salespeople's Ethical Problems', *Journal of Retailing* Vol. 59, pp. 46–66
- Li, Wanxian, Xinmei Liu and Weiwu Wan (2008), "Demographic Effects of Work Values and Their Management Implications", *Journal of Business Ethics*, Vol. 81, pp. 875-885
- Lii, Yuan-Shuh and Monle Lee (2012), "Doing Right Leads to Doing Well: When the Type of CSR and Reputation Interact to Affect Consumer Evaluations of the Firm", *Journal of Business Ethics*, Vol. 105, pp. 69-81
- Limbu Yam B; Marco Wolf and Dale L. Lunsford (2011), "Consumers' Perceptions of Online Ethics and its Effects on Satisfaction and Loyalty", *Journal of Research in Interactive Marketing*, Vol. 5 No. 1, pp. 71-89
- Lin, Grace Tyng-Ruu and Jerry Lin (2006), "Ethical Customer Value Creation: Drivers and Barriers", *Journal of Business Ethics*, Vol. 67, pp. 93-105
- Marnburg, E. (2000), "The Behavioural Effects of Corporate Ethical Codes: Empirical Findings and Discussion", *Business Ethics: A European Review*, Vol. 9 No. 3, pp. 200-210
- Mazzola, P.; D. Ravasi and C. Gabbioneta (2006), "How to Build Reputation in Financial Mrkets", *Long Range Planning*, Vol. 39, pp. 385-407
- Mc Cabe, A. Catherine; Rhea Ingram and Mary Conway Dato-on (2006), "The Business of Ethics and Gender", *Journal of Business Ethics*, Vol. 64, pp. 101-116.
- Mc Nichols, C. W. and T. W. Zimmerrer (1985), "Situation Ethics: An Empirical Study of Differentiators of Students' Attitudes", *Journal of Business Ethics*, Vol. 4, pp. 175-180
- Mulki, Jay Prakash and Fernando Jaramillo (2011), "Ethical reputation and value received: customer perceptions", *International Journal of Bank Marketing*, Vol. 29 No. 5, pp. 358-372

- Napal, Geetanee (2003), "Ethical Decision Making in Business: Focus on Mauritius", *Business Ethics: A European Review*, Vol. 12, No.1, pp. 54-63
- Nicholls, Alexander James (2002), "Strategic Options in Fair Trade Retailing", *International Journal of Retail and Distribution Management,* Vol. 30, No 1, pp. 6-17.
- Norris, Donald G. and John B. Gifford (1988), "Retail store managers' and students' perceptions of ethical retail practices: A comparative and longitudinal analysis (1976–1986), *Journal of Business Ethics,* Vol. 7, pp. 515-524
- Nygaard, Arne and Biong, Harald (2010), "The Influence of Retail Management's Use of Social Power on Corporate Ethical Values, Employee Commitment, and Performance", *Journal of Business Ethics,* Vol. 97, pp. 87-108
- Orlitzky, M.; F. L. Schmidt and S. L. Rynes (2003), "Corporate Social and Financial Performance: A Meta Analysis", *Organization Studies,* Vol. 24, pp. 403-441
- Oumlil, A. Ben and Joseph L. Balloun (2009), "Ethical Decision Making Difference between American and Moroccan Managers", *Journal of Business Ethics,* Vol. 84, pp. 457-478
- Park-Poaps, Haesun and Kathleen Rees (2010), "Stakeholder Forces of Socially Responsible Supply Chain Management Orientation", *Journal of Business Ethics*, Vol. 92, pp. 305–322
- Pettijohn, Charles, Linda Pettijohn and A. J. Taylor (2008), "Salesperson Perceptions of Ethical Behaviours: Their Influence on Job Satisfaction and Turnover Intentions *Journal of Business Ethics*, Vol. 78, pp. 547–557
- Rallapalli C. Kumar; Scott J. Vitell; Frank A. Wiebe and James H. Barnes (1994), "Consumer Ethical Beliefs and Personality Traits: An Exploratory Analysis", *Journal of Business Ethics*, Vol. 13, pp. 487-495
- Reynolds, J. Scott; Frank C. Schultz and David R. Hekman (2006), "Stakeholder Theory and Managerial Decision Making: Constraints and Implications of Balancing Stakeholders' Interests", *Journal of Business Ethics*, Vol. 64, pp. 285-301
- Robinson, Pamela K. (2010), "Responsible Retailing: The Practice of CSR in Banana Plantations in Costa Rica", *Journal of Business Ethics,* Vol. 91, pp. 279–289

- Roman, Sergio and Pedro J. Cuestas (2008), "The Perceptions of Consumers Regarding Online Retailers' Ethics and Their Relationship with Consumers' General Internet Expertise and Word of Mouth: A Preliminary Analysis", *Journal of Business Ethics,* Vol. 83, pp. 641-651
- Roman Sergio and J. L. Munuera (2005), "Determinants and Consequences of Ethical Behaviour: An Empirical Study of Salespeople*", European Journal of Marketing,* Vol. 39, No. 5/6, pp. 473-495
- Rowwas, Mohammed Y. A.; Scott J. Vitell and Jamel A. Al-Khatib (1994), "Consumer Ethics: The Possible Effect of Terrorism and Civil Unrest on the Ethical Values of Consumers", *Journal of Business Ethics,* Vol. 13, pp. 223-231
- Rowwas, Mohammed Y. A. (1996), "Consumer Ethics: An empirical Investigation of Austrian Consumers", *Journal of Business Ethics,* Vol. 15, pp. 1009-1019
- Ruegger, D. and S. W. King (1992), "A Study of the Effects of Age and Gender upon Students Business Ethics" *Journal of Business Ethics,* Vol. 11, pp. 179-186
- Sarma, Nripendra Narayan (2007), "Ethics in Retailing-Perception of Management and Sales Personnel", *(http:// dspace.iimk.ac.in/bitstream/2259/388/1/61-68.pdf),* last accessed on March 20, 2012
- Sasikumar, K. and Regina Sibi Cleetus (2008), "Impact of Corporate Retailing on Small Retail Outlets", *The Indian Journal of Commerce,* Vol. 61, No. 4, (October-December), pp. 68-77
- Sautar, Geoffrey; M. M. Mc Neil and Caron Molster (1994), "The Impact of the Work Environment on Ethical Decision Making: Some Australian Evidence", *Journal of Business Ethics,* Vol. 13, pp. 327-339
- Schwepker, Jr harles H. and Thomas N. Ingram (1996) Improving Sales Performance through Ethics: The Relationship between Salesperson Moral Judgment and Job Performance", *Journal of Business Ethics,* Vol. 15, pp. 1151-1160
- Sharma R. D. and Bodh Raj Sharma (2011), "Legal Provisions and Ethical Values in Retail Sector: Study of Convenience Goods", *Arash, A Journal of ISMDR,* Vol. 1, No. 1, January, pp. 1-9

- Sharma R. D. and Bodh Raj Sharma (2009), "Ethics in Retailing: Perceptions of Consumers", *Saaransh RKJ Journal of Management*, Vol. 1, No. 1, July, pp. 43-55
- Singhapakdi, Anusorn, Mahesh Gopinath, Janet K. Marta and Larry L. Carter (2008), "Antecedents and Consequences of Perceived Importance of Ethics in Marketing Situations: A Study of Thai Businesspeople", Journal of Business Ethics, Vol. 81, pp. 887-904
- Singhapakdi, Anusorn; Kenneth L. Kraft; Scott J. Vitell and Kumar C. Rallapalli (1995), "The Perceived Importance of Ethics and Social Responsibility on Organisational effectiveness: A Survey of Marketers", *Journal of Academy of Marketing Science*, Vol. 23, No. 1, pp. 49-56
- Singhapakdi, Anuson and Scot J. Vitell (1993), "Personal and Professional Values Underlying the Ethical Judgements of Marketers", *Journal of Business Ethics*, Vol. 12, pp. 525-533
- Singhapakdi, A and S. J. Vitell, (1990), "Marketing Ethics: Factors Influencing Perceptions of Ethical Problems and Alternatives", *Journal of Macro marketing* (Spring), pp. 4-18
- Stohl, Cynthia; Michael Stohl and Lucy Popova (2010), "A New Generation of Corporate Codes of Ethics", *Journal of Business Ethics,* Vol. 90, pp. 607–622
- Takala, Tuomo and Outi Uusitalo (1995), "Retailers' Professional and Professio-Ethical Dilemmas: The Case of Finnish Retailing Business, *Journal of Business Ethics,* Vol. 14, pp. 893-907
- Taylor, S. A. and, T. L. Baker (1994), "An Assessment of the Relationship Between Service Quality and Customer Satisfaction in the Formation of Consumers' Purchase Intentions", *Journal of Retailing*, Vol. 70, No. 2, pp. 163-78
- Thomas, James L., Scott J. Vitell, Faye W. Gilbert, Gregory M. Rose (2002), "The Impact of Ethical Cues on Customer Satisfaction with Service", *Journal of Retailing,* Vol. 78, pp. 167–173
- Trawick, I. Frederick, John E. Swan, Gail W. McGee and David R. Rink (1991), 'Influence of Buyer Ethics and Salesperson Behaviour on Intention to Choose a Supplier', *Journal of the Academy of Marketing Science,* Vol. 19 (1), pp. 17–23

- Trevino, L. K. and M. E. Brown (2004), "Managing to be Ethical: Debunking Five Business Ethics Myths', *Journal of Academy of Management Executive* Vol. 18, pp. 69–81.
- Valentine, Sean and Tim Barnett (2002), "Ethics Codes and Sales Professionals' Perceptions of their Organisations' Ethical Values", *Journal of Business Ethics*, Vol. 40, pp. 191-200
- Valentine, Sean and Gary Fleischman (2004), "Ethics, Training and Businesspersons' Perceptions of Organisational Ethics", *Journal of Business Ethics,* Vol. 52, pp. 381-390
- Valenzuela Leslier M., Jay P. Mulki and Jorge Fernando Jaramillo (2010), "Impact of Customer Orientation, Inducements and Ethics on Loyalty to the Firm: Customers' Perspective" *Journal of Business Ethics*, Vol. 93, pp. 277–291
- Verbeke, William; Cok Ouwerkerk and Ed Peelen (1996), "Exploring the Contextual and Individual Factors on Ethical Decision Making of Salespeople', *Journal of Business Ethics*, Vol. 15, pp. 1175-1187
- Vitell, Scott J.; Kumar C. Rallapalli and Anusorn Singhapakdi (1993), "Marketing Norms: The Influence of Personal Moral Philosophies and Organisational Ethical Culture", *Journal of the Academy of Marketing Science*, Vol. 21, No. 4, pp. 331-337
- Vogel, D. (1992), "The Globalisation of Business Ethics: Why America Remains Distinctive', *California Management Review* (Fall), 30–49
- Whysall, Paul, (2000) "Retailing and the Internet: A Review of Ethical Issues", *International Journal of Retail & Distribution Management*, Vol. 28 (11), pp. 481 – 489
- Whysall, Paul (2000), "Addressing Ethical Issues in Retailing: A Stakeholder Perspective", *International Review of Retail, Distribution and Consumer Research,* Vol. 10 (3), (July), pp. 305–318
- Whysall, Paul (2000), "Stakeholder Mismanagement in Retailing: A British Perspective*",* *Journal of Business Ethics*, Vol. 23, pp. 19-28
- Whysall, Paul (1998), "Ethical Relationship in Retailing: Some Cautionary Tales", *Business Ethics: A European Review*, Vol. 7 (2), pp. 103-110

- Yoo, Boonghee and Naveen Donthu (2002), "The Effects of Marketing Education and Individual Cultural Values on Marketing Ethics of Students", *Journal of Marketing Education,* Vol. 24 No. 2, pp. 92-103
- Yücel, Recep; Halil Elibol and Osman Dagdelen (2009) "Globalisation and International Marketing Ethics Problems", *International Research Journal of Finance and Economics*, Vol. 26, pp. 93-104
- Zolingen, Simone J. van; Hakan Honders (2010), "Metaphors and the Application of a Corporate Code of Ethics", *Journal of Business Ethics*, Vol. 92, pp. 385–400

Books

- Bajaj, Cretan; Rajneesh Tulip and Niche V Srivastava (2007), Retail Management, Seventh Edition Oxford University Press, New Delhi, pp. 3, 4 and 9
- Beauchamp, Tom L. and Norman E. Bowie (1983), 'Ethical Theory and Business', Second Edition, Prentice Hall, Inc., Englewood cliffs, N. J.
- Berman, Berry and Joel R. Evans (2007), Retail Management, Tenth Edition, Prentice Hall of India Pvt Ltd, New Delhi, pp. 44
- Boatright, John R. (2009), Ethics and the Conduct of Business, Fifth Edition, Pearson Education, New Delhi
- Cox, Roger and Paul Brittain (2006), Retailing, Fifth Edition, Pearson Education, New Delhi, pp. 32.
- De George, Richard R. (1982), 'Business Ethics' Second Edition, Macmillan Publishing, New York
- Fernando, A. C. (2009), Business Ethics, An Indian Perspective, First Impression, Dorling Kindersley, Pearson Education, New Delhi, pp. 4, 5, 6
- Kotler Philip (2005), Marketing Management, Eleventh Edition, Pearson Education Indian branch, Delhi, pp. 411
- Mitchell, Charles (2009), International Business Ethics, Third Edition, Atlantic Publishers and Distributors, World Trade Press, New Delhi, pp. 9, 10
- Pradhan, Swapna (2007), Retailing Management, Second Edition, Tata McGraw Hill, New Delhi, pp. 4
- Sivananda, Swami (2004), Ethical Teachings, Sixth Edition, The Divine Life Society, Uttarakhand, India, pp. 3
- Vedamani, Gibson G. (2008), "Retail Management", Third Edition, Jaico Publishing House, Mumbai, pp. 3-4.

ANNEXURE I
Schedule for Customers

General Information:

1. Age: ---------------------
2. Gender: -----------------
3. Qualification: ----------
4. Marital Status: --------
5. Religion: ---------------
6. Occupation: -----------
7. Family Size: ------------
8. Family Expenditure (per month in Rs): -------------
9. Family Income (Per month in Rs): -------------------
10. Most of the purchase decisions are taken by: -----

Note: On the basis of your recent experience with regard to the following three types of products viz. Convenience, Shopping and Specialty. Please write 5, 4, 3, 2 or 1 against each statement.

Here: 5 means Strongly Agree
        4 means Agree
        3 means neither Agree nor Disagree
        2 means Disagree
        1 means Strongly Disagree

CG = Convenience Goods: Which are easily and frequently purchased with less time requirement. e.g. Soap, Toothpaste, Medicine and Other eatable products

S_HG = Shopping Goods: The goods for which you take some time for buying and have different choices. e.g. Clothes, Kitchen appliances etc.

S_PG = Specialty Goods: Which are infrequently purchased, need more time and efforts. e.g. Jewellery, Vehicle, Laptop etc

Legal Provisions:

	CG	S$_H$G	S$_P$G

1 Retailers provide genuine quality products
2 They do not sell the low standard products
3 They do not adulterate the goods supplied
4 They provide the products which are safe and fit for intended uses
5 They do not dump the products
6 They do not hoard the gifts which are meant for customers
7 They replace/repair the products during the period of guarantee/warranty
8 They sell the unbranded products by claiming them as superior
9 They offer excessive discounts by increasing the price of the same product
10 They become angry and refuse after sale service even when it is part of sale
11 They do not under weigh the products
12 They charge fair prices
13 They do not practice price discrimination
14 They use deceptive pricing where actual price is higher than the advertised one
15 They do not charge higher rate of VAT
16 They maintain proper records in case of sales on credit
17 They do not indulge in misleading and false labeling
18 They do not practice false packaging
19 The packages contain the printed quantity
20 They do not indulge in deceptive advertising with false claim or induce misleading beliefs.
21 They provide true and accurate information about the quantity, price and quality of products.
22 They do not use deceptive and manipulated sales promotion
23 They do not employ minors in their stores
24 They do not exploit customers
25 They do not breach the product guarantee/warranty/after sale contracts
26 They do not create environmental pollution
27 They do not sell the expired date products
28 They issue the bills on purchases

Ethical Values:

	CG	S$_H$G	S$_P$G

1 Retailers provide adequate after sale services to you
2 They recognise you as customer
3 They give due cognizance to your complaints
4 They do not disparage competitors
5 They treat all customers equally and fairly
6 They claim something beyond their control, when it is not
7 Salesmen have knowledge of all the products

8 They do not conceal their limitations			
9 They do not exploit the customers whose bargaining power is not strong			
10 They provide accurate information			
11 They provide access to all varieties of products			
12 They deal with customers politely and patiently			
13 They are truthful, sincere and honest			
14 They are courteous, respectful and helpful			
15 They show products according to the type of customers			
16 They impress upon customer needs instead of their sales motive			
17 They do not sell the more expensive products when less expensive products are better for customers			
18 They do not make excuses for the product which is not in stock			
19 They tell the complete truth about the product features			
20 They do not ignore customers who are less profitable			
21 They do not pressurise customers for making a purchase			
22 They assist only those customers who are likely to buy			
23 They do not give preferential treatment to certain customers			
24 They protect your rights as consumers			
25 The retailers are ethical in dealing with customers			
Customer satisfaction:	CG	S_HG	S_PG
1 You get the good quality products from retailers			
2 The quantity of products printed is authentic			
3 The product packing is proper and safe			
4 You get the desired brands of products			
5 They charge fair and printed price			
6 They supply goods on delivery date			
7 After sale services are provided by them			
8 Store location is convenient to you			
9 Sitting arrangement is proper			
10 Proper parking space is available			
11 Stores have long queue for shopping			
12 Window displays are attractive			
13 They are helpful			
14 They provide correct and timely information			
15 They are always available on the store			
16 They help you in the buying decision process			
17 They provide the needed assistance			
18 They do not discriminate with you			
19 They implement your suggestions			
20 The overall performance of retailers is good			
Other Issues	CG	S_HG	S_PG
1 Age fosters polite behaviour.			

2 Retailers who are senior in age are honest, punctual, humble and respectful
3 Young retailers indulge more in unfair retailing practices.
4 Retailers senior in age control the unethical behaviour of their salesmen.
5 Education contributes to ethical behaviour.
6 Educated retailers abide by prescribed norms and regulations.
7 Educated retailers are humble, respectful and more helpful.
8 Less educated retailers indulge in unfair retail practices.
9 Highly educated retailers deal fairly.
10 Less educated retailers do not discriminate with customers relating to price, tone of language and quality of products.

ANNEXURE II
Schedule for Retailers

General Information

1. Age: ---------- 2. Qualification: --------------- 3. Type of Store: ----------------

4. Number of Employees: ------------ 5. Experience: ---------------------------

6. Monthly Sales (Rs): ---------------- 7. Monthly Profit (Rs): ------------------

8. Whether a member of any association? Yes / No If yes, please specify-------

9. Whether your association has framed a code of ethics for you? Yes / No

10. How frequently to get your measures checked? ---------------------------------

11. Name two wholesalers from whom you purchase products:

(i) ---------------------------------- (ii) ---

12. Name two manufacturers from whom you directly buy products:

(i) ------------------------------------ (ii) ---

13. Name the government departments with whom you have dealings:

(i) ----------------------- (ii) ------------------------------ (iii) ---------------------------

(iv) ---------------------- (v) ------------------------------ (vi) ---------------------------

14. Name two financiers with whom you have dealings: (i) ----------- (ii) --------

Note: Please tick 5, 4, 3, 2 or 1 against each statement. Where 5 means Strongly Agree; 4 means Agree; 3 means Neither Agree nor Disagree; 2 means Disagree and 1 means Strongly Disagree.

Statements

In relation with Consumers	SA	A	N	D	SD
1 You provide the goods demanded by the consumers	5	4	3	2	1
2 Adulteration of goods is common these days	5	4	3	2	1
3 Your packing is proper and safe	5	4	3	2	1
4 You inform your consumers about product usage	5	4	3	2	1
5 You repair/replace the products within warranty/guarantee period	5	4	3	2	1
6 You charge printed price	5	4	3	2	1
7 You have knowledge of VAT rates on different products	5	4	3	2	1
8 Advertising without deception results to nothing	5	4	3	2	1
9 Preference to some consumers is must for making them loyal	5	4	3	2	1
10 You issue bills on purchases made by the consumers	5	4	3	2	1
11 You give the needed information to your consumers	5	4	3	2	1
12 You treat all your consumers equally	5	4	3	2	1
13 You help your consumers in choice making	5	4	3	2	1
14 Your focus is on customer satisfaction than on sales or profit	5	4	3	2	1
15 Telling truth in all matters is difficult in present business	5	4	3	2	1

16 You protect consumer rights	5	4	3	2	1
17 You are fair in dealing with your consumers	5	4	3	2	1

In relation with Salesmen/employees

1 You treat all your employees equally	5	4	3	2	1
2 The employees' complaints are dealt with immediately	5	4	3	2	1
3 Employees are paid for overtime work	5	4	3	2	1
4 You help your employees as and when needed	5	4	3	2	1
5 You protect employees' rights	5	4	3	2	1

In Relation with Suppliers

1 You provide the needed information to your suppliers	5	4	3	2	1
2 You deal truthfully with your suppliers	5	4	3	2	1
3 You pay the bills on proper time	5	4	3	2	1
4 You follow the terms and conditions of your suppliers	5	4	3	2	1
5 You build long term relations with your suppliers	5	4	3	2	1
6 You give due respect to your suppliers	5	4	3	2	1
7 You help your suppliers as and when needed	5	4	3	2	1
8 You focus on both own and suppliers' interest	5	4	3	2	1
9 You return expiry dated products to your suppliers	5	4	3	2	1
10 You are fair in dealing with your supplier	5	4	3	2	1

In Relation with Competitors

1 You follow the rules of fair play with your competitors	5	4	3	2	1
2 You never criticise your competitor	5	4	3	2	1
3 You readily cooperate with competitors	5	4	3	2	1
4 You do not hire the employees of competitors	5	4	3	2	1
5 You give respect to your competitors	5	4	3	2	1

In Relation with Government

1 You comply with the legal rules and regulations	5	4	3	2	1
2 You provide the needed information to authorities	5	4	3	2	1
3 Governmental officials demand money from you	5	4	3	2	1
4 You fill the tax return on time	5	4	3	2	1
5 You pay the actual rates of tax	5	4	3	2	1

In Relation with Financers

1 You cooperate with your financers	5	4	3	2	1
2 You give the needed information to your financers	5	4	3	2	1
3 You pay interest at agreed rate	5	4	3	2	1
4 You pay the loan on maturity date	5	4	3	2	1
5 You give due respect to your financers	5	4	3	2	1

In Relation with Community

1 You try to protect the environment	5	4	3	2	1
2 You do not employ minors in your store	5	4	3	2	1
3 You give due respect to children and women	5	4	3	2	1
4 You participate in trade exhibitions	5	4	3	2	1
5 You are ethical in dealing with all the stakeholders	5	4	3	2	1

ANNEXURE III
Schedule for Wholesalers

General Information:

1. Age--------------------------------
2. Qualification: -------------------
3. Religion:------------------------
4. Experience---------------------
5. Type of Products: -------------
6. Number of Employees: -------
7. Monthly Sales (Rs): -----------
8. Monthly Profit (Rs) : ----------
9. Name two Manufacturers: ----

Note:-Please tick 5,4,3,2 or 1 against each statement. Where 5 means Strongly Agree; 4 means Agree; 3 means Neither Agree nor Disagree; 2 means Disagree and 1 means Strongly Disagree

Statements	SA	A	N	D	SD
1 You get the required information from retailers	5	4	3	2	1
2 Retailers follow your instructions	5	4	3	2	1
3 They are truthful in their dealings with you	5	4	3	2	1
4 They co-operate with you	5	4	3	2	1
5 They pay the bills on proper time	5	4	3	2	1
6 They pay the exact amount as agreed	5	4	3	2	1
7 They agree with your terms and conditions	5	4	3	2	1
8 They demand excessive commission from you	5	4	3	2	1
9 They demand more gifts from you	5	4	3	2	1
10 They build long term relations with you	5	4	3	2	1
11 Retailers deal with you politely and patiently	5	4	3	2	1
12 They are honest in dealing with you	5	4	3	2	1
13 They undertake their responsibility as a retailer	5	4	3	2	1
14 They give due respect and recognition to you	5	4	3	2	1
15 They criticise other retailers with you	5	4	3	2	1
16 They are loyal to you	5	4	3	2	1
17 In case of less commission retailers shift to other wholesalers	5	4	3	2	1
18 You trust your retailers	5	4	3	2	1
19 Retailers are committed to you	5	4	3	2	1
20 You are satisfied from your retailers	5	4	3	2	1
21 They help you as and when required	5	4	3	2	1
22 Sometimes they become irritable	5	4	3	2	1
23 They do fair business practices with you	5	4	3	2	1
24 They focus only on their interest	5	4	3	2	1
25 They give excuses for keeping inventory in the retail store	5	4	3	2	1

26 Retailers are humble to you	5	4	3	2	1
27 They are sincere	5	4	3	2	1
28 They charge the printed price	5	4	3	2	1
29 Your retailers are straight forward	5	4	3	2	1
30 They return expired dated products	5	4	3	2	1
31 They keep their promises	5	4	3	2	1
32 They don't deceive you	5	4	3	2	1
33 They introduce new brands of product	5	4	3	2	1
34 They demand excessive promotion expenses	5	4	3	2	1
35 Your retailers are ethical in dealing with you	5	4	3	2	1

ANNEXURE IV
Schedule for Manufacturers

General Information

1. Age--------------------------------
2. Qualification---------------------
3. Type of Business-----------------
4. Experience-----------------------
5. Number of Employees: --------
6. Monthly Sales (Rs): ------------
7. Monthly Profit (Rs) : ----------
8. Number of retailers to whom you directly supply products:-------------
9. Whether you have framed a code of ethics for your retailers   Yes / No

Note: Please encircle 5,4,3,2 or1 against each statement. Where 5 means Strongly Agree; 4 means Agree; 3 means Neither Agree nor Disagree; 2 means Disagree and 1 means Strongly Disagree.

Statements	SA	A	N	D	SD
1 Needed information is provided by the retailers	5	4	3	2	1
2 Retailers follow your instructions	5	4	3	2	1
3 They are truthful in dealing with you	5	4	3	2	1
4 They co-operate with you	5	4	3	2	1
5 They give the needed space to your products	5	4	3	2	1
6 The pay the bills on proper time	5	4	3	2	1
7 They pay the exact amount as agreed	5	4	3	2	1
8 They agree with your terms and conditions	5	4	3	2	1
9 They demand excessive commission for selling your products	5	4	3	2	1
10 They demand more gifts for selling your products	5	4	3	2	1
11 They build long term relations with you	5	4	3	2	1
12 They deal with you politely and patiently	5	4	3	2	1
13 They are honest in dealing with you	5	4	3	2	1
14 They undertake their responsibility as retailers	5	4	3	2	1
15 They give due respect and recognition to you	5	4	3	2	1
16 They criticise other retailers with you	5	4	3	2	1
17 They are loyal to you	5	4	3	2	1
18 In case of less commission and gifts they shift to other firms	5	4	3	2	1
19 You trust your retailers	5	4	3	2	1
20 They are committed to you	5	4	3	2	1
21 You are satisfied from your retailers	5	4	3	2	1
22 They help you as and when required	5	4	3	2	1
23 Sometimes they become irritable	5	4	3	2	1

24 They do fair business practices with you	5	4	3	2	1
25 They focus on their interest only	5	4	3	2	1
26 They threaten you to keep the products of your competitors	5	4	3	2	1
27 They give excuses for keeping inventory in the retail store	5	4	3	2	1
28 They are humble to you	5	4	3	2	1
29 They are sincere	5	4	3	2	1
30 They introduce your products to consumers	5	4	3	2	1
31 They force you to set higher price of the product	5	4	3	2	1
32 They charge the printed price	5	4	3	2	1
33 Your retailers are straight forward	5	4	3	2	1
34 They return expired dated products	5	4	3	2	1
35 They don't deceive you	5	4	3	2	1
36 They keep their promises	5	4	3	2	1
37 Your retailers are ethical in dealing with you	5	4	3	2	1

ANNEXURE V
Schedule for Regulatory Bodies

1. Name of the Department----------------------------------

2. No. of visits to retail stores:

    (a) Yearly (b) Half Yearly (c) Quarterly

    (d) Monthly (e) Weekly

3. Tick the ethical values retailers maintain in their dealings with you.

    (a) Honesty (b) Fairness (c) Truthfulness (d) Openness

    (e) Responsiveness (f) Accountability (g) Respect & Recognition

4. Mention the measures you take for reducing unfair retail practices.

    (a)---

    (b)---

    (c)---

    (d)---

Note: Please tick 5, 4, 3, 2 or 1 against each statement. Where 5 means Strongly Agree; 4 means Agree; 3 means Neither Agree nor Disagree; 2 means Disagree and 1 means Strongly Disagree.

Statements	SA	A	N	D	SD
1 Retailers provide the needed information	5	4	3	2	1
2 The information is accurate and authentic	5	4	3	2	1
3 The information is given on proper time	5	4	3	2	1
4 They hide some facts about the retail business	5	4	3	2	1
5 Retailers give proper respect to you	5	4	3	2	1
6 They co-operate with you	5	4	3	2	1
7 They are truthful to you	5	4	3	2	1
8 Retailers follow your instructions	5	4	3	2	1
9 They try to offer some money for doing unfair practices	5	4	3	2	1
10 The are humble and sincere	5	4	3	2	1
11 They are honest	5	4	3	2	1
12 The are straight forward	5	4	3	2	1
13 They are responsible	5	4	3	2	1
14 They follow the legal norms	5	4	3	2	1
15 They criticise their competitors with you	5	4	3	2	1
16 Retailers are ethical in dealings with you	5	4	3	2	1
Taxation Department					
1 Retailers maintain proper books of accounts	5	4	3	2	1
2 They show actual sales	5	4	3	2	1
3 They disclose actual profit	5	4	3	2	1
4 The fill the tax return on time	5	4	3	2	1
5 They pay the tax on prescribed rates	5	4	3	2	1
6 They evade tax	5	4	3	2	1

Food and Supply Department
1 Retailers do not adulterate the products | 5 | 4 | 3 | 2 | 1
2 The products are safe and hygienic | 5 | 4 | 3 | 2 | 1
3 Packages are good | 5 | 4 | 3 | 2 | 1
4 The quantity is authentic | 5 | 4 | 3 | 2 | 1
5 The quality of products is genuine | 5 | 4 | 3 | 2 | 1
6 They do not sell outdated products | 5 | 4 | 3 | 2 | 1
7 They have accurate measures of weight | 5 | 4 | 3 | 2 | 1
8 They charge the printed price | 5 | 4 | 3 | 2 | 1

Labour Department
1 They do not employ minors in their stores | 5 | 4 | 3 | 2 | 1
2 They close their shops on the last Sunday | 5 | 4 | 3 | 2 | 1
3 They give reasonable salary to the employees | 5 | 4 | 3 | 2 | 1
4 Employees are not harassed at retail store | 5 | 4 | 3 | 2 | 1
5 Retailers are doing fair retailing practices | 5 | 4 | 3 | 2 | 1

Retailers Association
1 Your members follow price list | 5 | 4 | 3 | 2 | 1
2 They give you needed information | 5 | 4 | 3 | 2 | 1
3 They pay the membership fee | 5 | 4 | 3 | 2 | 1
4 They attend the meetings called by you | 5 | 4 | 3 | 2 | 1
5 They sell standardised products | 5 | 4 | 3 | 2 | 1
6 They do not practice price discrimination | 5 | 4 | 3 | 2 | 1
7 Their promotion is not deceptive | 5 | 4 | 3 | 2 | 1
8 You guide them for fair retail practices | 5 | 4 | 3 | 2 | 1
9 You cancel the membership of those who do unfair practices | 5 | 4 | 3 | 2 | 1
10 You have developed a code of ethics for your members | 5 | 4 | 3 | 2 | 1